Playtime!

MARK JURY

Playtime!

AMERICANS AT LEISURE

A HARVEST BOOK

HARCOURT BRACE JOVANOVICH

NEW YORK AND LONDON

Special thanks to Dan Jury who began this project by helping me on the long drives (during high-school vacations) and ended up taking some of the best pictures in the book.
M.J.

Introduction

On July 3, 1970, the wheels of a giant Military Air Transport DC-8 hit the cement runway at Travis Air Force Base, California, and the load of returning Vietnam veterans broke into a spontaneous cheer. The stewardess grinned broadly and said, "Well, you guys made it."

After a year in Vietnam and Cambodia, I was home, safe and sound, in the United States of America.

After the turbulent decade of the sixties, the America to which I returned was a strange place indeed: The war was winding down; campuses were quiet; the inner cities had cooled; the counterculture was history.

The news, instead, was that the Biggest Leisure Boom Ever had gripped the country; an unprecedented explosion of leisure spending was coupled with an increasing amount of time for Americans to spend it in.

That America was preoccupied with fun, fun, fun was almost unbelievable to me. As a photojournalist, I had focused on many of the "significant" events of the sixties—a kaleidoscope of civil rights, hippies, alternative lifestyles, ghetto riots, and antiwar demonstrations. Yet there was always the nagging awareness that these events actually involved an extremely small percentage of Americans. What matters, I always wondered, to those millions of people *out there?*

Obviously, those millions had given scant notice to the shellshocks of the sixties. They had diligently pursued The American Dream and the assurances of a good job, a nice house, two or three automobiles, reasonable health, and an abundance of gadgets. With material possessions taken for granted, people had moved on to a new Dream—how to "get away from it all."

I began crisscrossing America, talking with and photographing Americans having fun. At that time, I had no idea I'd become involved in a six-year journey. However, I also thought leisure meant "killing time."

Nothing could be farther from the truth.

The intensity, commitment, and zeal that Americans bring to their leisure reflects a basic shift in our society: the work ethic is giving way to the pleasure principle. We have entered the Age of Leisure.

From $58.3 billion in 1965 to $160 billion in 1977, leisure spending rose on a steady curve through Vietnam, an oil embargo, runaway inflation, an energy crisis, unemployment, and a recession. In fact, whenever a crisis arose, spending for fun became even more frenzied in an effort to spend while one still could.

I began this project by randomly searching out leisure events and activities and talking with the participants. After several years and hundreds of rolls of exposed film, I don't think there's any leisure activity—no matter how bizarre—that would surprise me. As Alvin Toffler observed in *Future Shock*, ". . . the realm of leisure, unlike that of work, is little constrained by practical considerations. Here imagination has free play—and the mind of man can conjure up incredible varieties of fun."

In an era when scientists warn about the danger of "chronic brain overloading" from information bombardment, Americans *must* have substantial doses of leisure; and people will undoubtedly continue to develop innovative ways to "get away from it all." These new activities by no means edge out the old standbys of American leisure—watching television, playing golf, attending sporting events. It's just that Americans today have enough leisure time to enjoy traditional spare-time activities—and then *still* have time left over.

A forty-seven-year-old steelworker underscored the need to become involved in an activity. Near retirement, he was about to have, under his union contract, a four-months' paid furlough of sorts. Lately he'd been thinking about buying a camper and hitting the road, or joining a CB radio club.

"You can't bowl every day for four months," he said, "you'll go nuts."

Mark Jury
Easter Sunday 1977

Playtime!

The Biggest Leisure Boom Ever

"Of course, the newspapers say this is the biggest leisure boom ever," said Jim Vinson of New Haven, Indiana, "and there's sure been a boom in trailers since I got my first one in nineteen-sixty-nine."

"It's getting bigger all the time," he added, "because people are retiring earlier. Guys in these shops—it's thirty years and out. If they went to work there when they were sixteen or seventeen years old, they retire at forty-six or forty-seven. So they're buying trailers."

Jim Vinson retired from a foreman's position at the International Harvester Company and settled into a traditional retirement of television, his garden, and a cottage at a nearby lake. "I was out looking for a second car one evening," he recalled, "and there was a camper sitting there. I looked at it and kind of got the fever. So I went back that night and bought one."

Jim and his wife, Vera, now travel about eight months out of the year, and have visited every state except Hawaii. "If anyone had ever told me I'd end up traveling around the country in a trailer, I'd have told them they were crazy," said Jim, "but it's been great. Trailering is just a different life, that's all, and you meet such nice people. Campers are all one big family.

"My first trailer was a twenty-footer, then I got a twenty-seven-footer—that's the one I pulled to Alaska. Then I traded and got a twenty-four-footer and kept that only ten or eleven months and then I traded for this fifth wheel. I've got a big easy chair in the fifth wheel and it's just as comfortable as my living room at home. I can sit there and watch television and lean back—there's very few trailers that have room for a big easy chair."

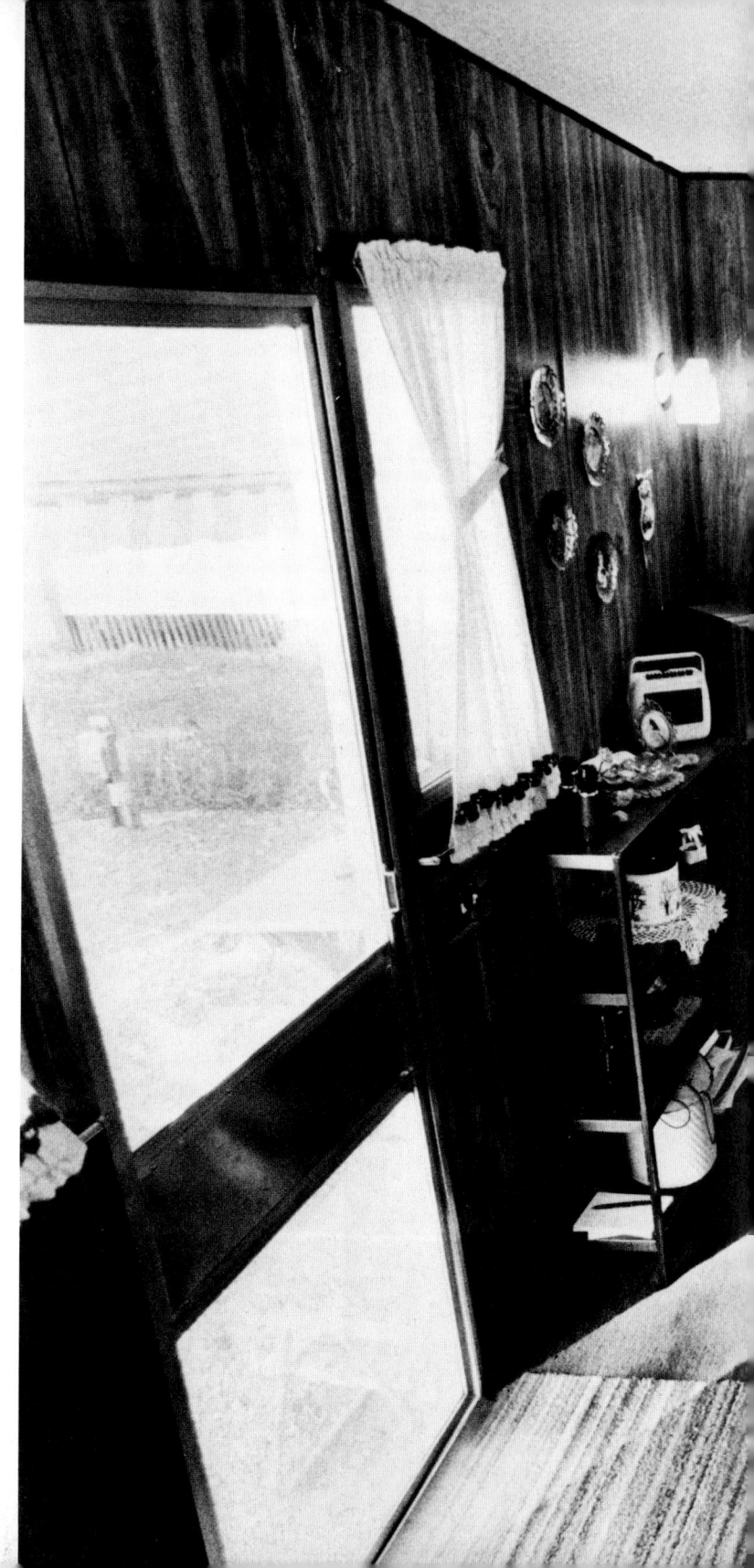

For backpacking enthusiasts Dave and Stella Emery of Eugene, Oregon, the biggest leisure boom ever has severely cramped their activity.

"Each year you find more people up there, which means each year the quality of the backpacking experience is degraded a bit from what you've experienced previously," says Dave, a copy editor at the Eugene *Register-Guard,* "or you've got to go back in farther or be more cagey about how to get away from people. We've found places that I wouldn't disclose on a torture rack because we plan to go again and we don't want to find people when we get there.

"There's a phrase about the wilderness areas: they're 'in danger of being loved to death.' It's very true. The *National Observer* just had an article about the system used in Yosemite, which relies on computers to program people into different areas to try to help them avoid each other as much as possible in the back country. That's really a travesty. I don't want a computer to have anything to do with my backpacking experience. To hell with them. Yet that's what's happening.

"A few years ago in Kings Canyon National Park they had to close a trail because more than fifteen thousand people a season were using it and it was just being pulverized. That kind of thing is the antithesis of what we're looking for when we go backpacking.

"Mountain climbers have a hell of a time, too. People have to stand in line now—literally—to climb many of the popular peaks. And that's very sad."

To "get away from it all," the Emerys now search out places like a lava field, five thousand feet up in the Willamette National Forest.

"For us, backpacking today means making some compromises," says Dave. "Sometimes we shun the most attractive backpacking areas and scenic wonder spots because they're so glamorous they attract scads of people. We've also abandoned fishing in our search for solitude, because fishermen will go to great lengths to get to a good fishing spot."

At Devil's Eye, in the Suwannee River near Branford, Florida, the spring was overflowing with scuba divers.

"It's like this on the weekend," said a diver from Valdosta, Georgia. "You know, it's really sort of ironic that we drive all the way down here to dive in crystal-clear water and then it's so muddy from all the divers in it that you can't see anything."

He assured me that during the week the springs returned to a magnificent natural state. I pressed him on what the diving was like then.

"Well, actually, I've never been able to get down here during the week," he said.

Even genuinely remote leisure attractions have been discovered by Americans eager to find diversion. One Sunday afternoon we drove to Old Mill Village, an isolated collection of attractions and shops in the Endless Mountains of Pennsylvania, that I had visited as a child.

On this day, however, a nearby field had been turned into a parking lot to accommodate the overflow of cars—with license plates from New York, New Jersey, Virginia, Connecticut.

"How do people find this place?" asked a man who was waiting to buy popcorn. "Look at the people. You must be making a lot of money."

"People have to be doin' something nowadays," said the popcorn lady, ignoring his comment. "Doin', doin', doin'. And if there's nothing for them to be doin', then they think something up."

'Barhopping' Event Set for Archbald

If you drive along Main Street in Archbald Saturday you will see a serious case of barhopping with men running from tavern to tavern but only stopping in for seconds.

The occasion will be the Archbald 500—an event sponsored by the Borough Centennial Committee.

It is a test of both endurance and capacity because the contestants not only have to run 1.7 miles, but stop in the eleven taverns along the way and gulp down eight ounces of beer in each.

Ed Casey, committee chairman, said so far more than sixty persons have paid seven dollars each to take part. Additional entries will be taken Saturday at 1:30 P.M. in the parking lot of St. Thomas Aquinas Church—the starting point.

In addition to eighty-eight ounces of beer, each contestant will receive a mug and the top three will be given trophies.

Casey admitted the idea is not original for the borough, explaining that it is a tradition at Penn State.

Assisting him are James McDonough, Robert Jones, Robert Gerrity, Sam Motts, and John Scwartztrauber.

The Scranton Tribune
Scranton, Pennsylvania

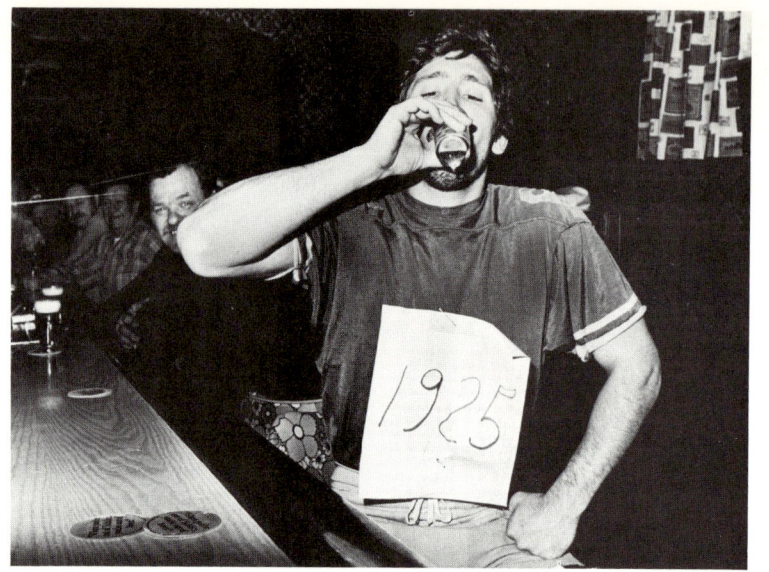

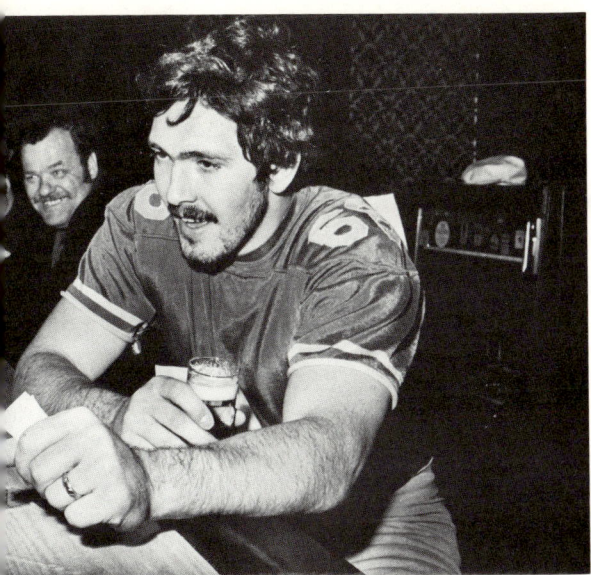

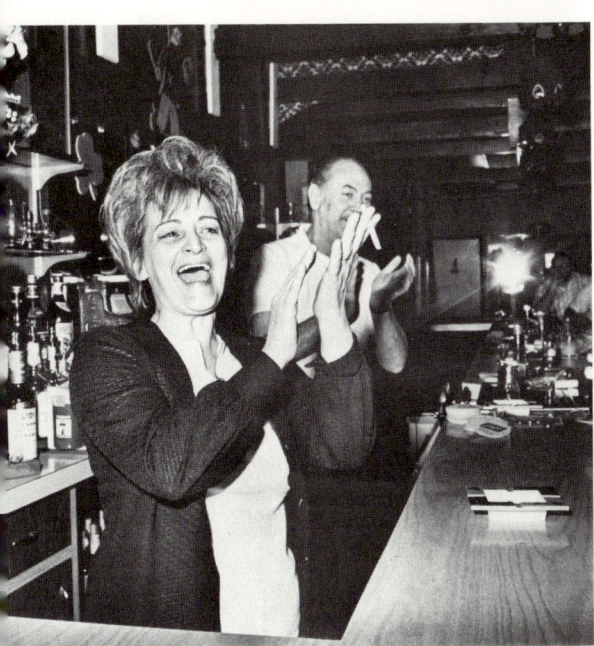

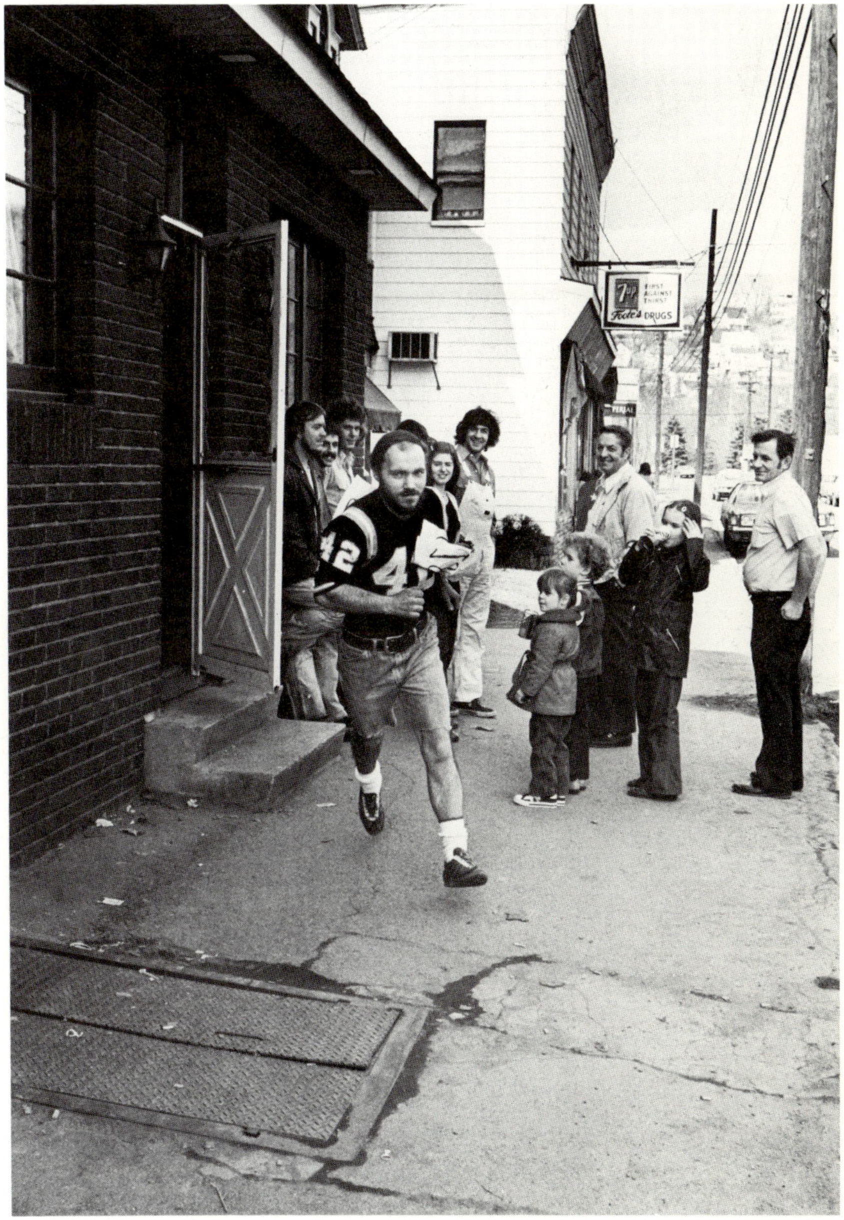
7up
FIRST AGAINST THIRST
DRUGS
42

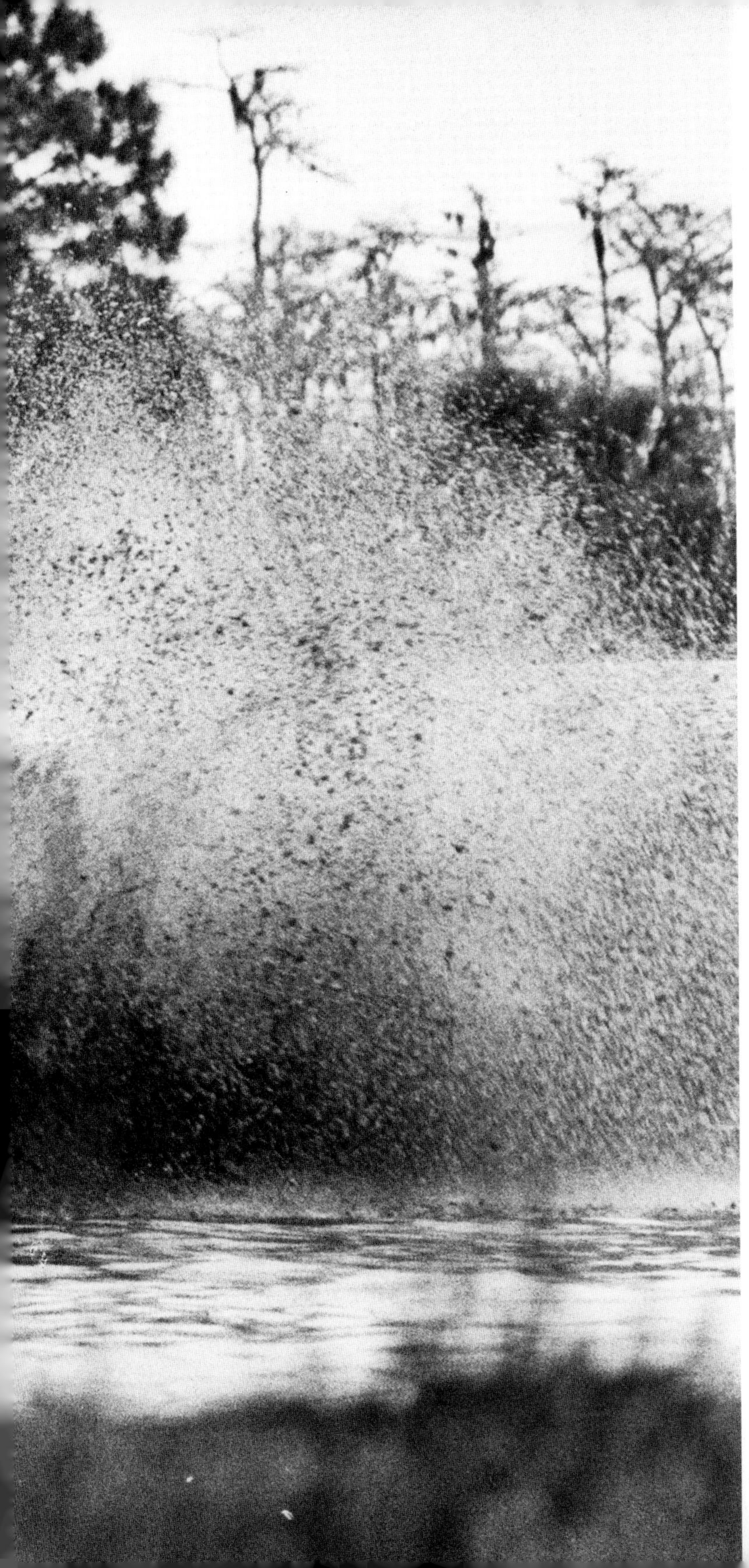

In the fall of 1972 I was driving north from Miami after attending the Republican National Convention. While stopping for gas in Naples, Florida, I asked the attendant, "Who do you think will win?"

"Lee Hancock," he replied.

"I beg your pardon?"

"Well, Lee's got that big ole supercharged Pontiac engine in his machine."

Forget the Presidential race, the attendant was talking about *the* race—the World Championship Swamp Buggy Race held each spring and fall in Naples.

Swamp buggies were originally built to traverse the Everglades. Today, they're used just as often for racing. Each contraption is unique, with huge airplane or tractor tires and powerful engines.

The Swamp Buggy Race is run on a muddy, water-filled track that has strategically placed potholes into which some of the smaller vehicles almost disappear.

"Oh, now isn't this the most ridiculous way to spend your time that you ever saw," one contestant, entered in the Powder Puff division of the Swamp Buggy Race, said.

Then, barely pausing, she added, "But I love it! I love it!"

In Pittsfield, Maine, visitors are lured to the town fairgrounds where members of the Athenaeum Club and the Arts Club cook over ten thousand eggs, seventy-five pounds of ham, one hundred pounds of sausage, and one hundred-fifty pounds of bacon in the "World's Largest Frying Pan"—the focus of the Central Maine Egg Festival.

"Getting the frying pan was no big deal," said Prentice Strong, Jr., an originator of the event. "We needed a gimmick so I said, 'Hey, how about a ten-foot frying pan.' On a bet I picked up the telephone and called Alcoa in Pittsburgh.

"At the same time, I said, 'If we're going to have an aluminum frying pan, it should be Teflon-coated,' so I did the same thing, called up Dupont in Wilmington, Delaware.

"To sum it up, they did it. Alcoa manufactured it and shipped it to DuPont, where it was Teflon-coated and on display for a while and then shipped up here.

"This is what's so much fun about the thing. You sit in your office and come up with a little promotion to fry a few eggs in Pittsfield, Maine, that summer and all of a sudden you're getting worldwide publicity and eight to ten thousand people show up."

Local events like the Egg Festival are burgeoning as record numbers of Americans take to the road looking for something to do.

In June, 1976, *Time* magazine reported, "According to a benumbed corps of travel statisticians, more than 99 million Americans—nearly half of the nation—will be taking vacations in the U.S. . . . Their spending will be above $85 billion, up $10 billion from the previous year."

In late August, 1976, my brother Dan tried to take a burro ride into the bottom of the Grand Canyon. "No luck," said the lady at the burro booth, "all burros are reserved until the end of October."

He was welcome to wait and hope for a cancellation, she added, but these days, to "get away from it all" by burro required a reservation at least three months in advance.

Americans' growing preoccupation with leisure was the subject of a prophetic *Life* magazine issue on "Americans at Play" in September, 1971. In the introduction to the issue, the editors wrote:

"The weekend is a state of mind, betrayed by a vacant stare, that lasts till Tuesday and an anticipatory twitching that begins on Thursday. We talk fishing at the factory, surfing at the store, skiing in the office, and when we make new acquaintances, we identify ourselves less by what we do for a living than by what we do to loaf.

"Stuck at home, we busy ourselves waxing, oiling, and—best of all—just fondling the sporting paraphernalia that clutters our garages and encrusts our shelves. Or we immerse ourselves in the seductive prose of catalogs full of gorgeous power boats and alluring primus stoves. Wherever we are, inside our head, we're *out there.*"

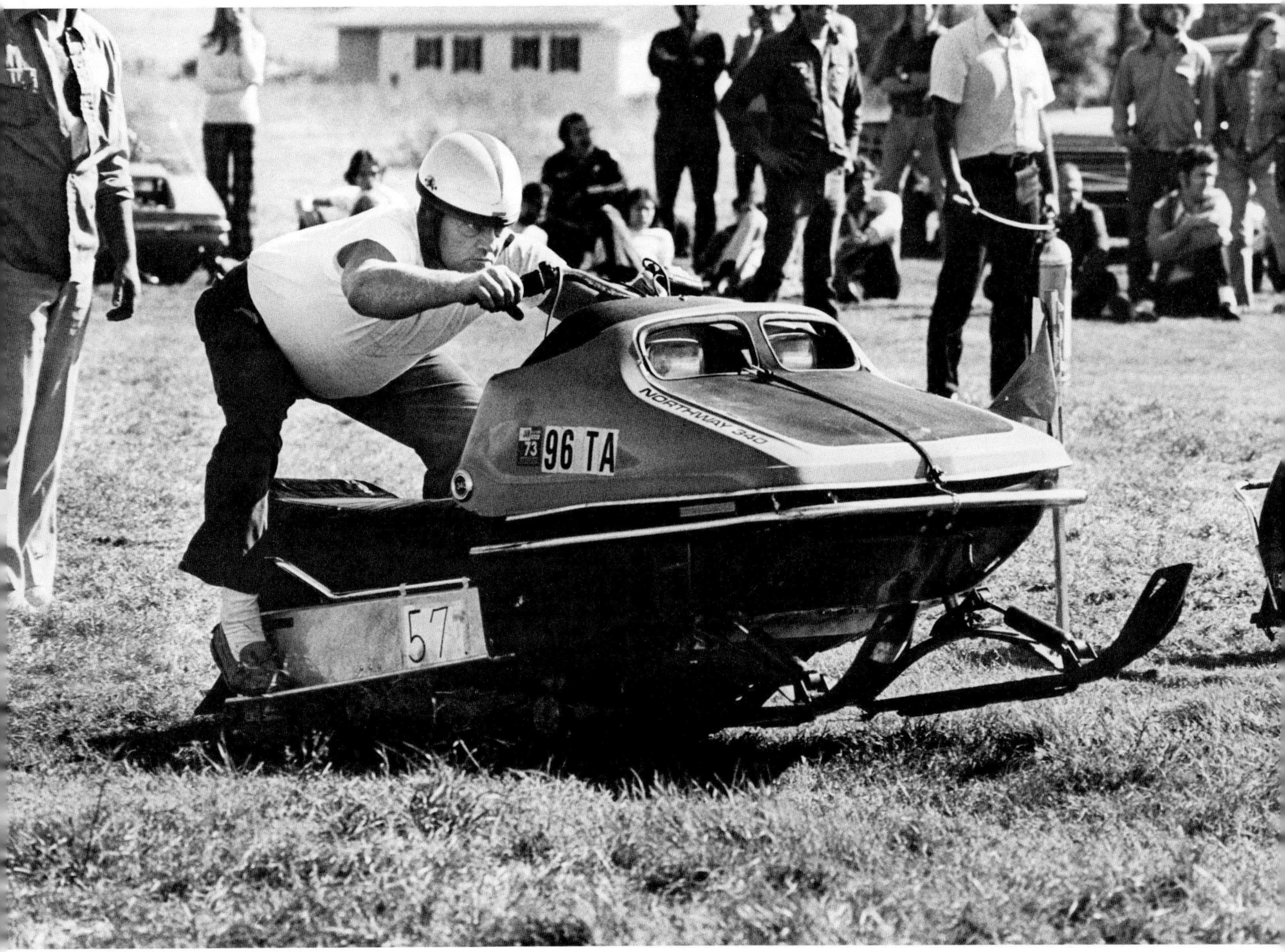
73
96 TA
NORTHWAY 340
57

"America Needs Leisure to Survive"

Why?

Why this unprecedented urge to get away from it all? The intensity, commitment, and zeal people were bringing to their leisure couldn't be explained simply by the reported reasons: a rapid rise in personal income, more time off the job, and earlier retirements.

In an attempt to find the answer, I visited Pete Vetch, who had been a leisure freak since the early sixties when the bug was particularly virulent in southern California.

After high school, Pete left Scranton, Pennsylvania, and moved to Los Angeles, where he dabbled as a movie extra. During one of his trips back home, he told me that he'd decided to give up acting and enroll in a school to become a women's hairdresser.

His reasoning was that a good hairdresser in Los Angeles could make twelve thousand dollars a year (including tips) by working *three days a week*. The other four days were then free to pursue a current passion—skydiving, bodybuilding, motorcycle racing, anything. His entire crowd lived for their leisure activities.

From Los Angeles, Pete moved to Downingtown, Pennsylvania (he'd left hairdressing and accepted a position with his father's company), and then to Saginaw, Michigan. I visited him there during the winter, and he was still gung-ho on leisure—participating in speed-skating meets, chairman of a winter carnival, and judge at an ice-sculpture contest. He was also considering investing in a snowmobile and motorcycle business.

43

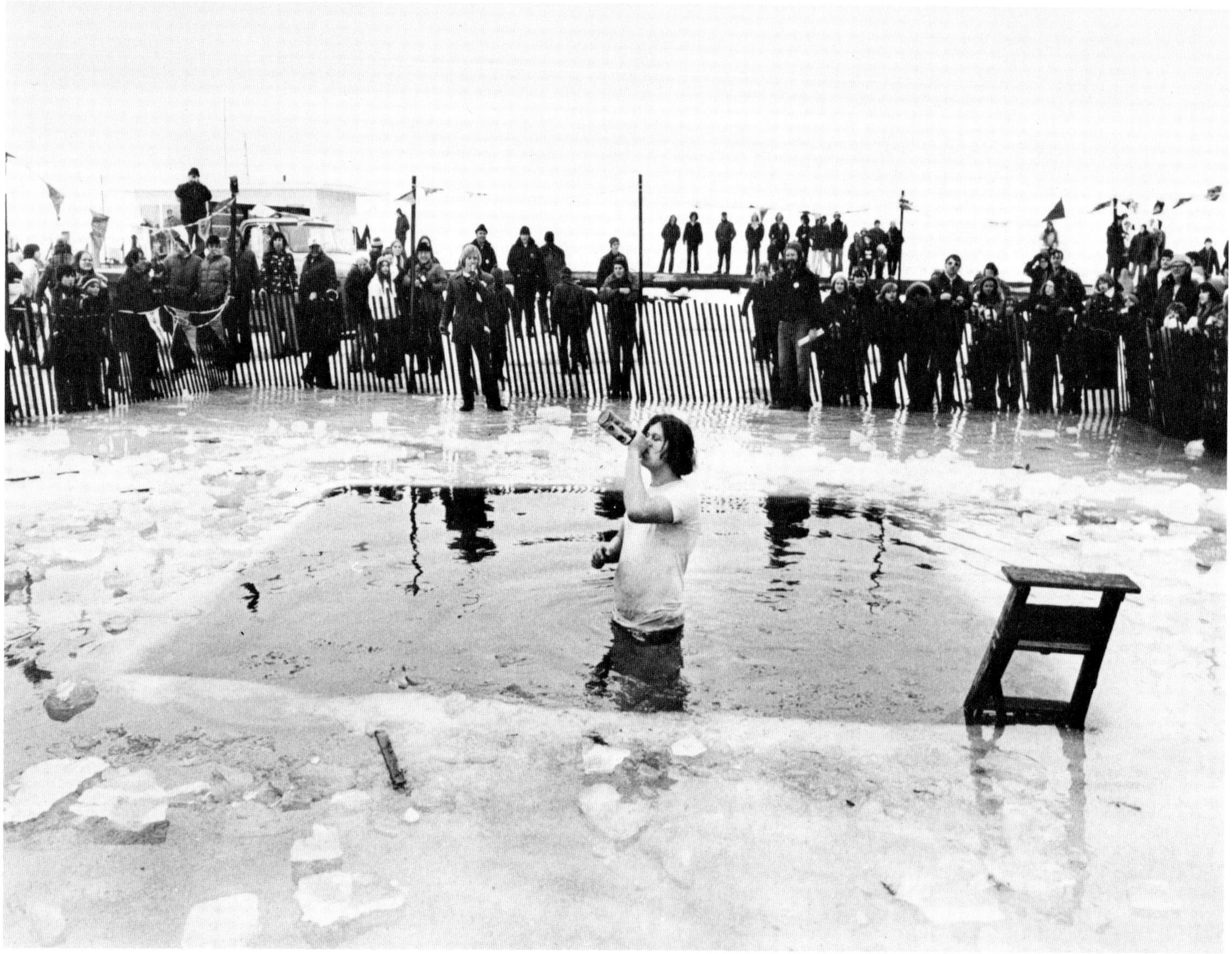

W e visited the "Perchville" Winter Festival in East Tawas, Michigan, which featured three days of events ranging from a Polar Bear Swim (left), to a fishing contest, to a Demolition Derby on the ice of Lake Huron (right). Over ten thousand people attended the event, which, according to a lady at the Chamber of Commerce, had "boomed in the past three years."

"The event keeps growing and we're always adding new events," said Tom O'Connor, president of Tawas Area Promotions. "We're planning now for next year and it should be tremendous."

Pete and I left "Perchville," trying to decide whether to check out the Enduro Snowmobile Races at Houghton Lake, the Tip-Up Carnival in Quincy, or the Winter Sports Festival at Gaylord.

"Hell, man, people want to feel good," said Pete. "The whole country's acting like southern California!"

45

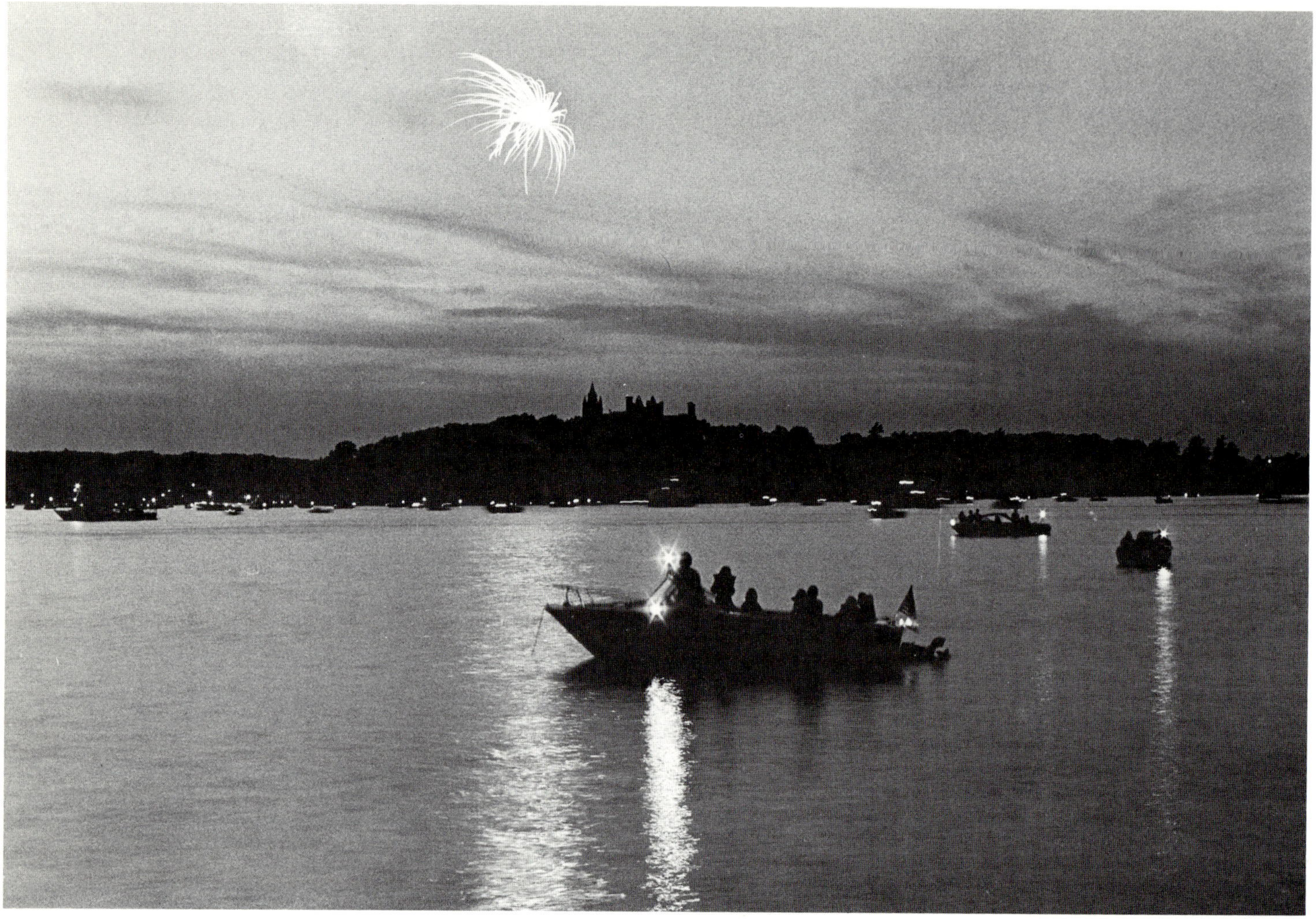

"Where do people get the money?" I asked Faye Babcock, who had left his position as manager of the local bank to join a marina. We were sitting on the banks of the St. Lawrence River watching a fireworks display over Boldt Castle. Hundreds of boats, ranging from quarter-million-dollar yachts to Sears "kickers," had converged to watch the event from the water.

"It's not your wealthy that's buying boats," said Faye. "I've noticed that in the past year your average middle-class person is coming in and finding, with the financing available, that he can afford that certain boat. Before, they've always been restricted to three years on a payo, but now you can give them seven, eight, nine years. It's almost getting like a home mortgage. All of a sudden it fits their pocketbook, so they buy it."

Rufus Hollinger, an official at Hershey Park, in Pennsylvania, was equally baffled by America's preoccupation with any leisure activity. The sprawling amusement complex had added a crafts barn where respected, professional craftspeople—representing broom-making to blacksmithing—each had a studio and worked just as they would in their own shop.

"I didn't realize how much these people are in demand until I tried to hire them for the crafts barn," said Hollinger. "Our crafts barn has been a complete success. I know you don't usually associate people who go to an amusement park as the kind who would be interested in a five-hundred-year-old craft, but the interest has been astonishing."

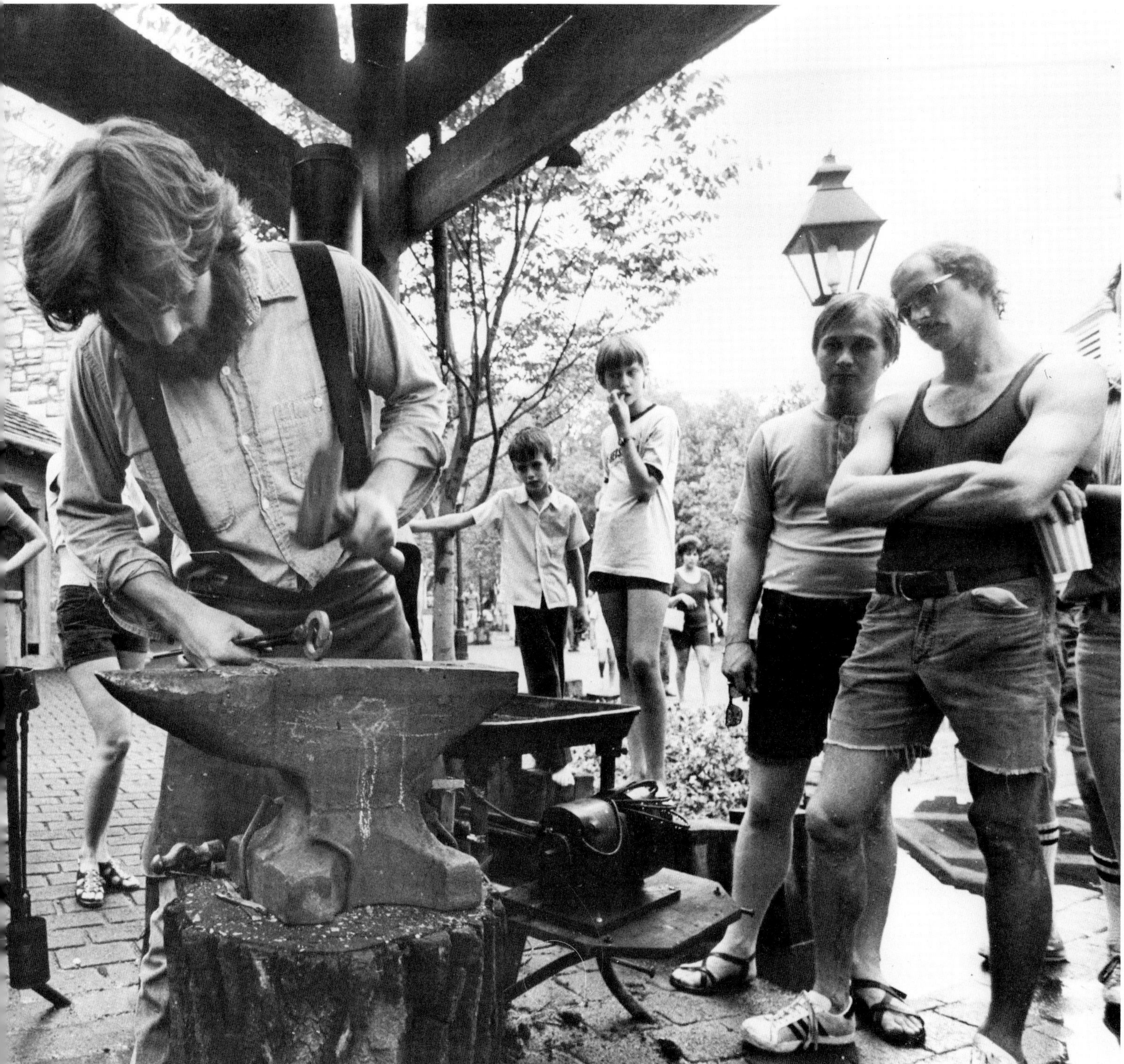

50

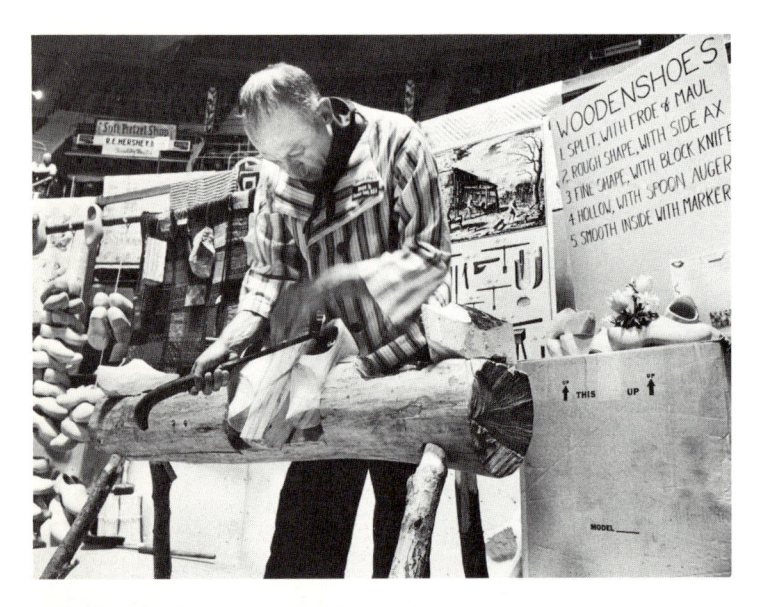

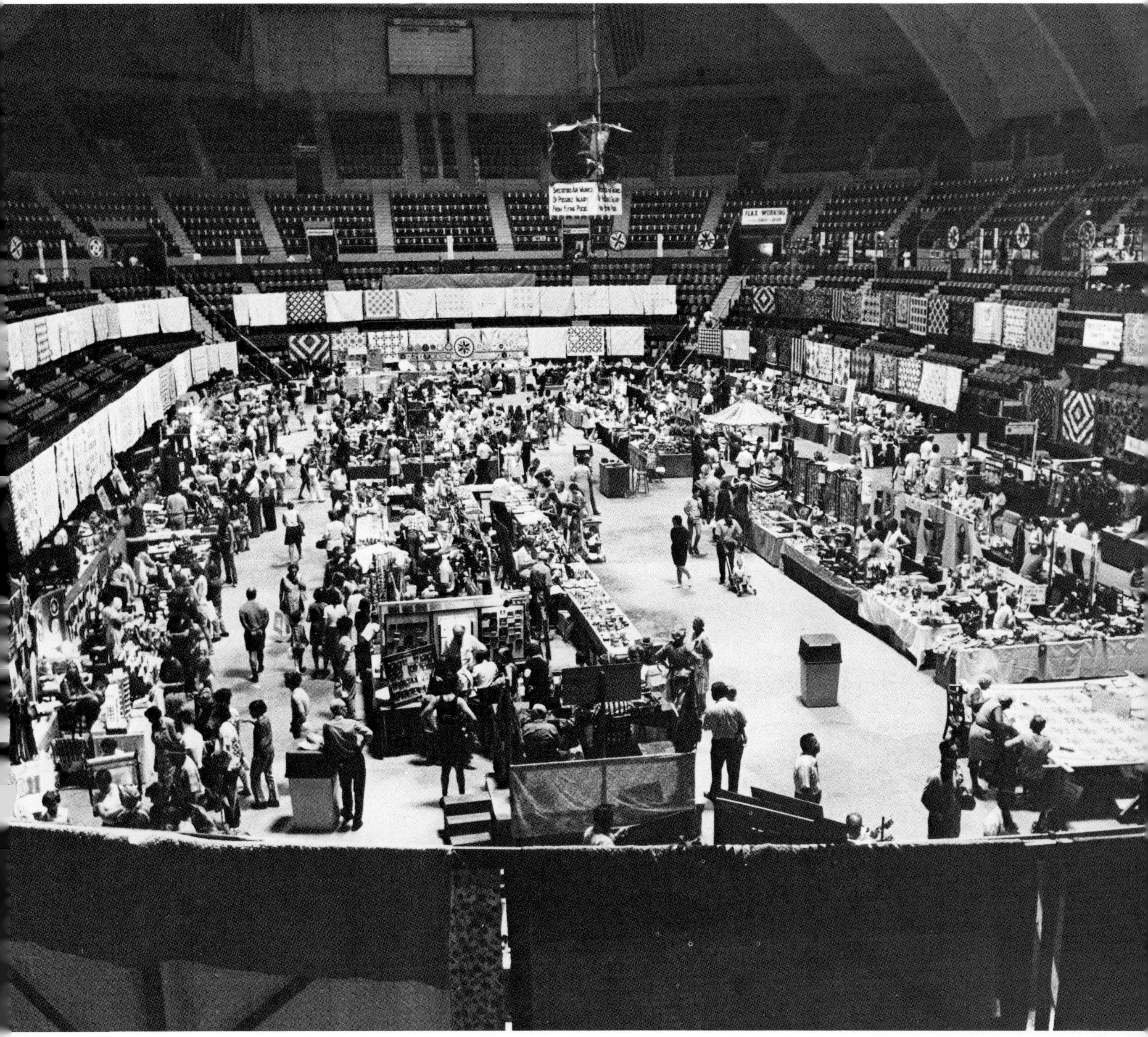
FLAX WORKING

"I got my job by being a good baseball player," says Larry Wichman, "Naked City" editor of *Screw* magazine, the New York City–based sex journal. "The second day I was working I came out and played and took over my position. My job security is that I'm a very good softball player."

Playing softball is treated quite seriously at *Screw*. "When we hire—on the employment form—we ask, 'Do you play softball?'" says Larry. "We don't ask them to throw a ball to us, but we do try to make sure that they play ball since we have such a small office."

The *Screw* team is a member of the Magazine and Book Publishers League in New York City. Teams from *The New Yorker, Time,* Random House, and other book and magazine publishers battle it out on the diamonds of Central Park with a surprising intensity.

"You work all week and it's ninety degrees and the dog manure is starting to ferment out in the gutters," says Larry, "and after the weekend you have to have something to look forward to on Monday morning. You can't look forward to a week of work, so you say, 'I only have a couple of days until softball and then it's only a couple days until another weekend, and then after the weekend I'll look forward to the softball game next week.' It's nice."

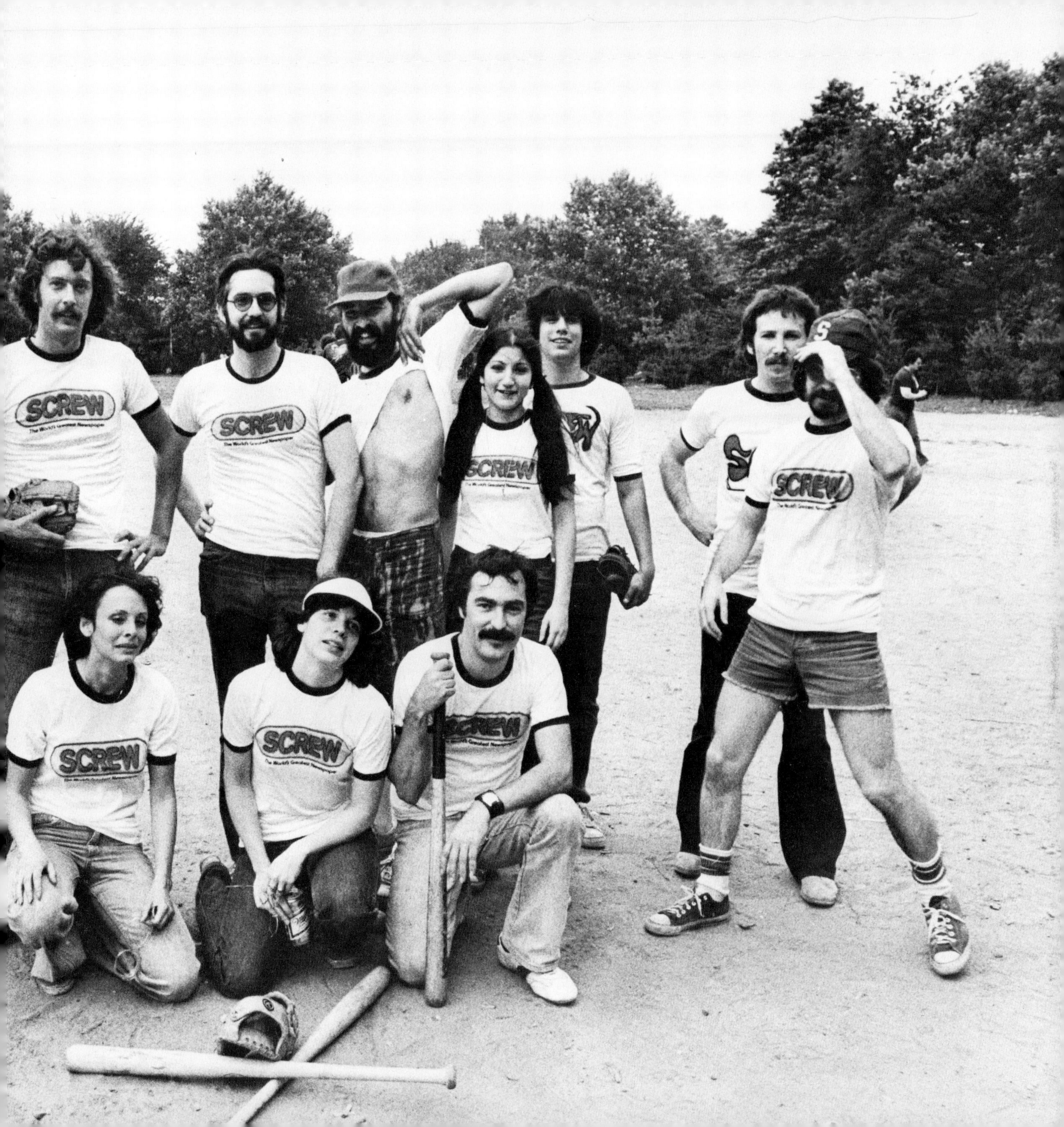
SCREW

The people I was meeting and talking with were remarkably loyal to their leisure activities.

Early one Sunday morning, after enjoying a walk through a marina in Daytona Beach, Florida, I shared a cup of coffee with a hospitable captain who had invited me aboard.

He was a former New York City banking executive who had retired after a near fatal coronary. His doctors had strongly urged a period of relaxation, so he had picked out a boat at the National Boat Show at the Coliseum and was now cruising down the intracoastal waterway.

He confided to me that, so far, the experience hadn't quite lived up to his expectations. Something was missing—he wasn't really enjoying himself.

He paused, thought about his dilemma, and then announced his solution:

"I think I'll have to get a different boat."

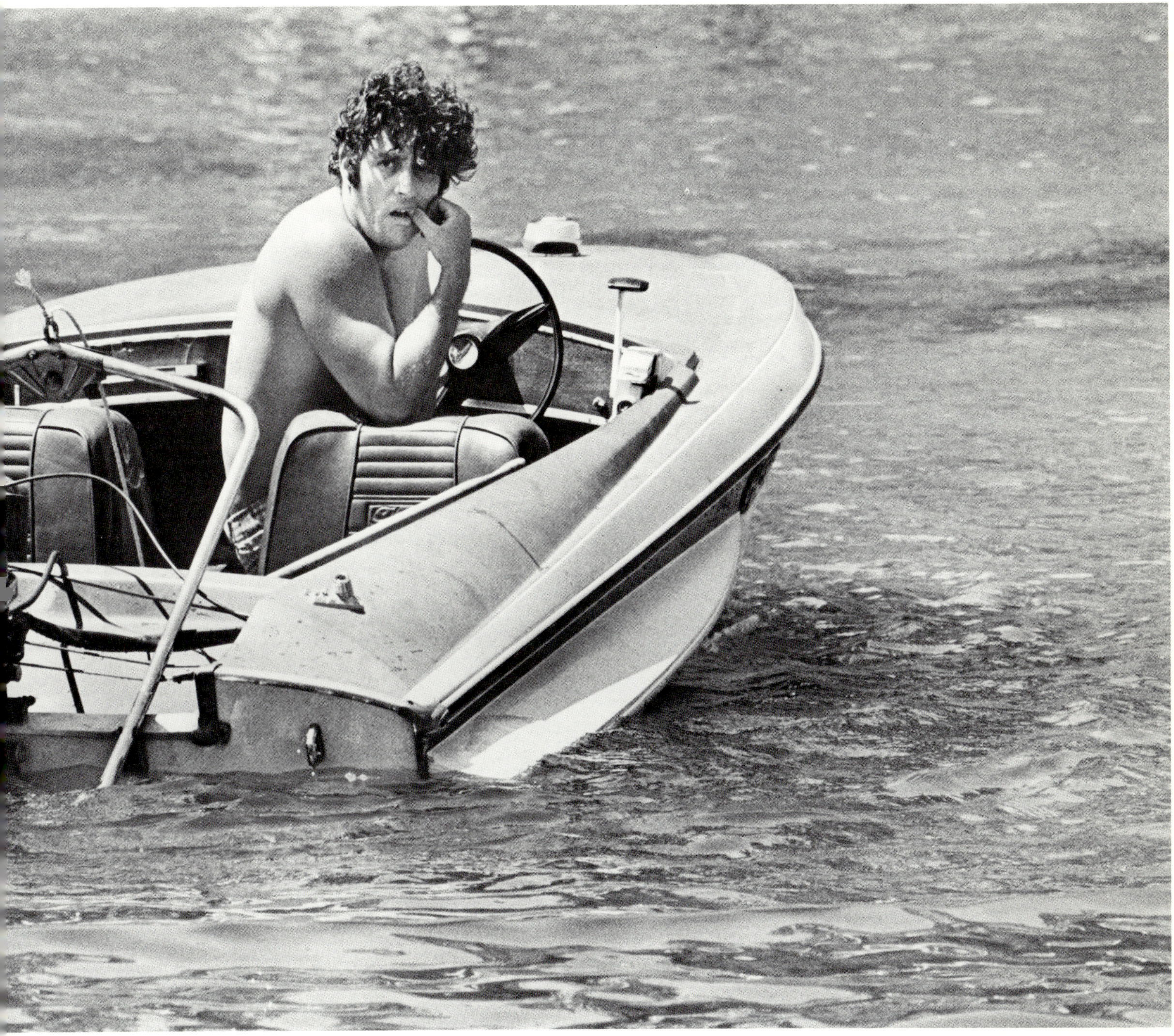

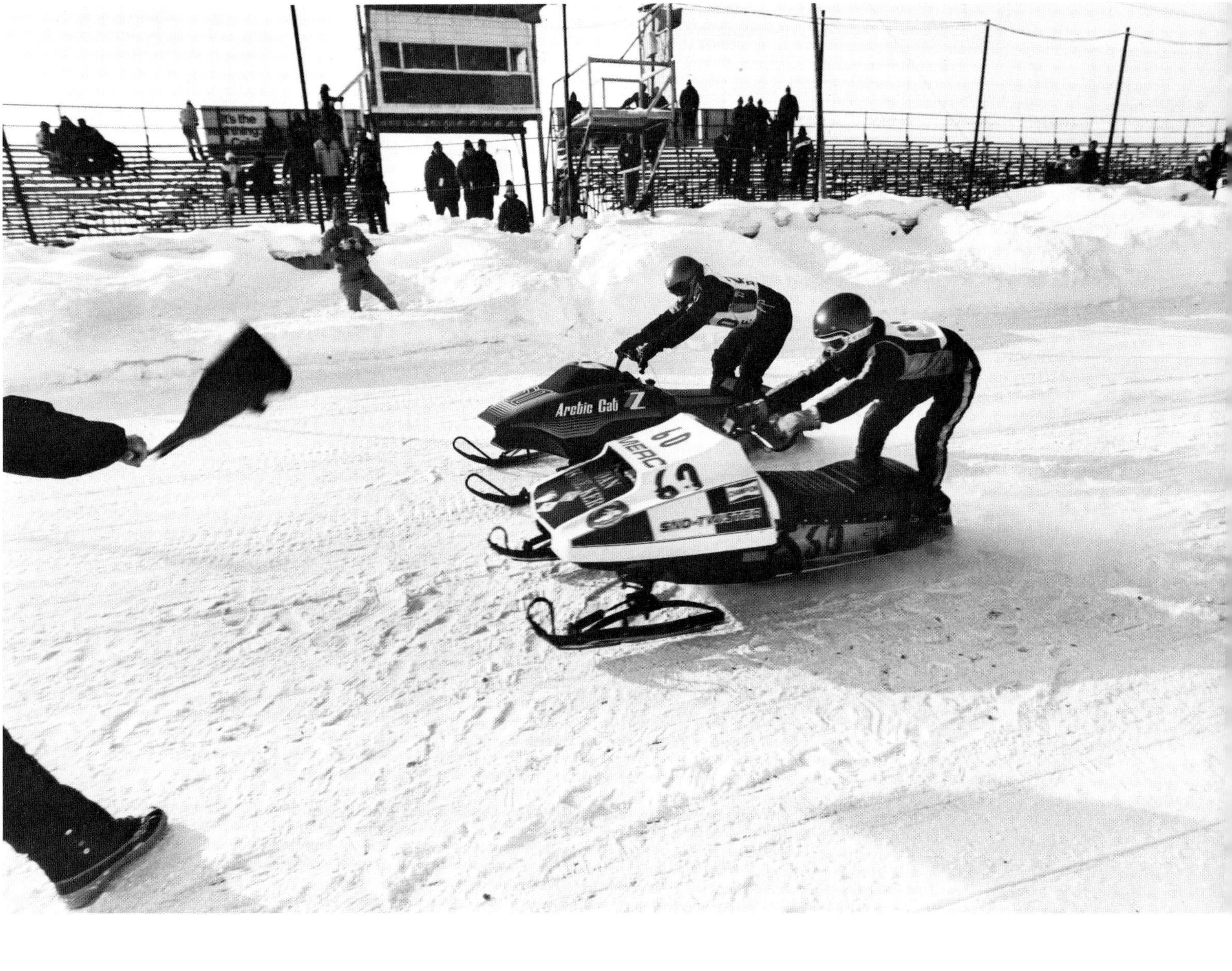
Arctic Cat
MERC
SNO-TWISTER

In Michigan I photographed a group of "snowjocks"—men wearing jackets with Union Carbide and Polaris patches whose passion was racing souped-up snowmobiles.

A girl in her mid-twenties, who had been watching the event, turned to her friend and said loudly, "I think this is *disgusting!* Grown men roaring around on their toys, while there's a war going on, the planet is being polluted to death, and most of the world is starving."

"I don't think you understand, young lady," said a middle-aged man nearby. He added firmly, "I'm not up here snowmobiling because I got nothin' better to do. Gettin' out in the clean air . . . the freedom . . . that's what makes me able to go back to being a welder on Monday morning. If I didn't have my weekends . . ." he trailed off, unable to articulate that snowmobiling to him was much more than just a way to kill time.

Then the local dentist spoke up. I'd talked with him earlier in the day and learned that in addition to snowmobile racing, he was also an avid dog-sled racer. He had proudly described his team of ten Alaskan Huskies, dogs bred strictly for racing, which weighed fifty to sixty pounds each and consumed an average of a pound of food per dog per day.

"My kid sister and her fiancé, or friend—whatever the proper terminology is these days—came up to visit us one weekend and they were appalled by the amount of food the dogs required," he said. "The fellow had spent time in the Congo with some relief agency and had really seen it all—things like a baby sucking on a shriveled, empty breast. His thing was that Americans should get rid of their pets, which he said consumed billions a year in food and care, and give the money instead toward alleviating starvation.

"I knew his idea was unworkable, but I consider myself a concerned individual and I really began thinking about it. His comments had me feeling pretty lousy.

"Of course, the reality is that my dogs are not denying the people in the Congo or anywhere else one mouthful of food. If I get rid of my dogs tomorrow, will one more person actually be fed? And for me, a small-town dentist in central Michigan, to worry about it and miss out on all the good things I get from my hobbies is pretty stupid.

"The end of this story is pretty funny," he added. "I was at Wayne State University about a year later to meet my sister and I actually ran into this fellow. Since I had resolved all this in my own mind, I was eager to discuss his views again, but as soon as I began, he said, 'Sorry, man, I'm not into that trip anymore' and hurried off!"

It wasn't until a session with a friend from my Vietnam Veterans against the War days, however, that I realized exactly what those Michigan snowmobilers were trying to say.

We met at a ski resort near Mansfield, Ohio. He now worked for a tire and rubber company and was decked out in new ski togs and had two "snowbunnies" in tow. He was especially proud of his bright yellow Corvette, which displayed decals for both skiing and sky-diving associations.

I commented wryly that he seemed to have overcome his post-Vietnam syndrome and successfully moved on to other things.

"Listen," he said, "if you think I'm going to sit around all weekend worrying about Vietnamese orphans or starving Biafrans and then go build tractor tires all week—you're crazy."

He banged his beer can down so the foam splattered high in the air and whooped, "America needs leisure to survive!"

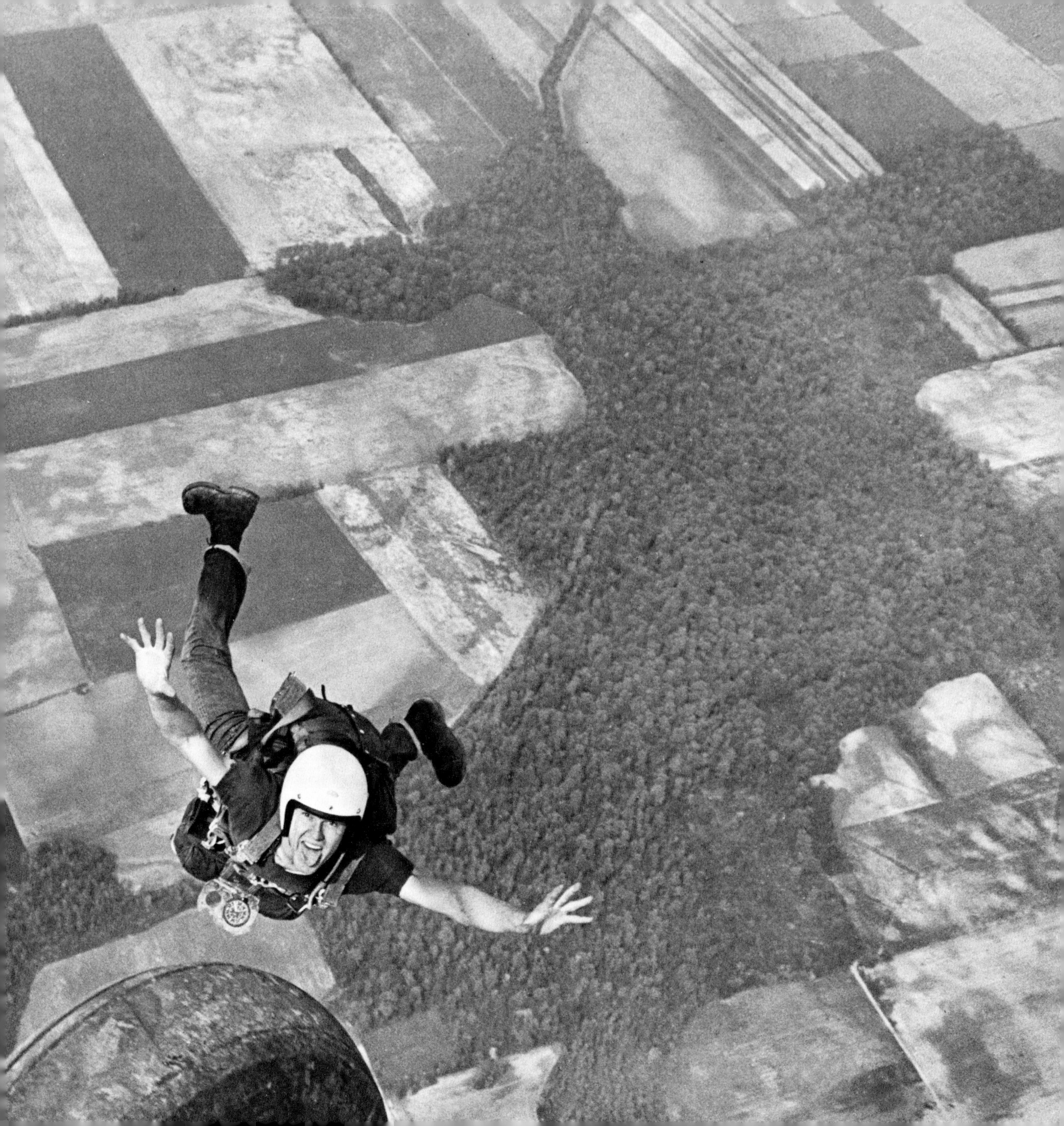

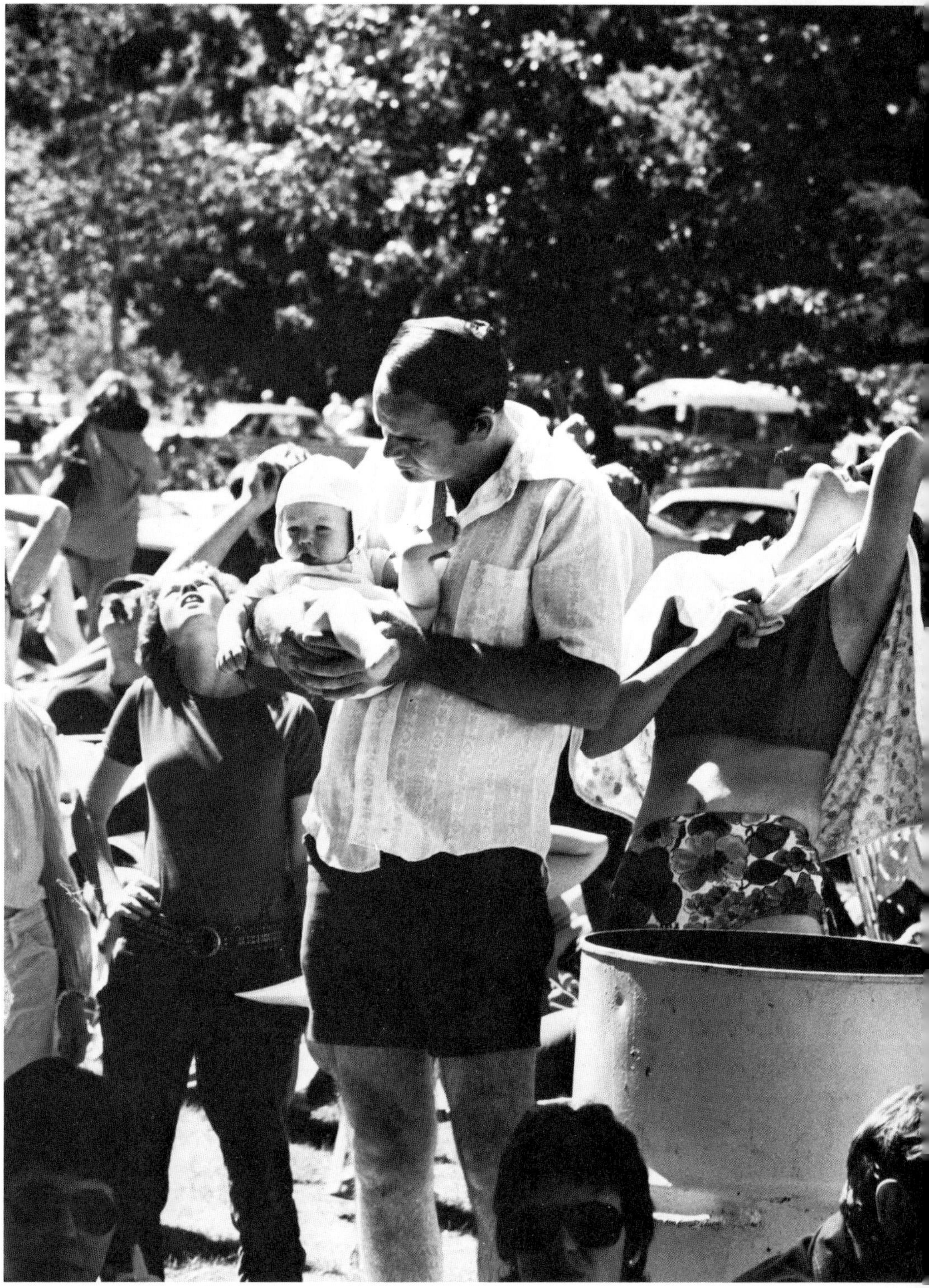

Leisure as Respite from Leisure

The next morning we overslept, and I missed the Bikini Race, the Ohio Winter Ski Carnival event that I had wanted to photograph.

"Skiing sucks anyway," said my friend. We hopped into his car and rumbled over to a nearby basement where he had merged his HO-gauge model train set with a co-worker's to make a spectacular room of mountains, villages, streams, and train stations. In the biggest leisure boom ever, having a number of active ways to escape is almost *de rigueur*.

On a beach near Newport, Rhode Island, I once met a fellow who was paddling a folding kayak in the surf. He'd actually traveled to Newport for a tennis tournament, but had become "fed up with tennis and decided I needed a break." Fortunately, he had packed his kayak.

At Lake Winnepausakee, New Hampshire, my brother, Dan, and I were sleeping on the beach when we were wakened by a commotion. Thousands of bathers were excitedly watching a team of Navy skydivers perform a spectacular skydiving exhibition; the men landed among the bathers to sign autographs.

According to one of the skydivers, the team spent the summer giving exhibitions at beaches and state fairs.

"It's really nice," said a middle-aged bather clutching an autographed 'Sailors Have More Fun' bumper sticker, "it breaks up your day at the beach."

62

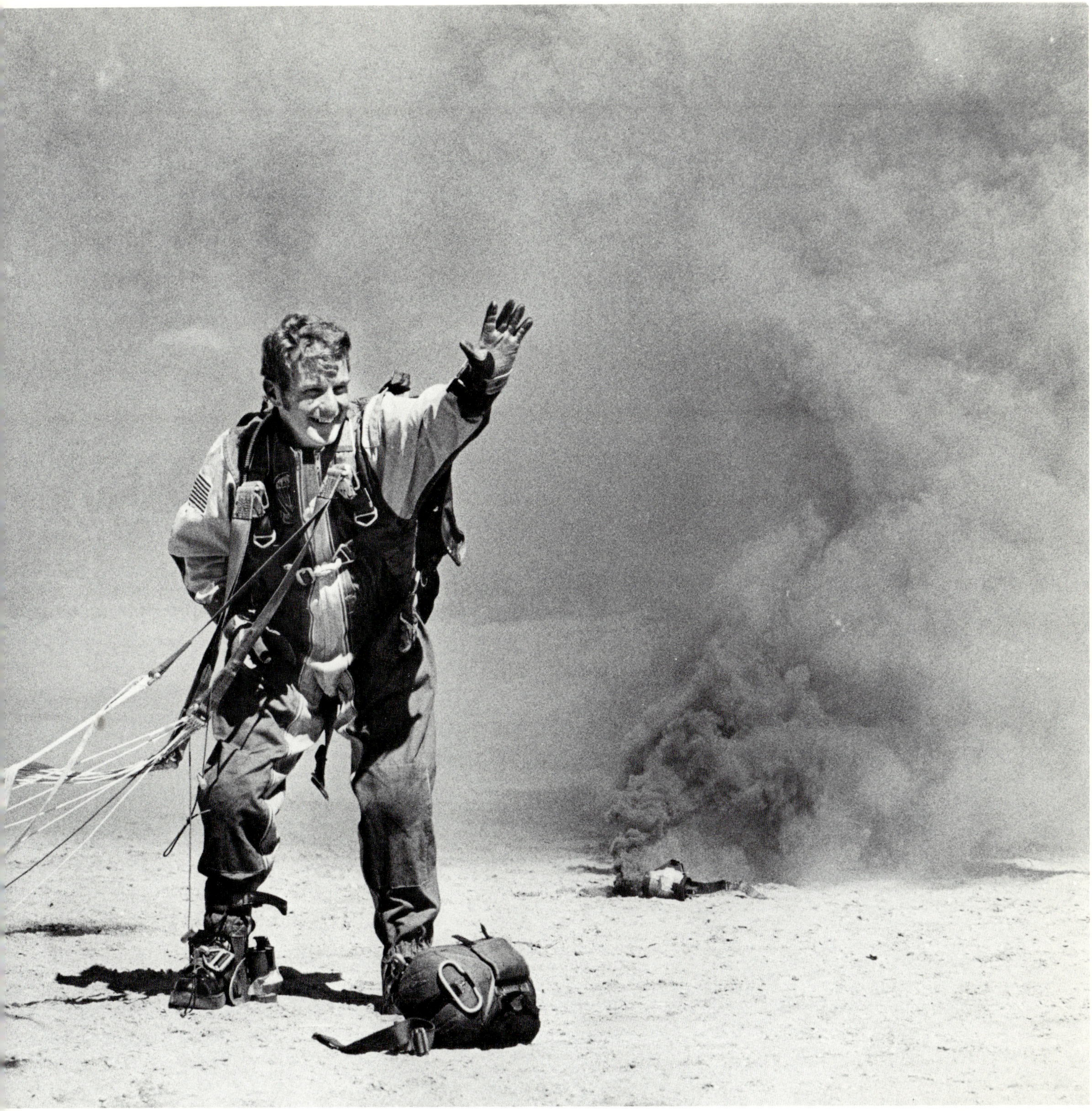

64

In Washington, D.C., the National Parks Service teamed up with the National Endowment for the Arts to sponsor an innovative program—the Strolling Troubadours.

"The Troubadours were created to entertain people who are waiting in line and just waiting around monuments in Washington," explained Margaret Anne Hanley, production manager of the group. "We perform at the Washington, Jefferson, and Lincoln monuments. At the Lincoln, for example, people often wait for more than an hour and a half to get in and it's quite hot. So we give them about a half hour of entertainment. It's been extremely successful, and we've had tremendous response. People tell us they've been waiting in line all day and this was the best thing that's happened to them."

"They're a captive audience," said Richard Morris, a professional actor with the troupe. "Why they wait an hour and a half in the hot sun is beyond me, but we bring some songs and theater skills that they've never seen before. That's what I like about it. We're showing little kids from all over America things they've never seen before."

*Mr. and Mrs. Caleb Shellfish
of Tepid Swamp, Louisiana
are pleased to announce the wedding of
their daughter, Mollie, to Martin Z. Mollusk,
relatively famous Hermit Tree Crab,
exact origins now under investigation.
The ceremony will be performed by
Mayor B. Thomas Waldman
somewhere in the vicinity of the
10th Street Beach
on Tuesday, August 19th,
nineteen hundred and seventy five
at 1 P. M.
A sand sculpting contest will precede
the wedding and the
Second World's Championship
Hermit Tree Crab Races
will follow the nuptials.
NO RSVP — Just Be There — Bring Rice
Also stale bread and cucumber rinds.*

The most incredible example of our need to be entertained may well be embodied in the above invitation.

I called Ocean City, New Jersey, and talked with Mark Soifer, director of public relations for the city. "By August," he said, "the bucolic life at the shore becomes boring for the summer residents. So why not marry two crabs on the beach in an elaborate ceremony as a diversion?"

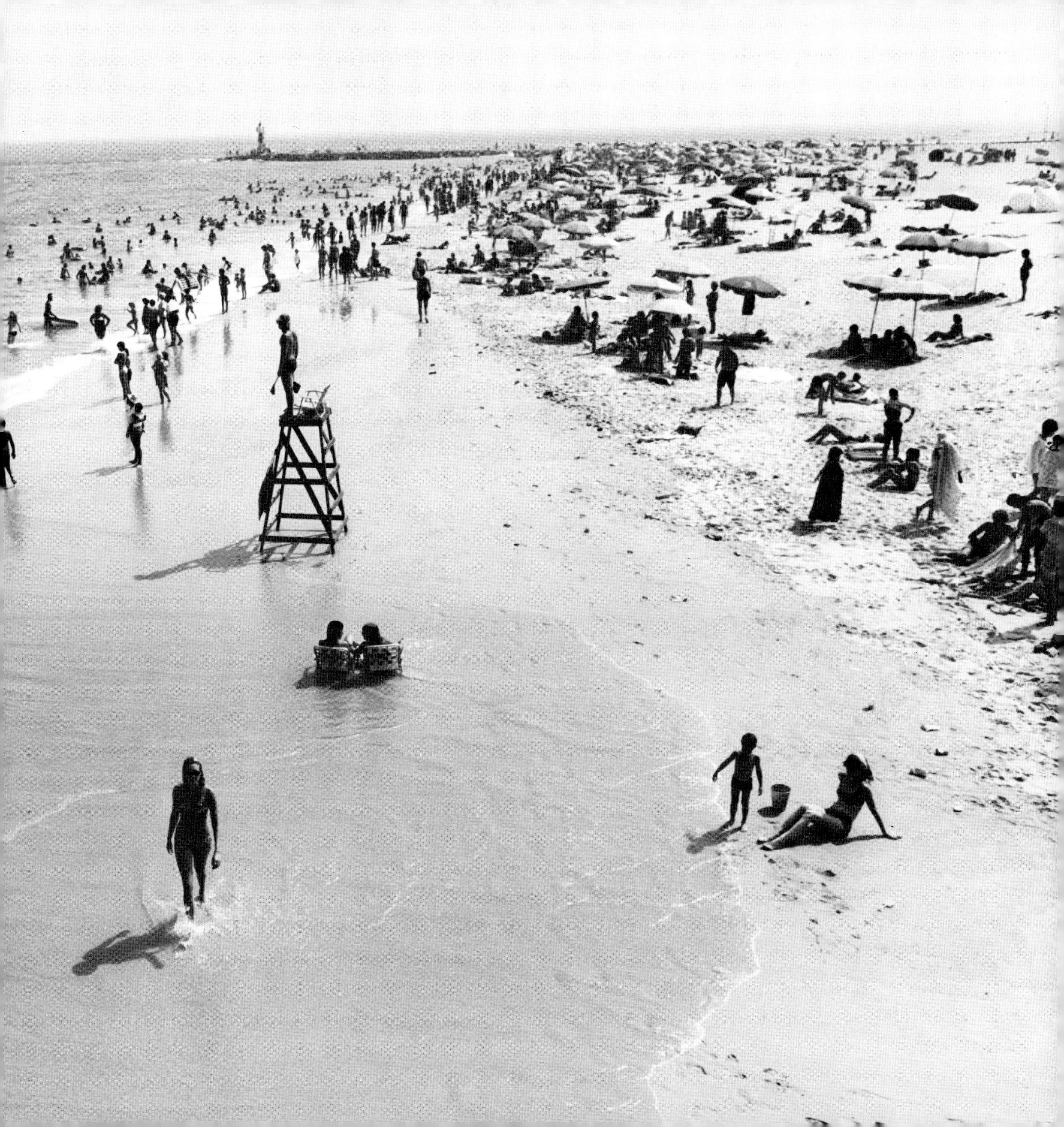

The wedding was held on the Tenth Street Beach at Ocean City with Mayor B. Thomas Waldman officiating. The mayor, incidentally, was making good on a campaign promise to marry Martin and Mollie.

At exactly 1:00 P.M. Else Berkstresser, a former Miss Ocean City, led the procession on to the beach, while flinging flower petals and cucumber rinds along the path.

"We wanted audience participation, so we had cue cards that were used for the wedding march and everybody joined going 'DA DA DA DA, DA DA DA DA'" said Mark Soifer, "and that added a little flavor."

Others in the wedding party included Smiley the Mouse (a fellow named Harry McIntire who works as a clown on the pier at night), Marilyn Moore (dressed in a mermaid costume), and Mrs. Joan McGuire, who works for a florist, and was wedding co-ordinator. She made the pallets of swamp petunias that Mollie and Martin rested on.

While the wedding party was taking their places, the Ocean City Mermaid Chorus, a civic club, sang "I Love You Truly." Then Mayor Waldman began the ceremony.

"It was written based on the original civil ceremony that the mayor uses," said Mark Soifer, "but all reference to God was taken out—we didn't want it to be sacrilegious—and humorous things injected so it wouldn't be offensive to anybody.

"My reason for getting so involved was the publicity," he added. "I wanted to do something a little different that would interest the television people—which it has. For example, I can easily take Martin to Philadelphia and have him appear on television. He's been on a number of television shows.

"Most people responded to the crab marriage. You know how people like pets in this country. They just think it's cute. Martin Z. Mollusk just caught on.

"Some people, though, just thought it was stupid. Humor, you know, is a funny thing. Some people thought two crabs getting married was just dumb. Who cares? Why marry two hermit tree crabs? But negative feedback was minimal and in the end, I think, we won some people over."

68

69

In December, 1975, we drove to Bloomington, Minnesota, for the Minnesota Vikings versus Dallas Cowboys NFL playoff game.

My interest wasn't the football mania. I knew all about football as a collective national experience, culminating in Super Bowl Sunday when crime declines, business drops off, and traffic dies down.

What piqued my interest was the parking-lot activities; a new breed of "tailgaters" had emerged at sporting events all over the country. With the boom in self-contained campers, fans were no longer restricted to a motel or the family station wagon. Now they were living in the parking lot for the day before and the day after the game. A mini-city developed, based on booze, fun, and a spectacular array of food.

At UCLA there were reports of elaborate table settings, with oysters jetted in from New Orleans, as well as clams, prime ribs, sausages, tossed salads and a fully stocked bar. In Columbus, Ohio, fans were dining on linen tablecloths with fresh-flower centerpieces; partaking of roast beef expertly carved by a hired chef, and washing it down with imported vintage wines. In Minnesota, we'd been in touch with a group that planned to roast a whole pig, complete with apple in the mouth.

One newspaper reporter wrote, "It's hard to tell if the games come with the parties or the parties come with the games."

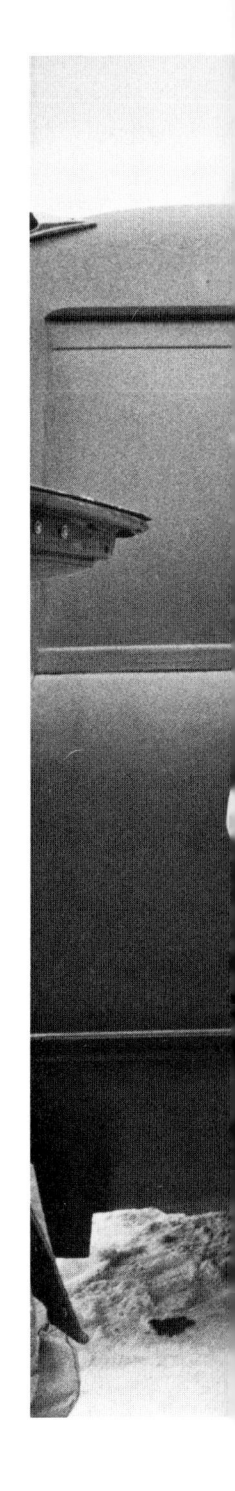

HAIL THE VIKINGS
RAISE YOUR GLASS
WATCH THE PURP
KICK THEIR...
75
12
V

72

After the game, we walked through the parking lot, futilely searching for the Galloping Gourmets—the pig-roasting group we had come to photograph.

While walking toward a cluster of campers, I noticed a lady lying in the snow while her husband hysterically accused the police standing nearby of not calling an ambulance.

Whack! I turned to see a young man get hit in the face with an ice-filled beer can and drop to the ground—which prompted his companions to begin a fist fight with the can-throwing group. Scattered fights were breaking out all over the parking lot.

It was now an hour after the game and people were still arriving for the parking-lot bash. A giant with a brilliant red beard came bounding out of his pickup truck shouting, "Where are the fights? Where are the fights?"

He stole the football from a group of players, grabbed another fellow by the shoulders and threw him to the ice, and even began baiting two Bloomington policemen until one of them fingered his mace can.

Clusters of drunks were clutching the bumpers of cars, while the equally plastered drivers tried to shake loose the unwanted passengers by spinning crazily on the glare ice that covered the parking lot. The tension resembled that of an urban riot. For the first—and only—time during my six years of photographing America at leisure, I was receiving threats simply because I had cameras.

It seemed prudent to stay near the cops, who had gathered in groups of a dozen or more. "I can't believe this," I said to one of the officers, "this is like combat."

The cop just smiled.

"This is nothing," piped up a fan, "you should have been in Pittsburgh last January after the Steelers won the Super Bowl. Thousands of people trashed the downtown. There were"—he ticked off the statistics like a sports announcer—"two hundred and thirty-three arrests and over sixty injuries, including a fractured skull suffered by a police officer."

The cops moved toward another fight. The owner of a twenty-six-thousand-dollar GMC motor home had just beaten his adversary to the ice. They were both bleeding. The cops made them break it up.

I began talking with a guest of the fellow involved in the fight. During the course of our conversation, I realized they hadn't been inside the stadium.

"I beg your pardon," I said, "you mean after coming here all the way from Nebraska, you watched the game on television in your camper?"

"You're damn right," he replied, "you go in there and you freeze your ass off. Can't see what's going on either. Every play, fifty thousand goddam people stand up in front of you. And we got our own special half-time entertainment." This he said with a wink at his wife.

I asked the next question timidly—not sure what triggers the violent streak in these men of the plains.

"But, uh, you traveled a long way?"

"Yeah," he replied, "I wouldn't miss a fucking Viking home game for anything."

74

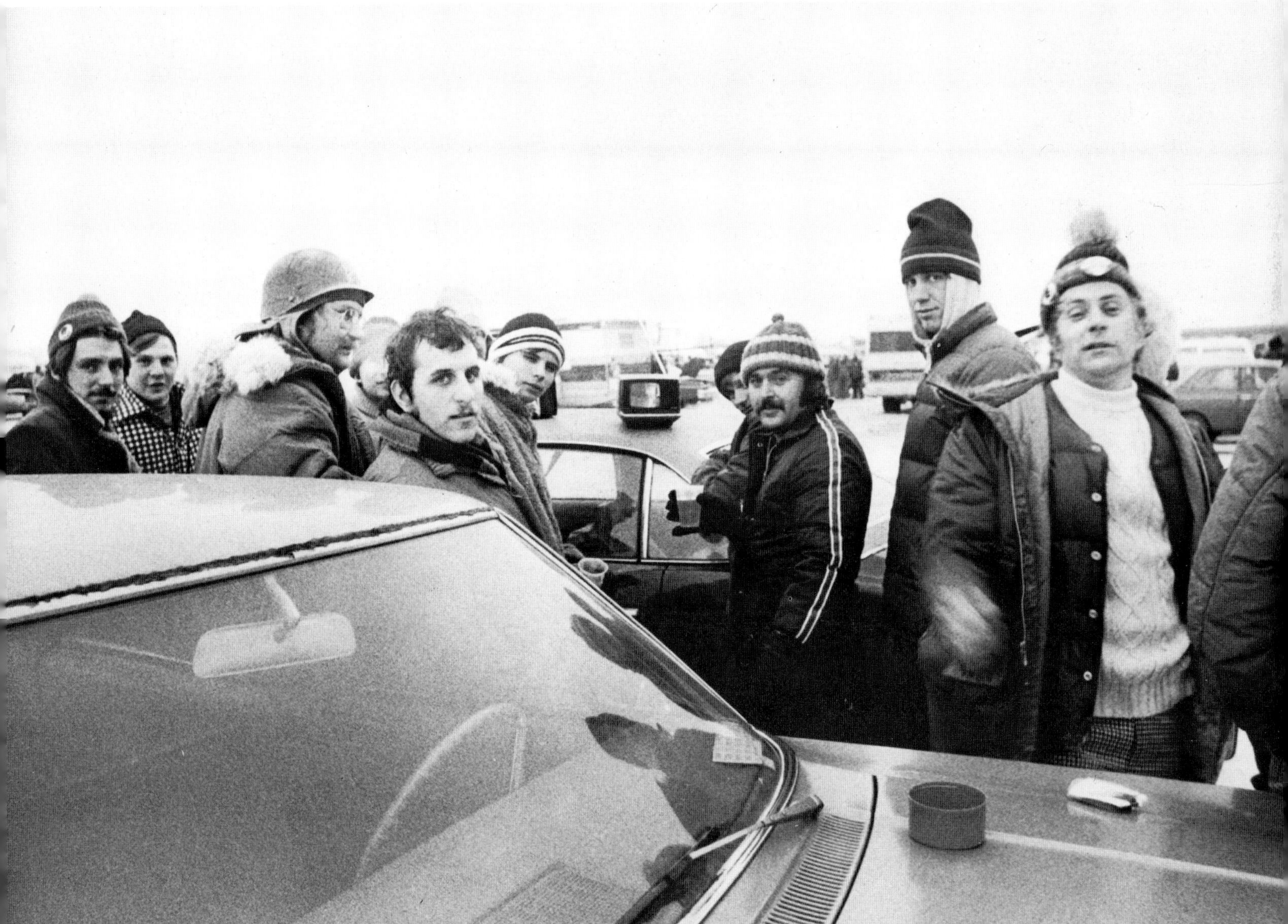

"What Do You Do in Your Spare Time?" "I Work."

At Pocono International Raceway, I attended a moto-cross seminar taught by Gary Bailey, the "Traveling Moto-Cross Professor" from California who crisscrosses the country spreading the gospel of moto-cross. The rain beating on the tin roof of the building, where we had taken refuge, had slowed down the session. One participant asked the other students if he could go first when the exercises resumed.

He explained that his wife was showing their cats at a feline beauty pageant being held at a nearby resort. He had to pick her up at 6:00 P.M. and then drive back to Philadelphia to watch his daughter compete in a baton-twirling contest. He would then return to the Poconos for the American Motorcycle Association qualifying race the next day—but he had to be back in Philadelphia in time for their monthly bridge game.

"What do you do in your spare time?" joked one of the cyclists.

"I work," replied the man.

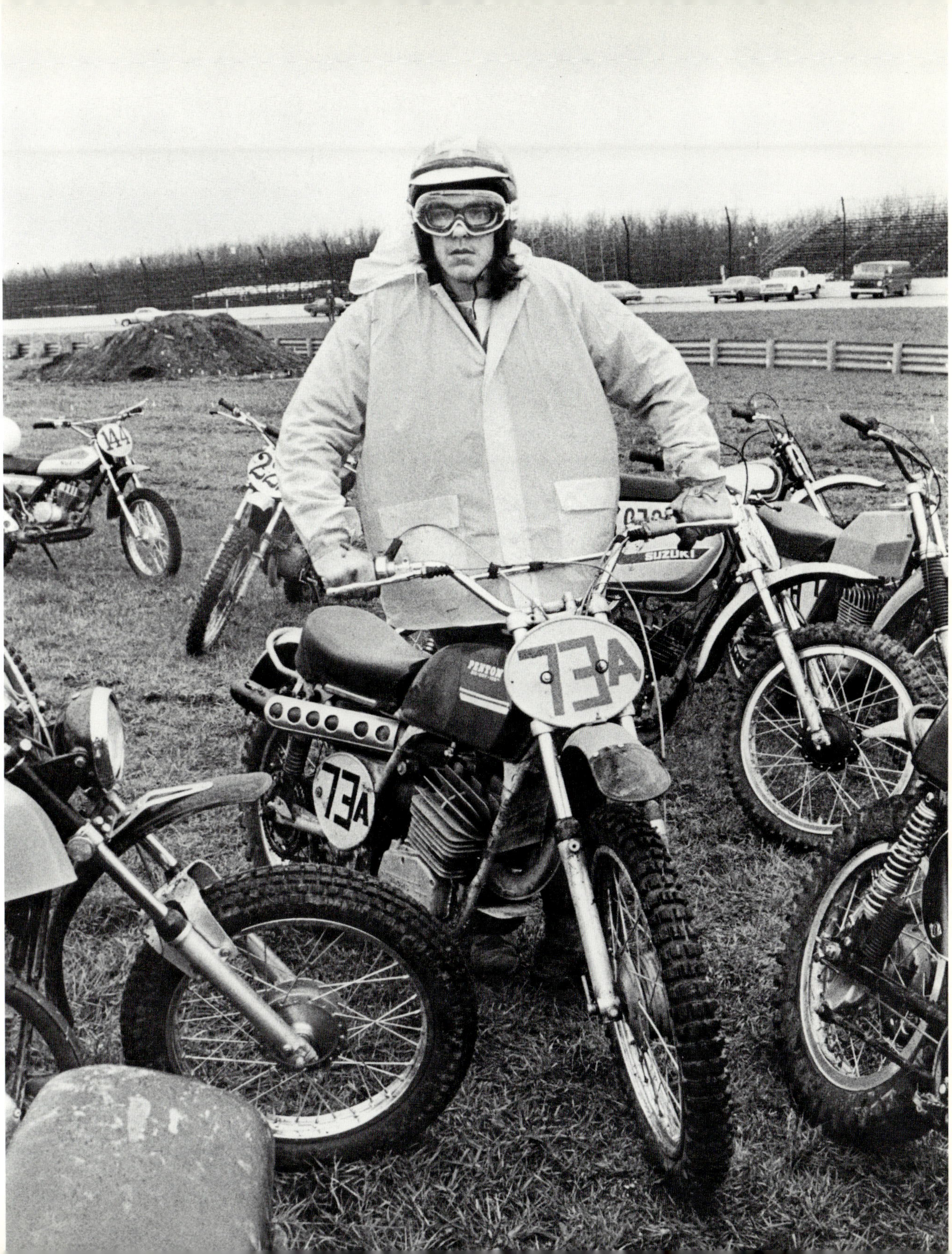
144
SUZUKI
73A

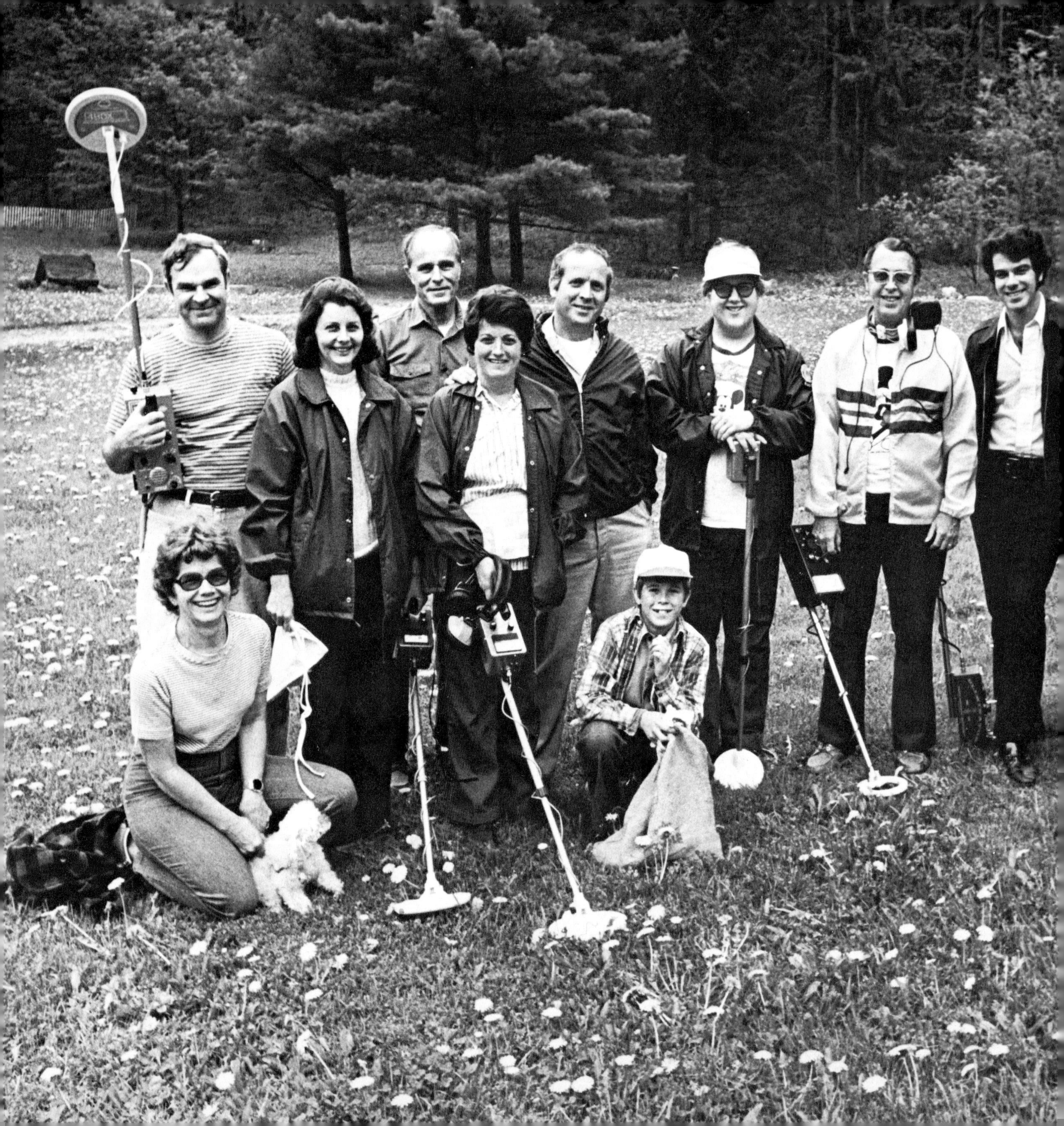

"I have a regular job," said Lee Couchman (second from right), of Richfield Springs, New York. "I'm a packer in the shipping room of a furniture manufacturer. It isn't the kind of job you would bounce out of bed in the morning and say, 'Boy, I can hardly wait to get there.' It's a job. That's that. It puts groceries on the table.

"Any seven-to-four or eight-to-five job has a degree of monotony to it, particularly when you do it day in and day out, year after year. You've got to have other things to help you keep your sanity. Of course, a lot of people can sit and watch television or sit and drink beer, but I'm a little more high-strung, I guess; I've got to be doing things."

Lee enjoys artifact hunting with a metal detector, a sport he's been doing for sixteen years, and he's a member of the Central New York Artifact Recovery Society (facing page).

"The appeal of metal detecting is that there's always the possibility of striking a real bonanza," said Lee. "But it's a real long shot. So you fall back to intrinsic values—something akin to finding the little token in the Crackerjack box when you were a kid. It's the satisfaction of finding something. I can dig a lot of gosh darn stuff that most people would call junk and because it's a little older or something, it's fascinating to me."

In addition to metal detecting, Lee and his wife enjoy a large number of other leisure activities. There's snowmobiling ("an activity that helps break up the winter") as well as water skiing, kayaking, and bicycling. The Couchmans also collect bottles, and Lee used to do a lot of flying.

"I've had a pilot's license for well over thirty years," he said, "but the expense of it now prohibits us from doing that. So I'm going to get into hang gliding. It's a cheaper way to do it.

"Back a few years we were a different kind of breed," he mused. "Now I find that a lot of people are getting into things that were kind of my sole territory. Like scuba diving. When I first really got into diving, I was considered a little crazy by the rank and file of people. But now most everyone understands that it isn't a novelty. It's an activity that a lot of people engage in."

Lee has also been into spelunking and mountain climbing—activities he particularly enjoyed with his oldest son.

"My kid has been ape over caving since he was twelve years old," said Lee. "Now he's into photography and has been heavily into macro-photography. He and his wife have been cataloguing all the wild flowers in the United States.

"They have quite an extensive slide collection, with the wild flowers catalogued according to the common name and the Latin name. He's now presenting the slides to groups, accompanied by a tape-recorded background—making quite a production out of it.

"This spring they traveled to the Smoky Mountains to get a shot of a certain wild orchid. He shoots a lot. He'll shoot dozens of exposures and pick out the best one."

"Is this a part of his job?" I asked.

"Oh, no, he's in the Army," said Lee, "a staff sergeant. He's a helicopter mechanic."

Millions of Americans have turned their leisure into work as a way of coping with the increasing amount of free time.

In fact, leisure activity is often referred to as "work." When I met with the artifact hunters near Ilion, New York, reference was made repeatedly to work: "Where will we work today?" or "I'm looking forward to working at the old stagecoach stop."

In a field near the Thousand Island Bridge in upstate New York, I photographed the Thousand Islands Highland Games competition. From all over the United States, hundreds of people dressed in kilts had converged on an open field for three days of competition in such Scottish activities as bagpipe playing and highland dancing.

82

The contestants were deadly serious. One corporate president left his island estate in the Seaway and flew by private helicopter to the event.

Dressed in a resplendent highland costume and cradling a custom-made pipe that gleamed, he made his way to the bagpipe competition, walked up on the stage, and played his selections.

His effort rated only a disappointing third place, however, and thoroughly crestfallen, he returned to his helicopter and flew back to his island.

For others, however, there was the heady feeling of being a winner. As the day concluded, those who had persevered proudly wore their ribbons.

"This can be loads of fun," said a contestant, "if you're willing to really work at it."

T he Mummy Dusters of Philadelphia, Pennsylvania, spend their leisure cleaning and repairing objects in the vast collection of the University of Pennsylvania Museum. Every Thursday evening, the group of volunteers meet to repair Peruvian pottery, sort Turkish carpets, polish metal weapons from Africa, catalogue American Indian artifacts, clean solid gold vases for display, and—occasionally—actually dust five-thousand-year-old mummies.

"I think the most memorable night was the session where we uncrated and moved to a new location some bodies of North American Indians found in the western part of the United States," said Dennis McClellan (right, shown identifying skulls). "They were preserved naturally, by being exposed to the elements, so they had much more realistic features than the wrapped Egyptian mummies do—something like beef jerky. The hair was intact, there were beads. I remember one especially, a mother holding a child. It gets you at first . . . but then it becomes so fascinating."

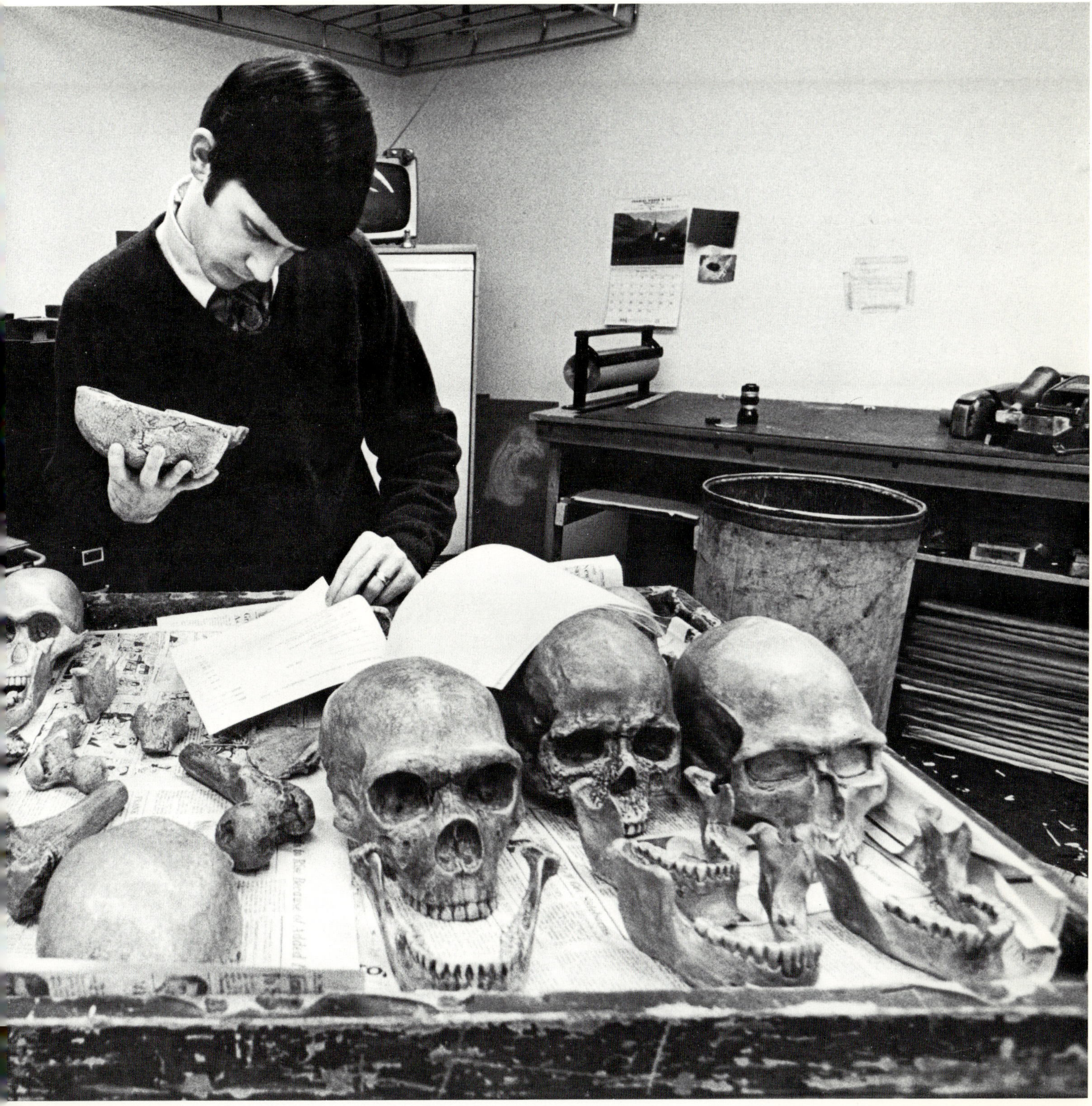

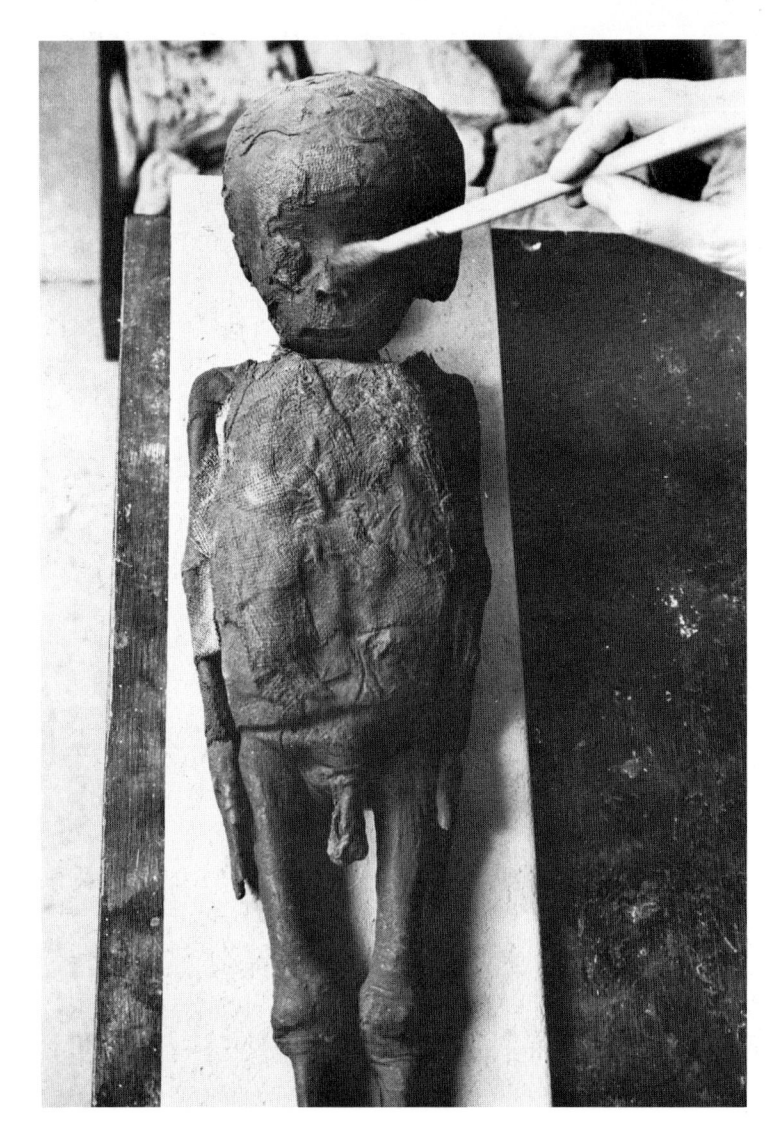

"The Mummy Dusters is not a student thing—it never was," explained Carolyn Dosker, assistant registrar of the museum. "Some of our people are in business, some are teachers, there's a nurse, a laboratory technician, a Pennsylvania state trooper, a career Navy man."

There's very little turnover among the twenty-five members of the group, and little interest in having part-time members. Potential members hear about the group from other members. "It's a situation where people have to be shown how to do things," said Mrs. Dosker; "we just couldn't handle a large group of people."

The Mummy Dusters work in many different areas of the museum, utilizing their particular skills and interests. D. W. Gould, a retired engineer, began cataloguing the museum's collection of tops and yo-yos, which had been gathered by archaeologists and anthropologists during their expeditions under the aegis of the museum. His interest in tops continued; today he's considered an authority on the subject, author of *The Top* (Clarkson N. Potter, New York, 1973).

The Mummy Dusters look upon themselves as a special group, very committed to their work at the museum. Come rain or sleet, the Dusters are at their post every week. After spending a night among the treasures of the past, the group gathers for refreshments and spirited talk about other cultures and other years.

A few, however, were discussing a different matter the evening I saw them. "We were talking about an emblem for our group," said Mrs. Dosker. "I've always thought the emblem could be a mummy with crossed feather dusters."

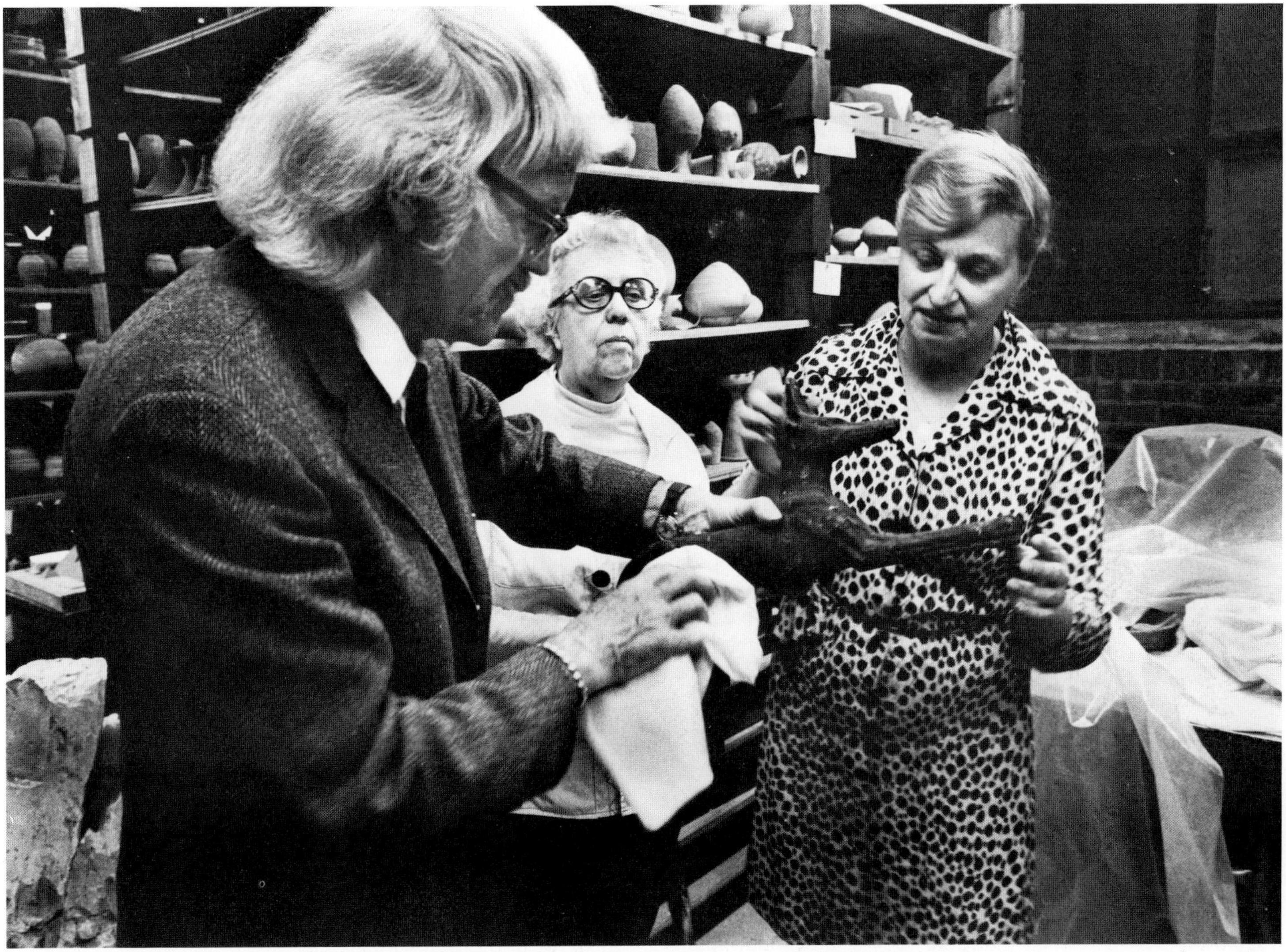

Leisure as Identity

Early in my documentation of America at leisure, I approached a smartly dressed young man at a resort in the Pocono Mountains. After chatting with him for a few minutes, and ascertaining that he skied with a passion, I asked him, "What do you do?"

"I ski," he replied, as if I were oblivious to the patch-festooned ski jacket he was wearing. And he began a litany of the slopes he had skied.

"No," I interjected, "I mean, what do you *do?*"

"Well, I'm into photography," he said. He tapped one of my Nikons and added, "But not like you are—ha, ha. And during the summer I shoot skeet."

"I mean what do you do for a living," I said.

"Oh," he replied, somewhat deflated, "I'm a computer systems analyst for the Carrier Corporation in Syracuse."

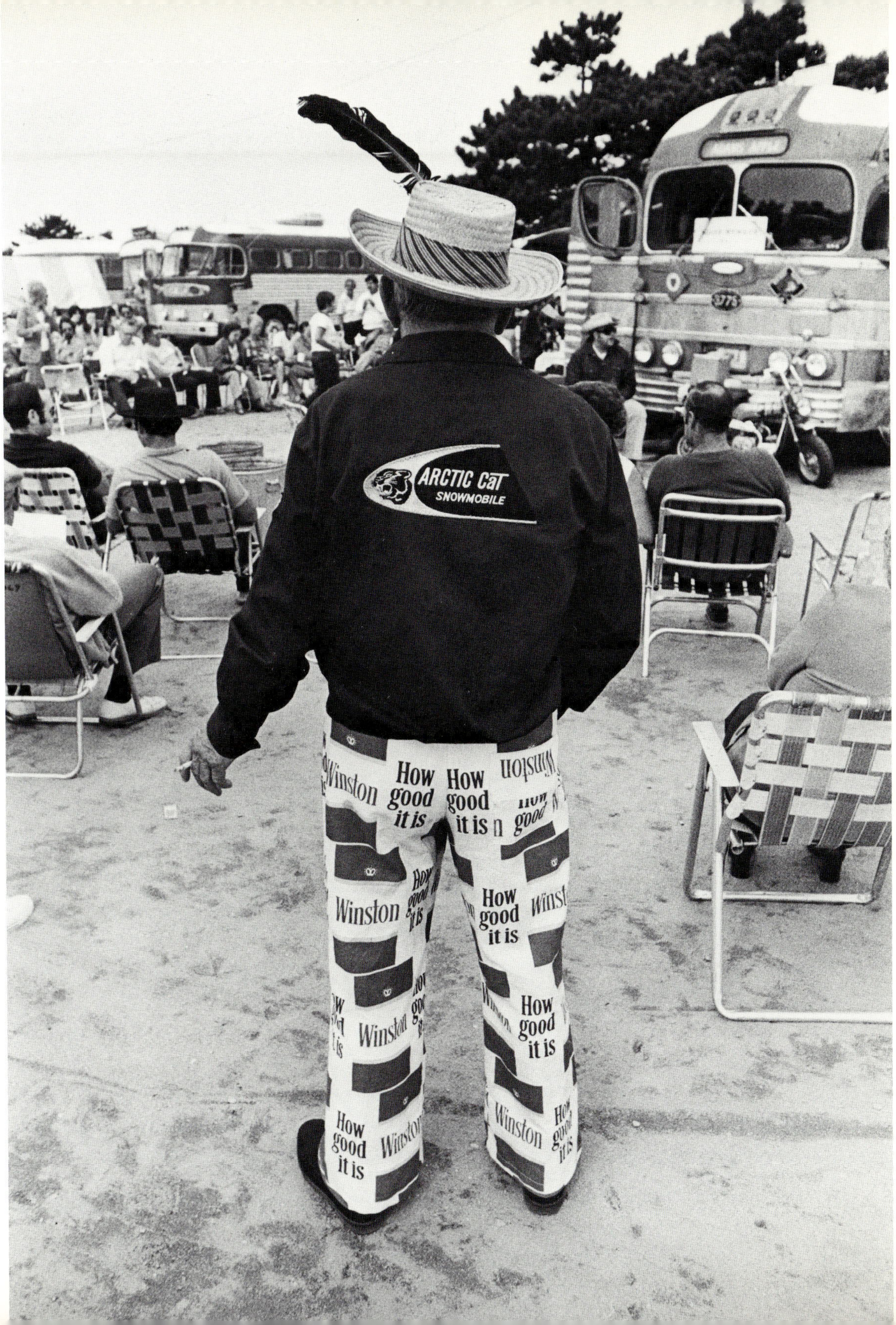
ARCTIC CAT
SNOWMOBILE
How good it is
Winston

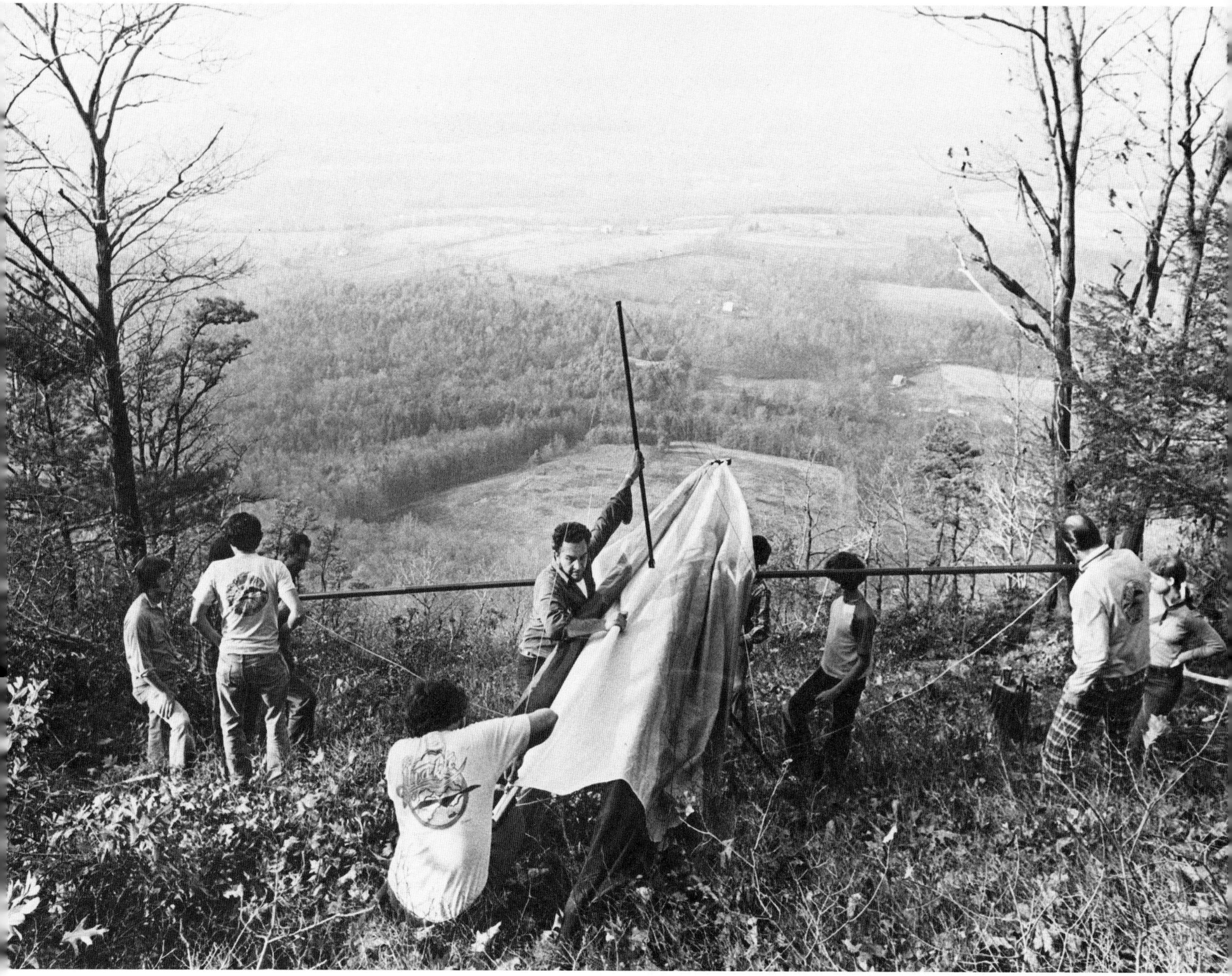

Ask Burton Aulisio (above) of Dalton, Pennsylvania, what he does, he'll reply, "I fly."

He's a hang-gliding fanatic (in the terminology of the sport it's simply called "flying"); professionally, he's a butcher. But he's a butcher so he can hang glide.

"I earn my living as a meat cutter—a butcher—with a large supermarket chain," says Burton. "It's not a bad job—it's a trade; and a universal job so I can get up and leave anytime I want and go hang gliding anywhere in the world.

"People have got to eat, so I believe I'm as safe as anybody. I can walk into a supermarket in Arizona or California and say, 'I'll work thirty hours a week' and the other hours I'll be on some mountain flying. I don't think I'll ever get tired of flying."

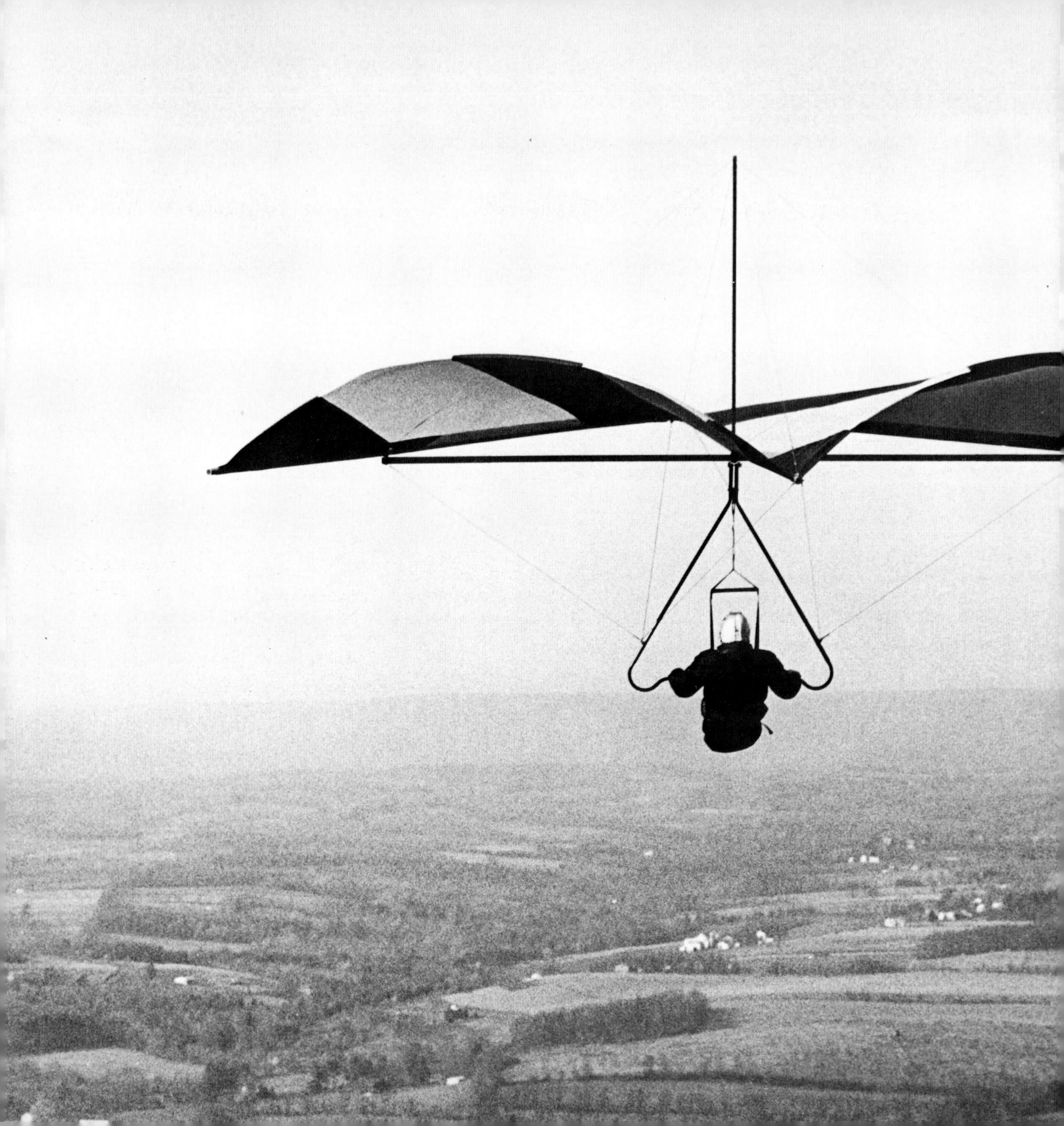

Burton's car displays United States Hang Gliding Association decals, he subscribes to hang-gliding publications, and he wears hang-gliding T-shirts.

"The appeal of hang gliding is almost unexplainable," he said. "Words can't describe the sensation of flying. It's a total sense of freedom, because you're so high. No one's going to bother you. And you're floating there—sitting there watching everything go by and all you feel is the wind. The appeal is the sense of freedom. At least that's my inspiration. There's nothing like it on the ground, and that's where I've been in the past twenty-one years.

"It's an addiction," he added. "To see this done before your very eyes is so flabbergasting you could talk the Pope into becoming a Protestant. It's that overwhelming. It's coming to the point where the wives are starting to learn themselves. It grabs you.

"My best flight to date was at a place called Wyalusing Rocks, which is about a thousand feet high. It's a cliff launch where you run off a rock, literally, fly over a river—which is nice—and land in the fields.

"The ultimate, I guess, would be being released from a balloon at thirty thousand feet and staying up in the winds for days."

James Russell of Kannapolis, North Carolina, created an identity by adding lights to his motorcycle until he had a unique vehicle. Wherever he goes (Daytona Beach, Florida, in these photos) a crowd immediately gathers. He's had postcards printed that have a color photo of himself and the cycle on the front. The back of the card reads: "8th original designed vehicle. 600 lights, operated on 4 special batteries. Lights increase weight of motorcycle to over 1000 lbs." Since the card was printed, he added a stereo, television, and various other amenities.

He told me that lately he'd been able to support himself on trips by selling autographed postcards to the crowds he attracted.

As I traveled around, I made a point of asking people at various events if they knew about the guy with the far-out motorcycle, and a remarkable number of people had either seen the rig or heard about it.

At a stock-car race in Darlington, South Carolina, a pit crewman confessed to his experience with James Russell's creation.

"I was driving toward Daytona late one night on interstate ninety-five," he said, "and that thing went around me and I damn near died. I heard this music and looked up and here come all these bright lights—I thought it was some damn UFO that was gonna suck me up and take me to outer space. I had to pull over and just sit there for darn near twenty minutes. My heart was goin' so that I was nearly too weak to drive."

94

95

96

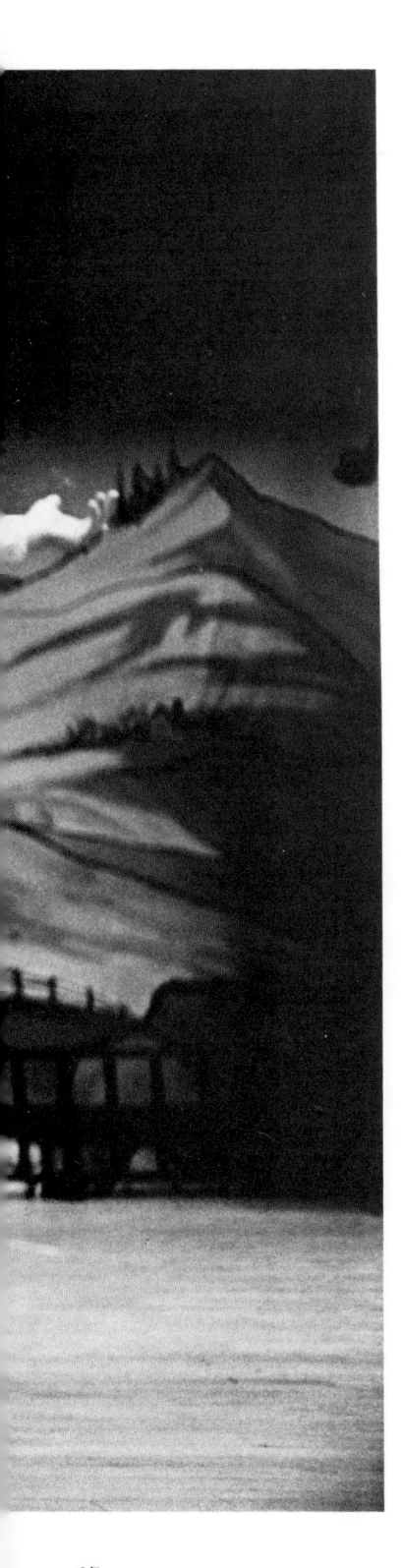

Identity through leisure is not limited to mastering a death-defying sport or building a unique motorcycle.

These people are the cast of *The Sound of Music,* a production staged by the Abington Players, a community little-theater group in northeastern Pennsylvania.

The Players have been performing continuously for twenty-five years; recent productions have included *Six Rms Riv Vu, Music Man, Lion in Winter, All My Sons,* and *Homecoming.* The group is open to all—it costs one dollar to join.

Rita Julius of Glenburn, Pennsylvania, directed *The Sound of Music.* "I've been doing theater since I was eight," she said. "I'm sixty now—that's a long time. I've always loved the theater, but after two summers in summer stock, I decided I didn't want a career in theater. I didn't want to live that way—you're either starving or dirty or tired—so I became involved in amateur theater and it's one of the nicest avocations there is.

"Little theater is stimulating recreation. You're trying within the confines of a play to get these people to work together and have a feeling for each other. It's exciting. It's like a group encounter session. You try to get people to bring to it what they have—to let them create a character within the role.

"I try to run rehearsals as professionally as I know how, and I make a lot of enemies this way. What's the point of doing it unless you can do it the best possible way? When we rehearse, we rehearse. I'm sort of a tyrant."

"I've always felt that most people like to act or are acting," she added. "This is what's fascinating. Once they've committed themselves to a part, everybody wants to excel. This is *hard work*. There's always a great *esprit de corps* that happens for every show. Regular professions have no meaning. It's just how much ability you have in stagecraft.

99

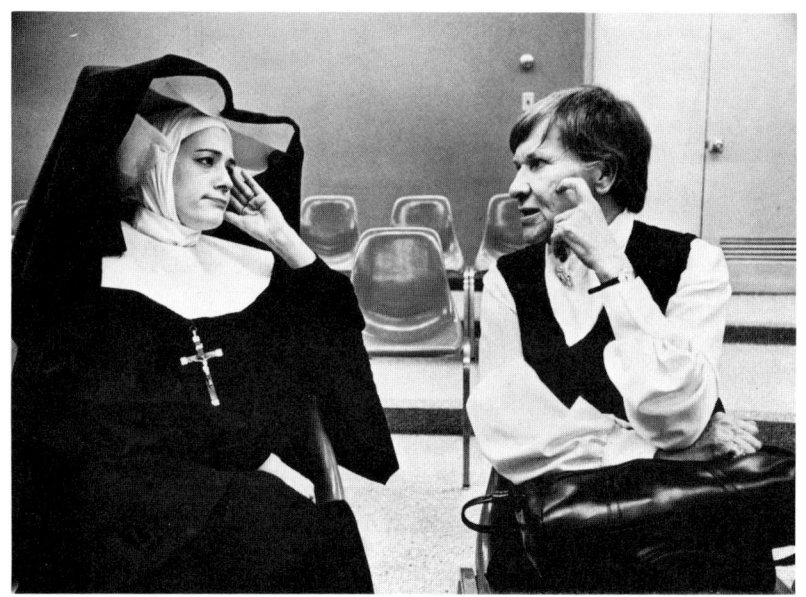

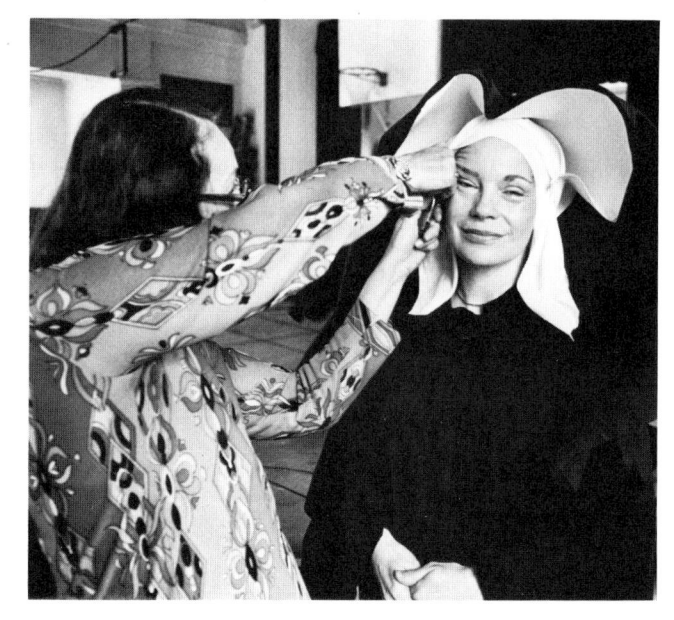

"People treat this very seriously. It's not a 'So what?' atmosphere," Rita said. "You feel terrible if you blow a line. And if you're going good, there's the glorious emotion when the audience is with you. It's very teary backstage."

100

101

102

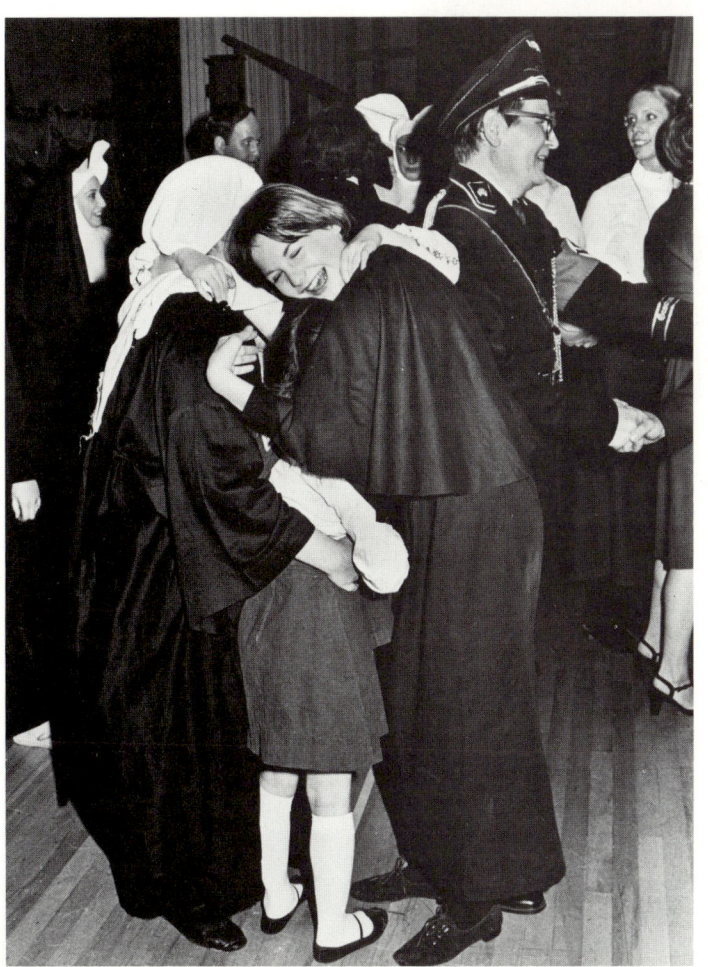

At the after-show party, a surgeon—who found little theater an ideal respite from the operating room—said to me, "It's a marvelous feeling to be able to 'be something' without going through years of study plus having to put up with the negative aspects of the specialty."

Indeed, "acting out a role" is an integral part of many leisure activities, but it wasn't until I visited the Fall Shoot of the National Muzzle-Loading Rifle Association in Friendship, Indiana, that I saw how the biggest leisure boom ever, the changing attitudes, the intensity of leisure activities and identity through leisure could coalesce into a way of life.

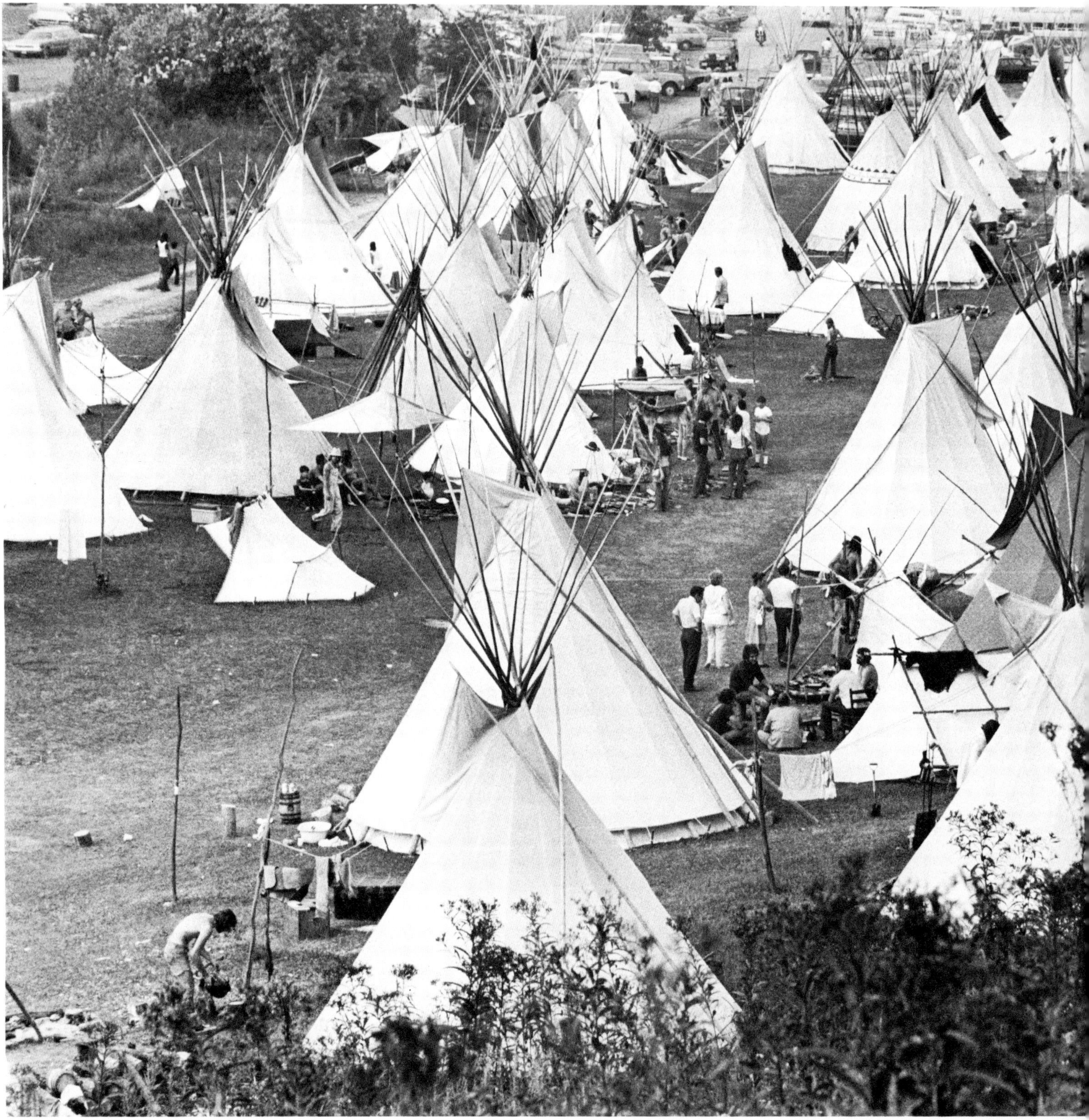

Leisure as Lifestyle

I had expected to find members of the NMLRA blasting away at targets with early American muzzle-loading firearms. I didn't expect to find a frontier village, as painstakingly re-created as a Hollywood movie set.

The muzzle loaders in the "primitive area" lived in tepees and dressed in authentic French and Indian war garb. In real life they were schoolteacher, photographer, electrician, salesman, architect, physician, truck driver, newspaperman, machinist. At Friendship, occupations were irrelevant—they were all just frontiersmen.

"You can't step out of an Airstream trailer and shoot a flintlock rifle. It just doesn't work," said Andy Baker of Cincinnati, Ohio, "so people began trying to master this whole other culture.

"We'd like to be part of a different era, I suppose. There's a lot of us that aren't particularly satisfied with what's happening in America today, and we think there were times in the past when it would have been more emotionally satisfying. So if we take a couple weeks off and do this, it gives a nice break before you go back to the grind.

"But the whole damn thing is just a game and it's just how good can you play it," he added. "You can play it to the absolute hilt or you can play it part way. We feel, up here, we're playing it to the hilt.

"The work that you have to do today is sometimes pretty repetitious and not too satisfying. Down here the same thing never happens twice in a day. It's a chance to play show and tell on a grown-up basis.

"Right now, our whole thing is kind of jumbled up. We are hoping eventually to have things in sections, so you'll be able to go from one century to another century and back and forth and then finally come home.

"And this will give you a kind of total environment. If you've read *Future Shock,* by Toffler, it talks about the 'enclaves of the past' and so forth. Well, you're sitting in the middle of one of them right now, in case you're interested in what they're going to turn out like."

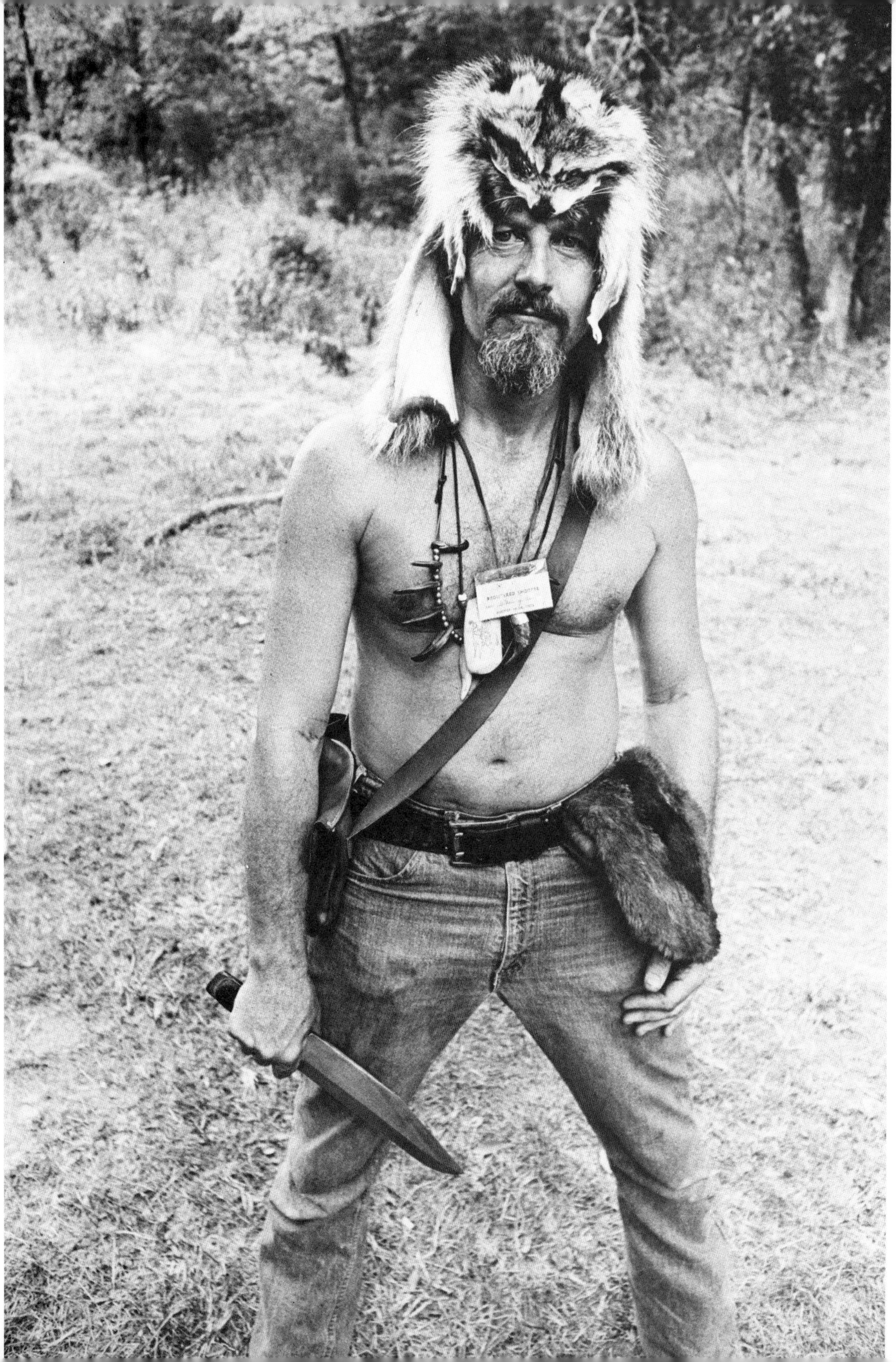

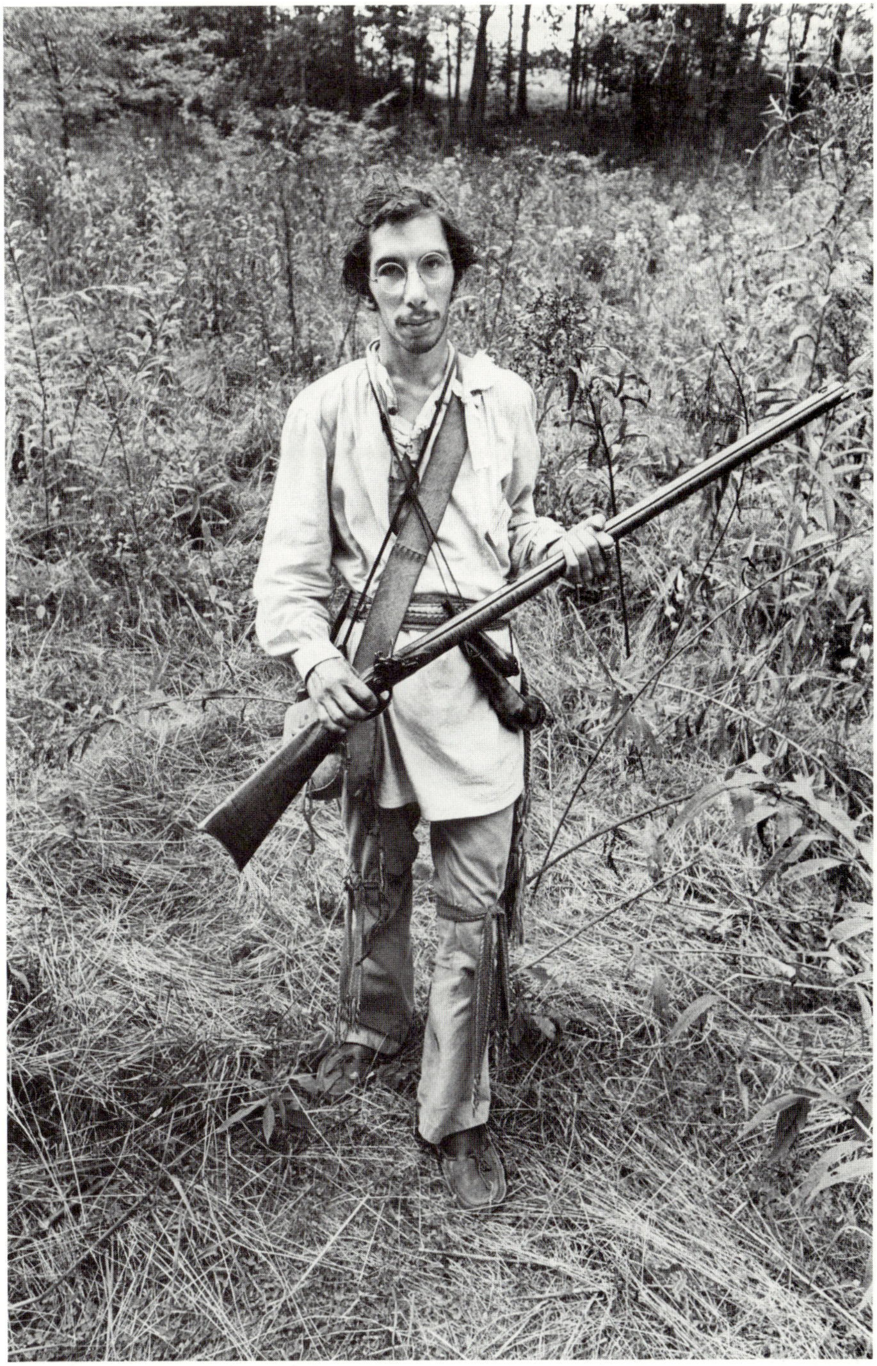

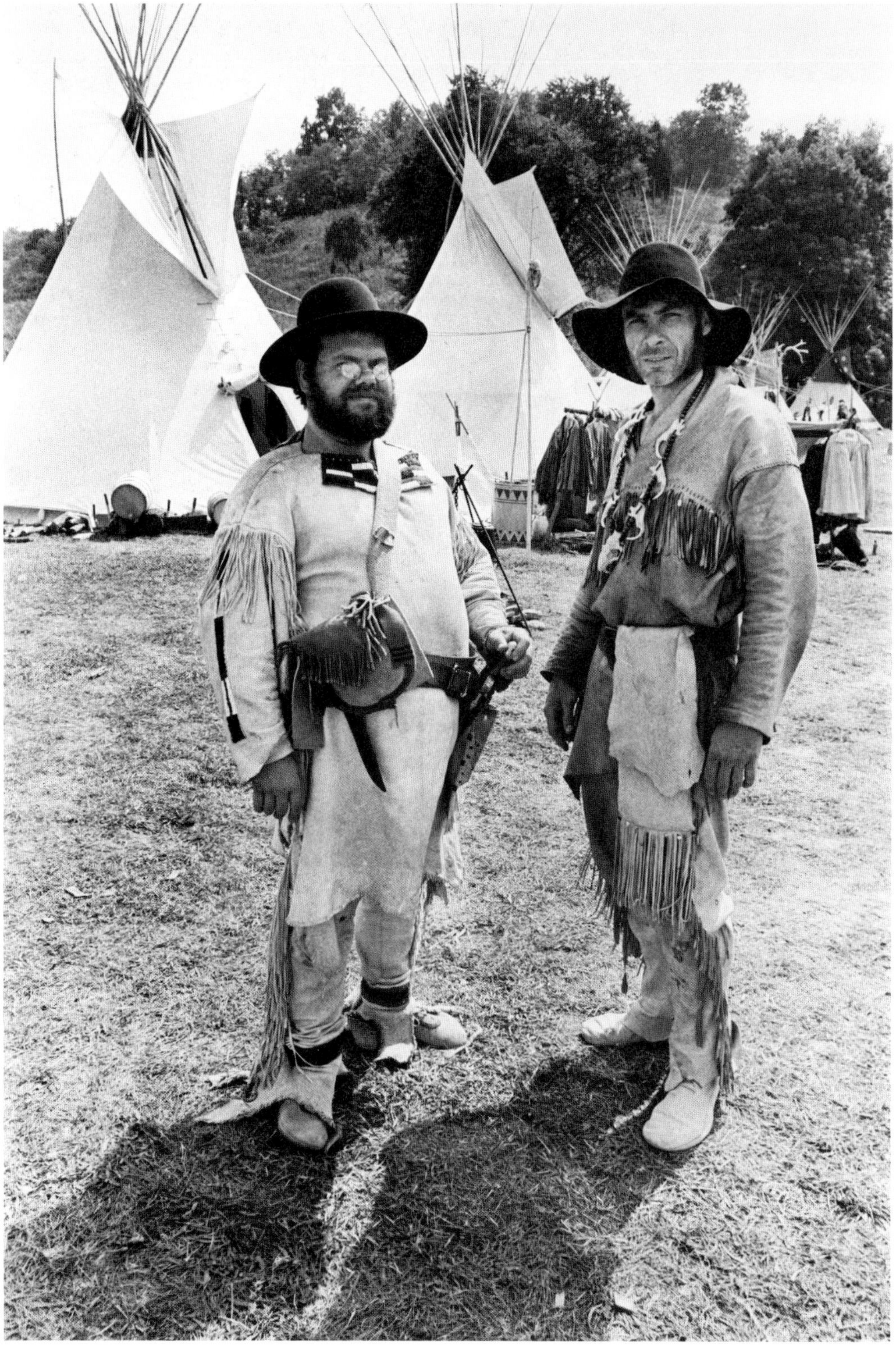

109

If the muzzle loaders were "still kind of jumbled up," another group we met had their act absolutely together. The Society for Creative Anachronism—whose members re-create the Middle Ages—consists of four "kingdoms" that cover the United States. The kingdoms are divided into a complex hierarchy of shires, baronies, provinces, and cantons ruled by an assortment of monarchs, seneschals, and princes.

The organizational expertise reflects the makeup of the SCA. "Basically, people in the society seem to be college or postgraduate people who are fairly well educated," explained one member. "A remarkable number of our people are professionals—especially in the sciences."

We met a group from Østgardr (Greater New York City) of the Eastrealm at Dick's Castle, an actual unfinished castle which sits high above the Hudson River directly across from West Point.

"The society almost is a lifestyle, because this is where all your emotional energy is being put," said Lady Catherine Fitzroy, Ambassadress of Bhakail (Philadelphia). "The job is something you do to make a living so you can afford to go to events and make fancy clothes. It almost gets like that. I'm a research technician in cancer research at Einstein Hospital in Philadelphia. That's a long way from the SCA!

"There's quite a difference between Karen Himmelsbach, the lady in a dirty lab coat and bluejeans, and Lady Catherine Fitzroy, the Ambassadress of Bhakail," she adds. "I actually stand up straighter when I'm Lady Catherine; but, of course, the clothes demand it. One's speech becomes more forsoothly, one's manners improve tremendously—it's much nicer.

"The culture shock isn't too bad, either. It's kind of hard to maintain this sort of thing for an awfully long time. Two-day events are about adequate, and then you start missing a hot bath.

"I suppose if I could get paid for doing something like the SCA, it might be interesting. But then it would be work."

From a simple beginning—the society started when a medieval-literature major in Berkeley decided she wanted to hold a tourney and invited all her friends—the SCA has

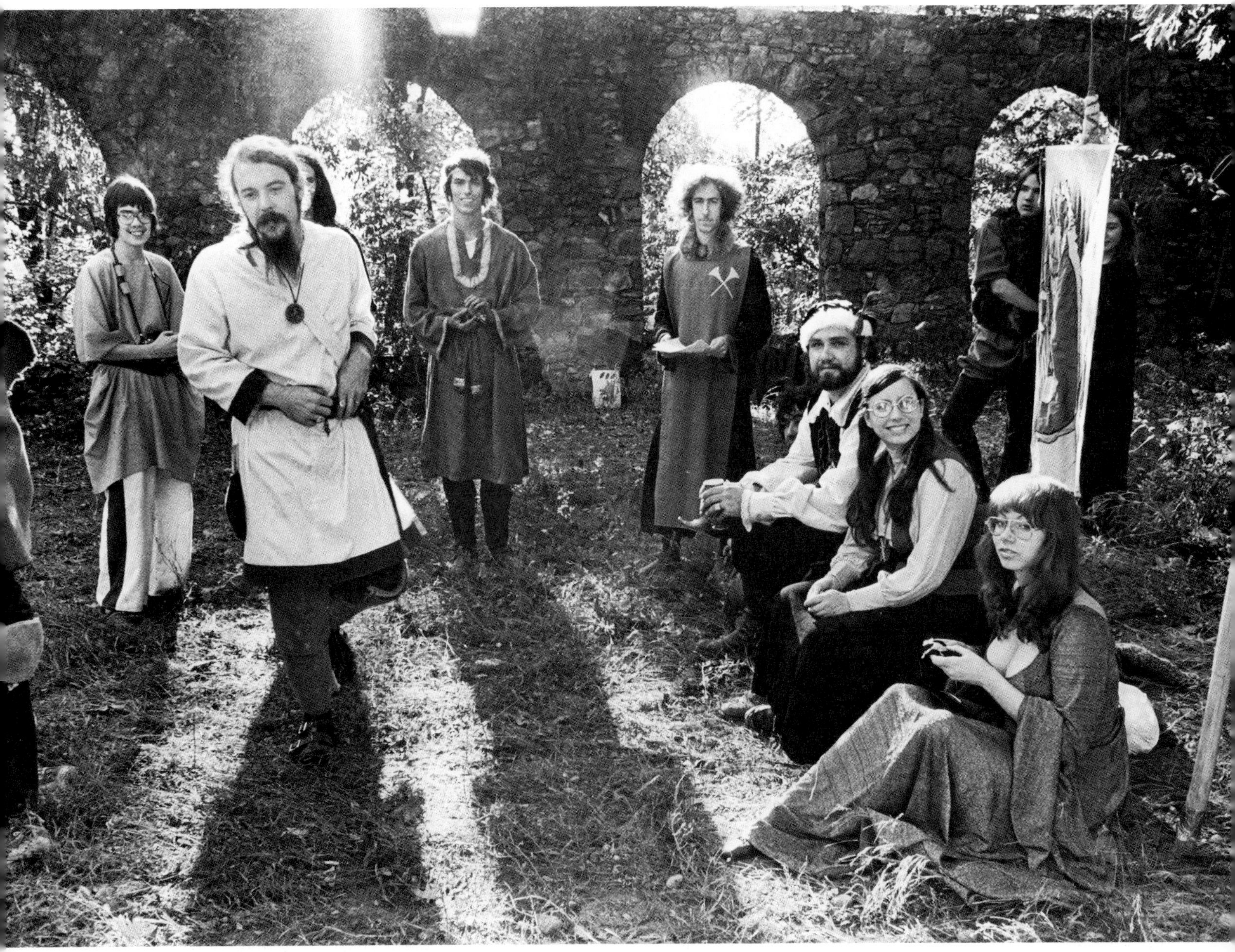

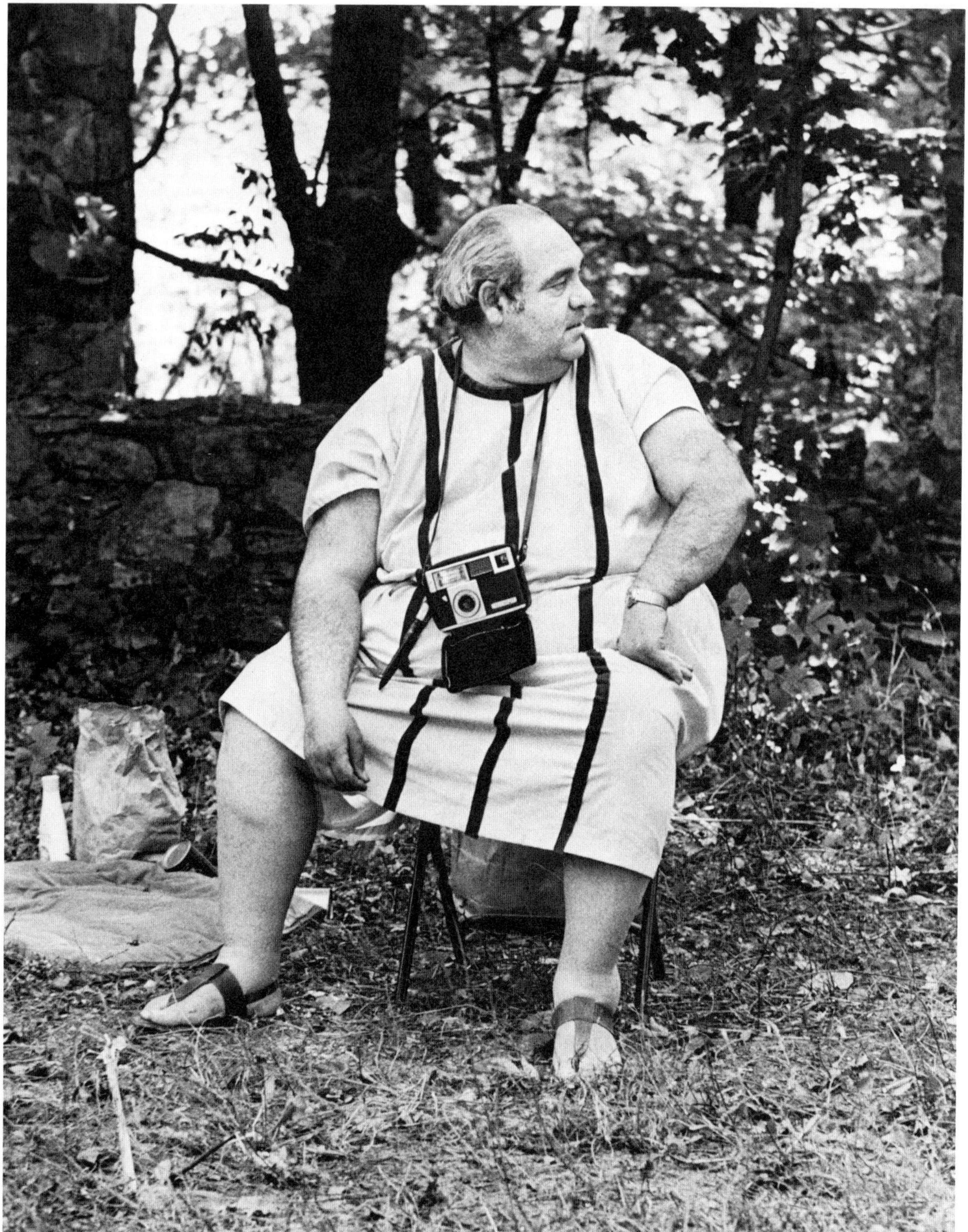

evolved into an organization that produces such elaborate events as a week-long, full-scale war between the kingdoms.

"I've been with the society going into seven years now," said Sir Garenhir of Ness (in the twentieth century, William Van Ness, a manager with the New York State Bureau of Unemployment). "I enjoy the fact that there's an actual life that I'm living. It's not just a simple activity like bowling where you go out and do it and then keep doing it if you enjoy it.

"It's a process of subcreation in a literary sense. You create your own character and then live his life through whatever adventures or nonadventures that he may run into."

Sir Garenhir started as a barbarian, then civilized himself. Later he became a freelance mercenary, was eventually knighted, and then settled down to running a feudal fief in the province.

"The society takes up every weekend and at least eight or so hours over the week," he said. "Since I'm in charge of the entire New York unit, we have various political and interpersonal things I have to be taking care of—like who's fighting with whom. What thing might develop into a problem if it's not stepped on very quickly. Where are we going to hold the next event? Who's going to be appointed to what vacant office?

"This is the first time I've found myself in a lifestyle. It wasn't intended when I joined the society, but here it is."

The essence of the Society for Creative Anachronism is the fighting, since rank within the group is determined through trial by combat.

"I like to fight," said Master Frederick of Holland (Fred Hollander, a structural chemist); "it keeps me in shape. I enjoy the feeling of skill in being able to maneuver my environment when I do fight. I like to win and do it fairly often—but that's not why I fight. I fight because a good fight just gets me so high, it's a good thing.

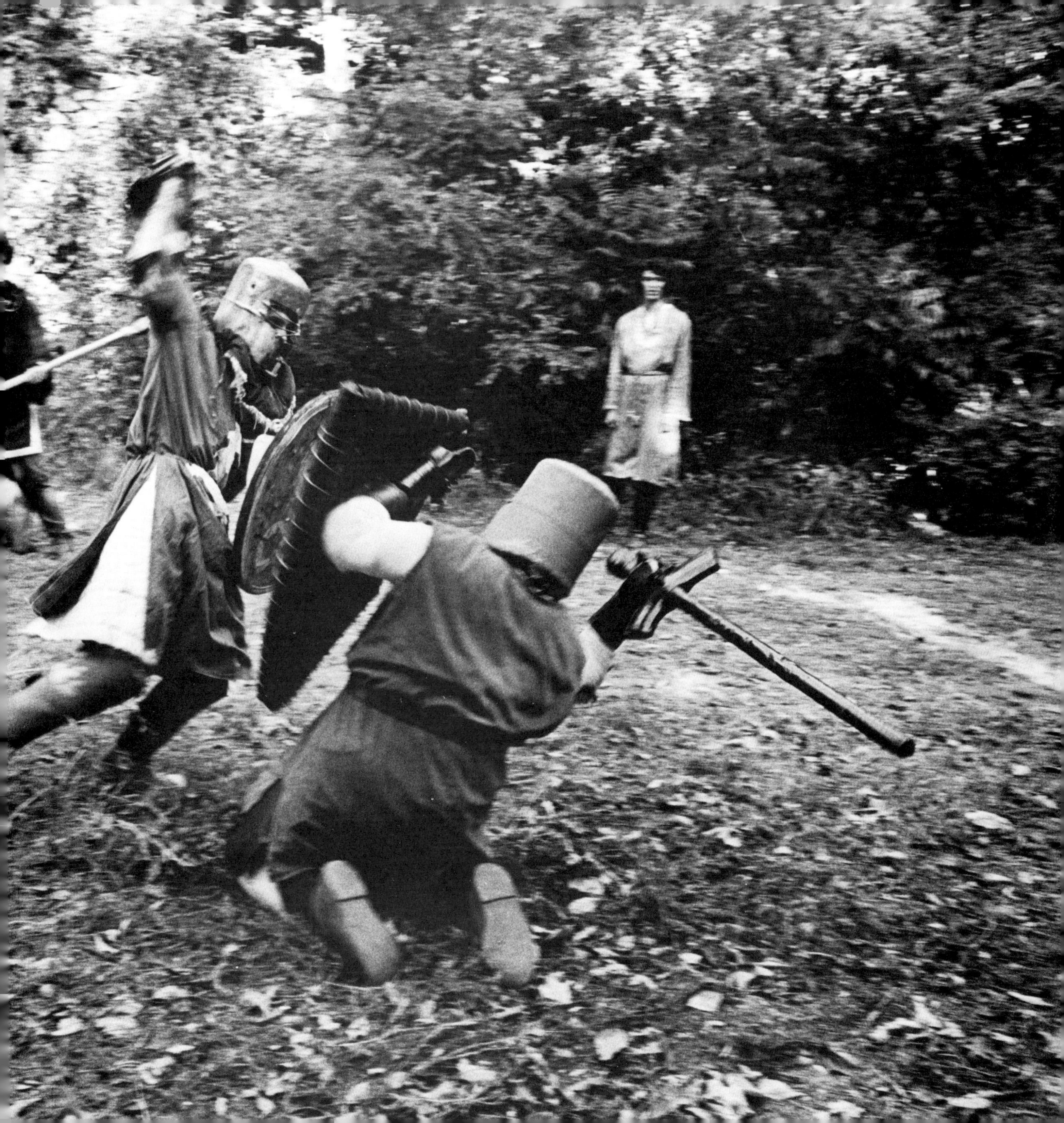

116

"But I don't think we bring an intensity to this that's unusual," said Fred. "Have you ever seen the people who go out for amateur baseball? They're very intense. I think people bring intensity to their leisure-time activities. People do take this seriously, but it's different only in form. I don't think there are any particular psychological differences between this and, say, the office baseball team—as far as the use of leisure time is concerned.

"Part of the fun is getting your game down right," he added. "It's a game. It's not like any other, but it's basically a game and as long as it's fun to play, you play it as deep as you want. And when it becomes not fun to play anymore, I, at any rate, find out what's causing it not to be fun anymore and do something about it.

"I'm going to be taking a break in a couple weeks. I've been to tourneys for over a month now every weekend. And in two weeks I am taking a break and am going to visit some friends in the twentieth century. Just relax for a whole weekend. I'm not going to do anything to prepare for a tourney, or clean up after a tourney, or anything to do with the Society for Creative Anachronism. I really want to relax."

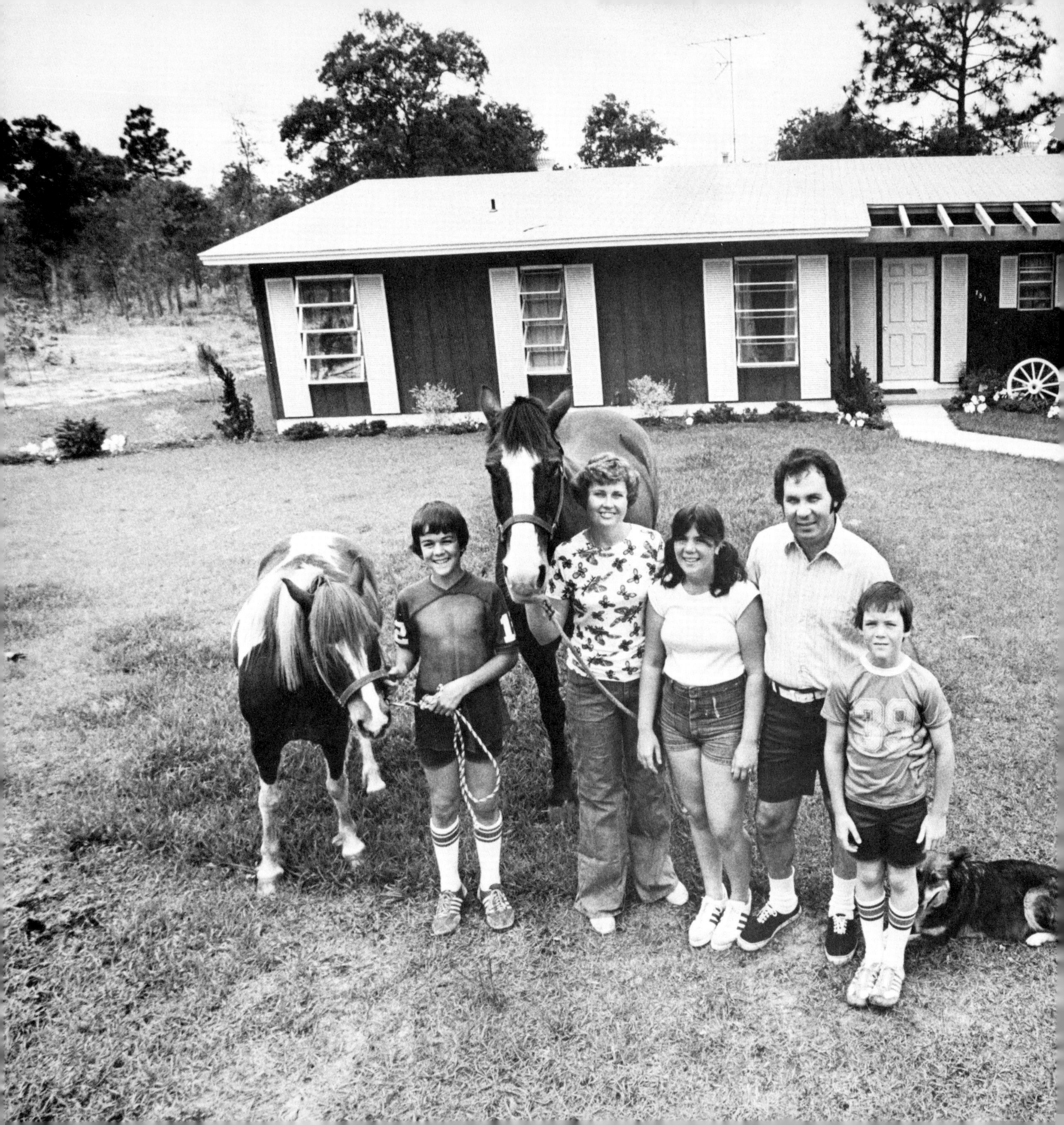

At Pine Ridge Estates, near Ocala, Florida, there is a development devoted to horses. Dubbed an "Equestrian Community," Pine Ridge has 4,800 homesites planned for eleven thousand acres. On the largest properties, a homeowner can stable up to six adult horses—smaller lots will accommodate two. There are twenty-eight miles of equestrian trails, ten parks, and a ninety-four-acre showplace that features an elaborate riding center, stables, tack room, show ring, and viewing terrace.

"We've built communities, such as Marco Island, in which golf and boating keynote the lifestyle," said Frank E. Mackle, Jr., president of the Deltona Corporation (which built Pine Ridge) and past president of the Horsemen's Benevolent and Protective Association. "At Pine Ridge the mainstream of community life will center around horses."

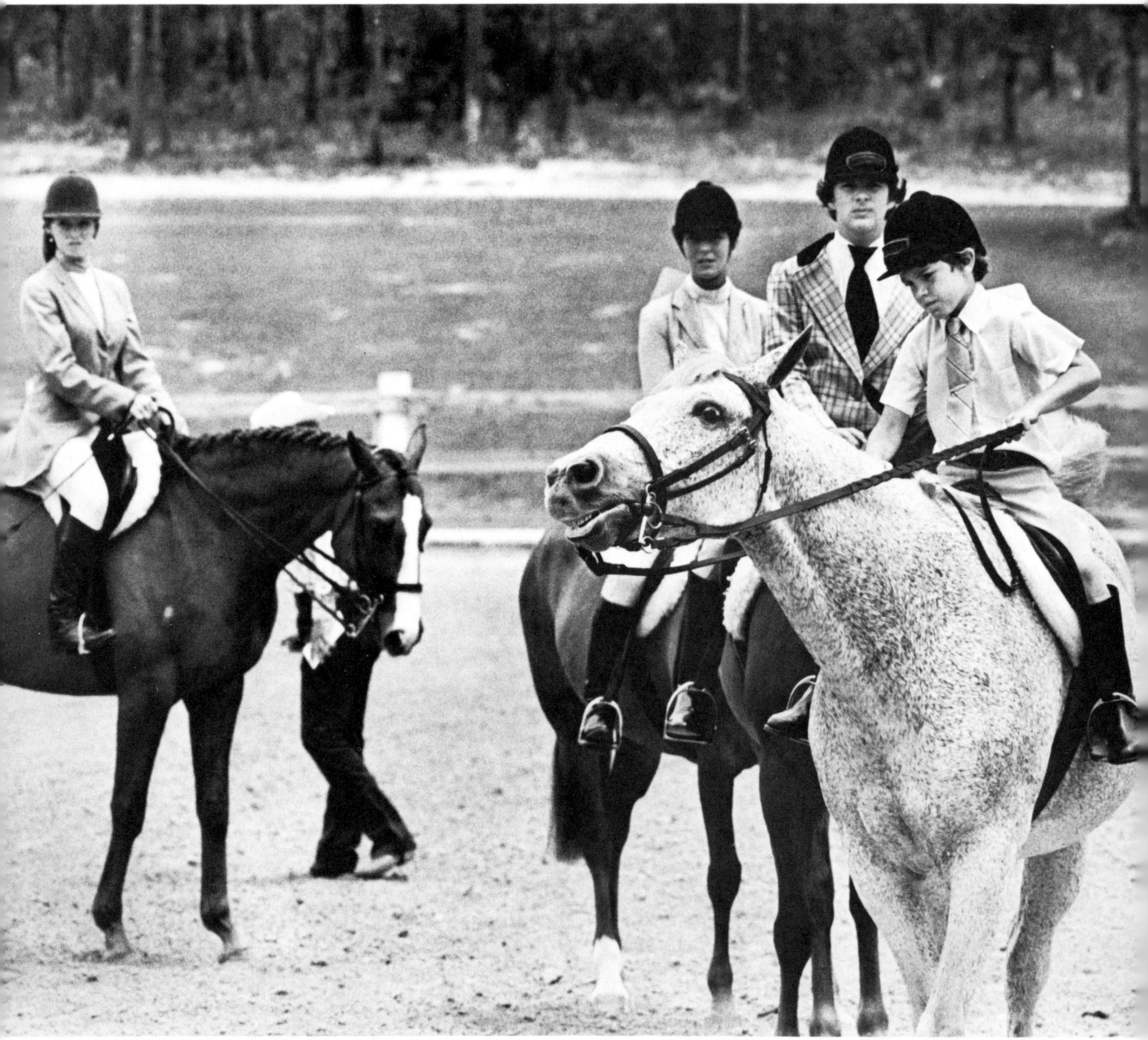

"Well, horses are my thing. I just love them," said Carol Webster, who lives on Pony Drive in Pine Ridge Estates. "I wouldn't move anywhere I couldn't take my horses. So we wouldn't have moved if we couldn't have come to Pine Ridge.

"At first, after we purchased the lot, we weren't going to live down here right away. But we liked it so much we decided to move down here *right now*. Get the kids out into the country where there was fresh air and sunshine and before they got into high school and got too attached to their friends and everything.

"We came here. We love it. The horses think they died and went to heaven. The climate is terrific all year round. We don't mind the warm weather and when it's cool here, it's only cold enough for a light jacket."

The Webster family (pp. 118–119) had tried boarding their horses at home in Stanton, Delaware, a suburb of Wilmington, with little success.

"We had our acre and a half, plus eighteen acres of park next to us," Carol said, "but if I wanted to ride, I had to put them in the trailer and drive to somewhere where there were horse trails or woods. There was really nowhere to ride unless I went to a lot of trouble. So I didn't ride very often."

Even though Billy had a thriving hairdressing salon, they decided to sell and move to Pine Ridge.

"Here, anytime I want to ride, I just get on my horse and I can travel for miles and miles on sandy roads," said Carol. "Our property borders on the formal equestrian trail; plus, there are eleven thousand and five hundred acres in Pine Ridge with miles and miles of roads. I got lost for five hours one day.

"I enjoy living where everything is horse. You can keep your horse on your property and, so far, everyone who's moved back here has horses. Not everyone has them on their property. Some are in the stable, which is absolutely the nicest place my horse has ever been. This is a terrific place for horse people."

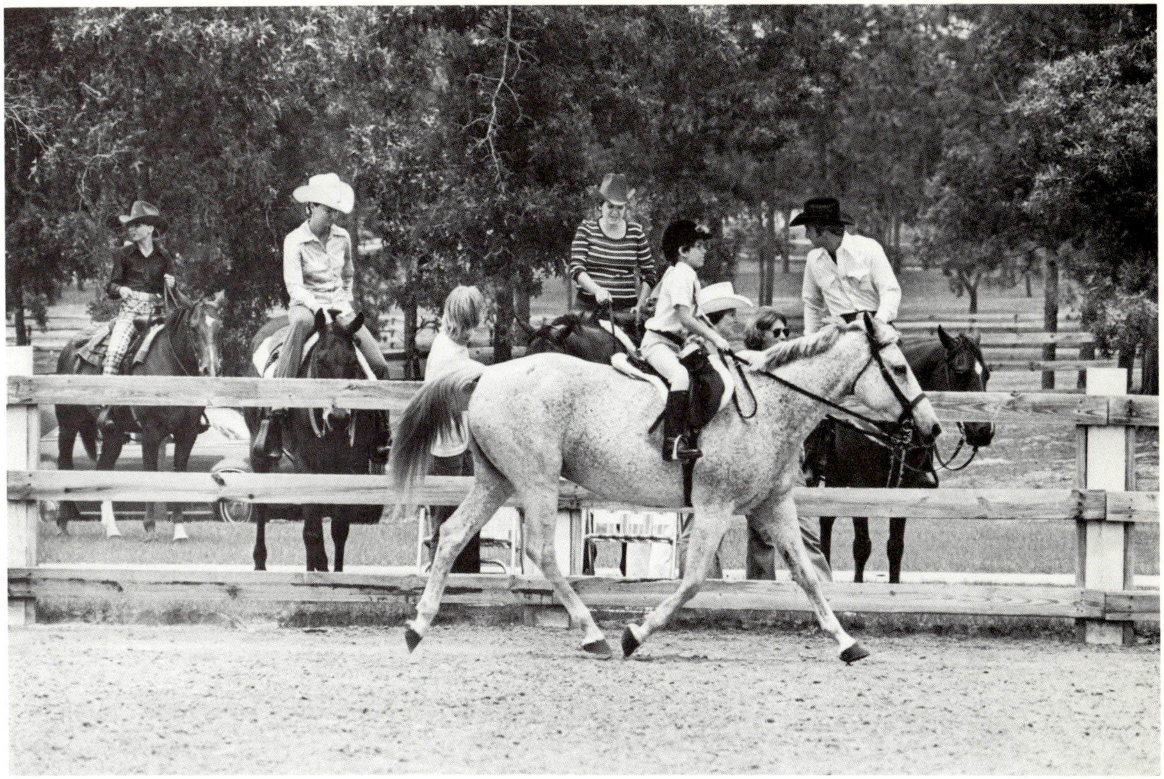

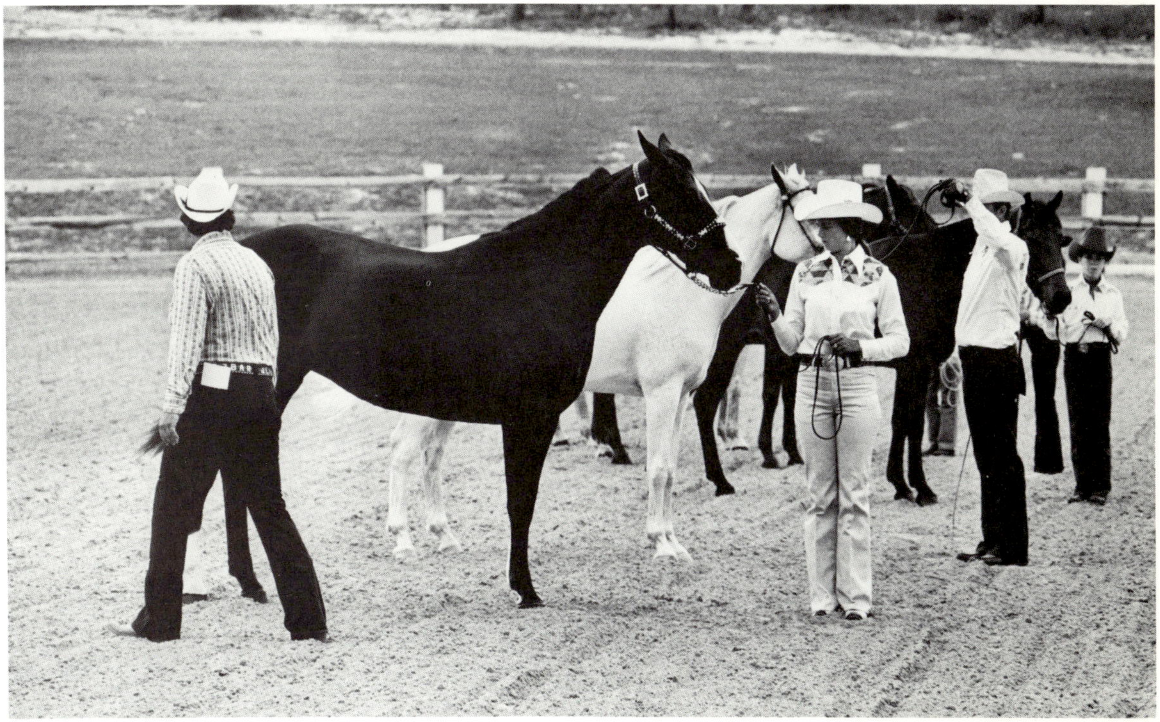

In the fall of 1975, we drove to Provincetown, Massachusetts, on the tip of Cape Cod, for the annual clambake of the Northeastern Chapter of the Family Motor Coach Association.

Before the festivities, the officers of the group held a business meeting in one of the converted buses.

The tiniest detail—like the size of proposed jacket patches—was discussed and considered at length. The men present considered their positions within the group a serious matter.

At work, in their communities, nationally, they might be shut out of the decision-making process. But here they were able to decide personally the things that would affect their lives in the FMCA.

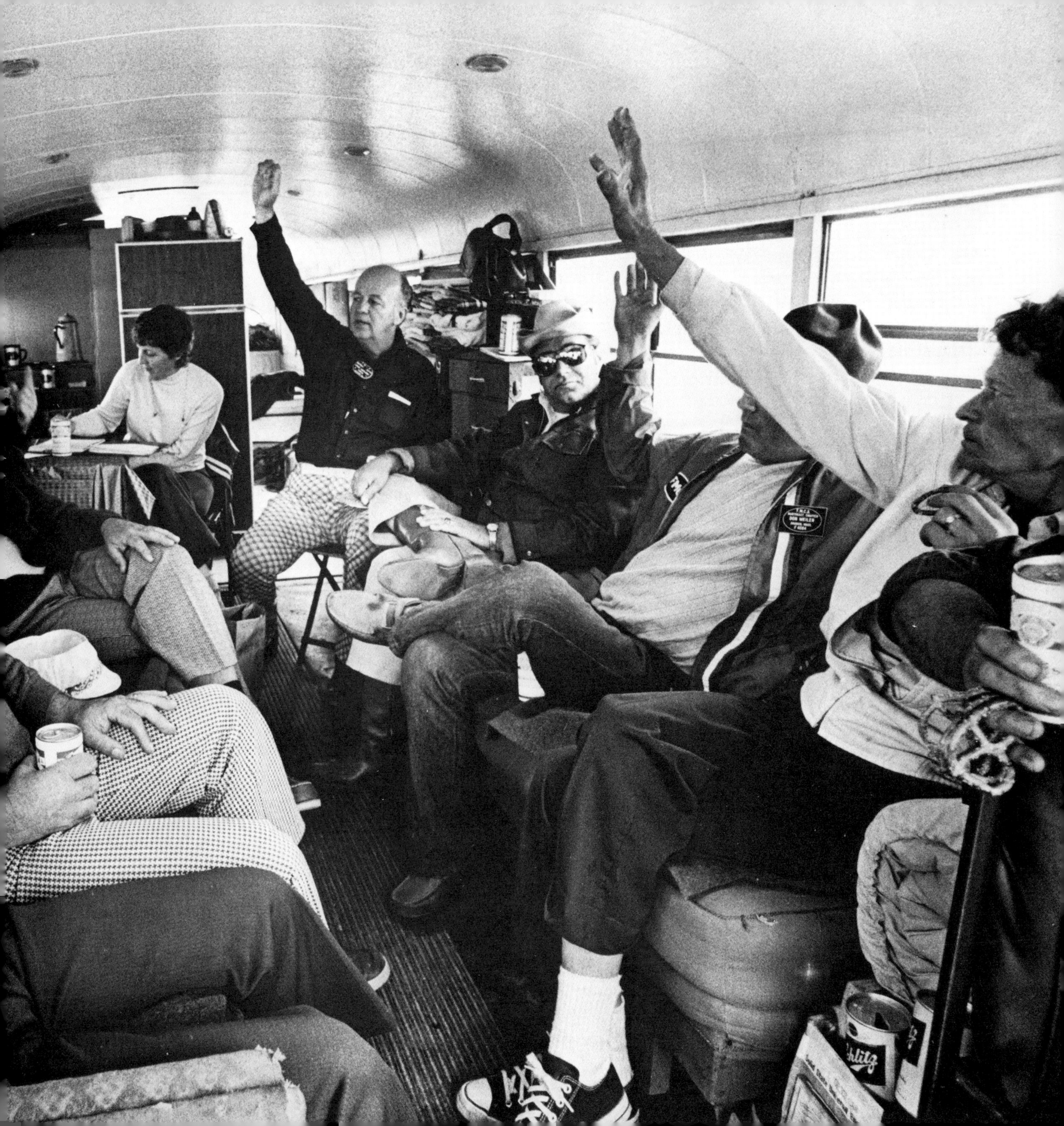

Later, I talked with Dave Garland, president of the chapter, who downplayed the emphasis on machinery. "More important than the value and size of the coach is the comradeship and friendships of the families involved. From camping and motor coaching a new breed of American nomad has evolved. These people spend several months of the year on the road—going to new places and visiting old friends and enjoying this wonderful country."

At the rally, a hundred-odd buses were parked along "streets" in one section of the Coastal Acres Campground. Awnings and picnic tables appeared, giving a look of permanence to the gathering.

The event didn't revolve around the motor coaches. In fact, the buses sort of blended into the background, to be used when it was time to sleep, cook a meal, use the bathroom. A group of fathers and sons were playing a rousing game of touch football, other groups met for drinks, one contingent returned from a fishing expedition.

I couldn't pinpoint exactly why the group gathered together every weekend. Even the "main event"—the lobster and clam dinner—was no big deal.

I mentioned this to an FMCA member. He concurred and added, "People certainly didn't drive all the way out here for a meal. They could have cooked lobster at home or gone to a restaurant. The appeal is the people you meet and the sense of belonging.

"We don't lock our doors," he continued, "and no one thinks anything of going in and out of each other's coaches. You don't have to worry about your children—if you don't see them all day you know they're with somebody else in the group."

"We share our family problems," said Dave Garland. "When a member passes on—a mother or father, husband or wife, or occasionally a child—we all feel sympathy for the family. We enjoy the birth of children and grandchildren into the group. We know so much about each other that it just makes our days in the club really exciting and worth while."

"My God," I said, "you're describing a small American town."

127

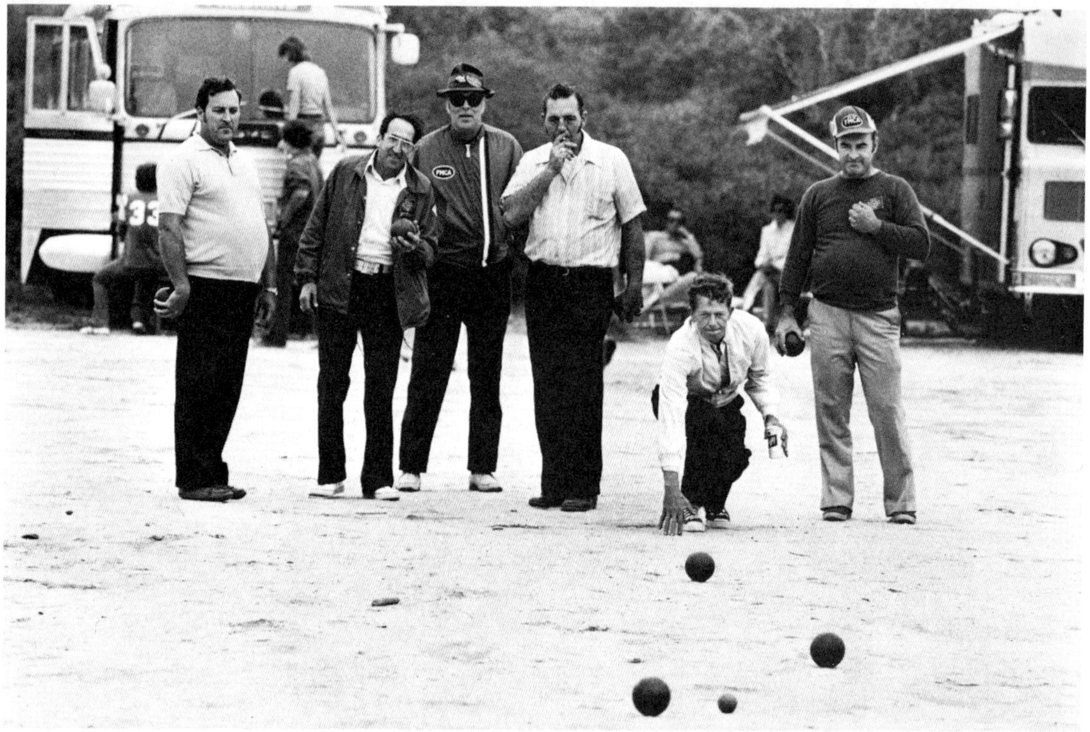

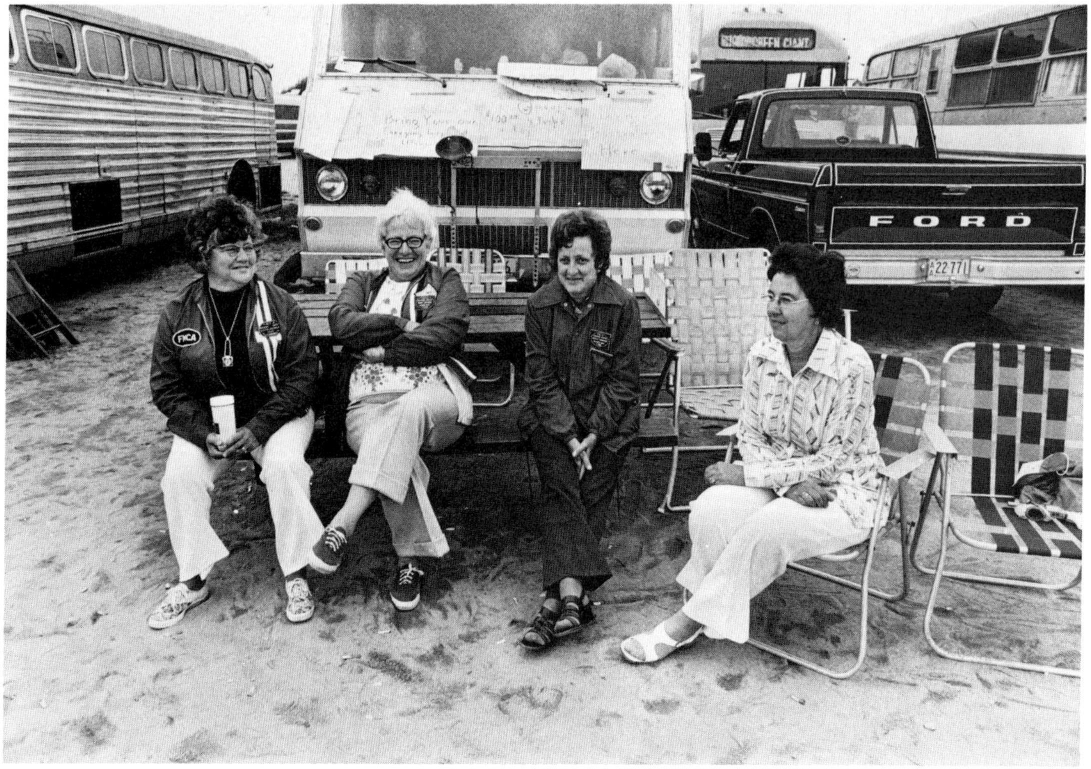
FORD

This group created their own instant village each weekend with the same people, the same slow pace, and values that were common to all. The fact that it was leisure time made it even better.

"You've got the tensions and pressures of work, the bills at home and that sort of thing is kinda pulling and tugging at you," said Dave Garland, "but when you get to a bus rally—that's fun! All those things are forgotten. This is good-time time. Relax and enjoy. Nobody's going to have any trouble with anybody because everyone is the ultimate in friendliness."

For many, the FMCA rallies have become a lifestyle. Dave Garland is deputy fire chief in Medford, Massachusetts, and swaps time with other firemen to get weekends off to attend rallies. Another couple told me that they'd been in a new house for six years and still hadn't got to know the neighbors on either side of them. ("We're either gone or thinking about going," said the man.)

The wife of an assistant manager for a large discount store said her husband had been transferred three times in four years, and to them—and their children—their friends in the FMCA were much more important than trying to make an entire set of new friends after each move.

The FMCA members also talked about how they "take care of their own" and, as if on cue, two wrecked buses pulled into the area. The lead bus driver had hit the brakes and his brother, following too close behind, had plowed into him. Immediately, the other FMCA members swarmed about the disabled coaches, planning repairs and making a list of replacement equipment they'd need from other buses; the families involved were given food and comfort.

"And it won't cost them a cent," said the man I'd begun talking with earlier, "what do you think of that?"

"I think it's a Pennsylvania Dutch barn raising," I replied.

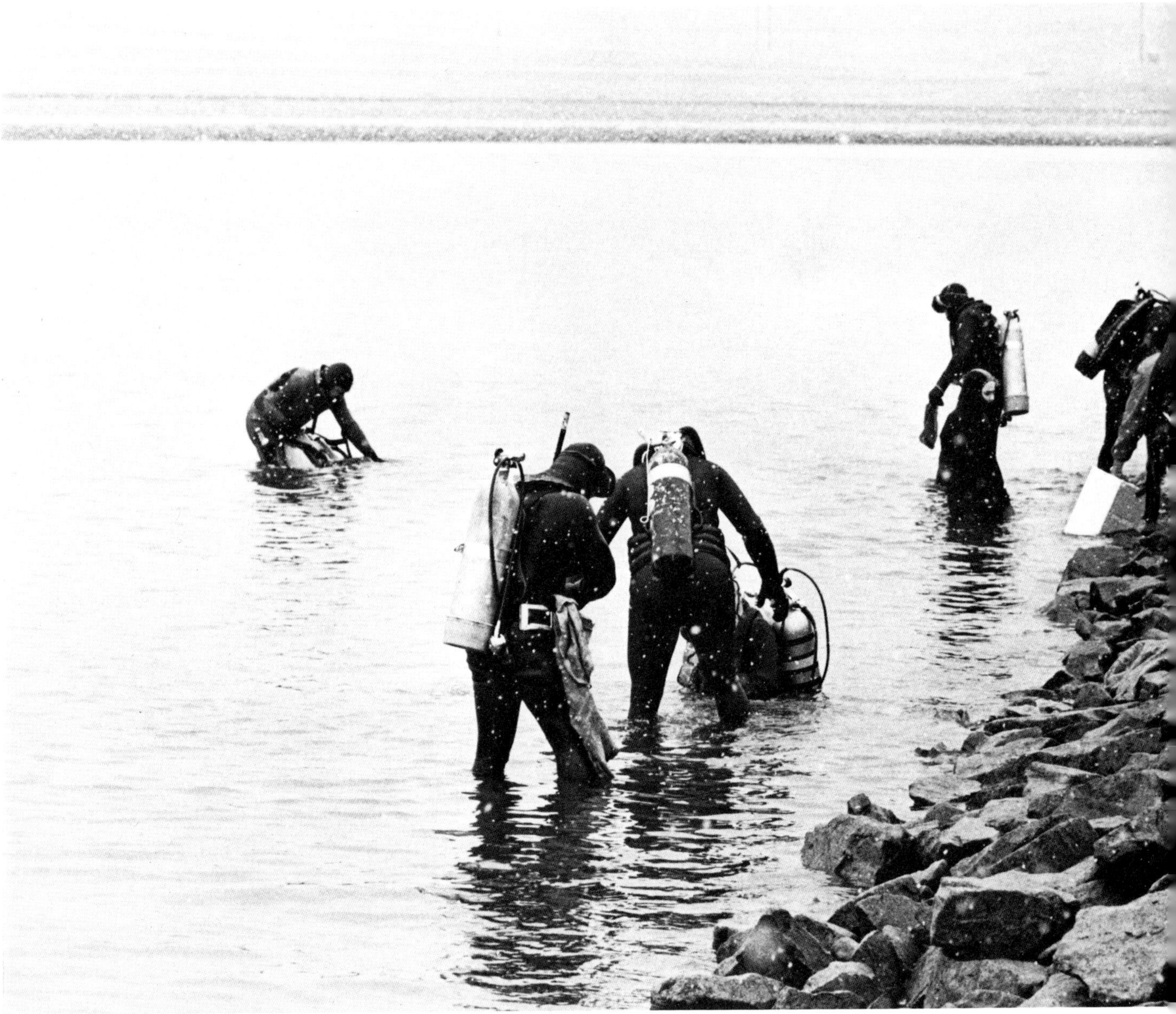

"Why Don't You Photograph Something Normal?"

While photographing a gathering of the Society for Creative Anachronism, I talked with Lady Gwynette du L'Orange (a keypunch operator in the twentieth century), who was spectacularly attired in long flowing robes and an ornate headdress. She asked me what other groups we had photographed and interviewed for the project, and I began naming some of them—like cave divers and bathtub racers.

All of a sudden, she exclaimed, "Oh no, you're not going to put us in with all those weirdos, are you?"

Her comment underscored a sentiment I heard frequently. After describing the activities and events I was attending to someone, I often received the impression that the other person felt I was concentrating on "weirdos and kooks."

Nothing could be farther from the truth. The people in this book represent the mainstream of American life. It's just that a specific leisure activity is determined not only by financial and psychological considerations but also by geography. But my editor felt I was concentrating on the esoteric.

"Why don't you photograph something normal?" he'd ask.

I'd try to explain that everything I'd done to date was normal, that leisure patterns were changing, and that everyone in America didn't live in a New York City environment—which left most of them free to develop their own activities.

"Where are you going next?" he asked.

"Pierre, South Dakota."

"What's in South Dakota?" he asked, the corners of his mouth beginning to turn up.

"Uh . . . the Oahe Winter Dive. Bunch of scuba divers have a gar-grabbing contest. They go underwater in this dammed lake and see how many of these big ugly fish they can grab in an hour."

My editor was standing in the doorway grinning as I left.

I attended the Third Annual Oahe Winter Dive with Tom Bowers, the owner of Skin and Scuba Oahe Dive Shop (it's a part-time business; he's also an IBM representative) and the moving force behind the event.

On the day of the dive it was below freezing with a blustery wind. The water temperature was thirty-two degrees and it was snowing intermittently. About sixty divers had registered and their equipment was strewn along the bank. They were all eager to get in the water.

I approached Cliff Jorgenson, a diver from McLaughlin, South Dakota, and asked, "Why do you come out and dive in the middle of winter?"

"Well, it's too far to go to California.

"We have a lot of money tied up in equipment," he continued, "and we want to use it. Besides, a winter dive is a lot of fun."

Chuck Heck, of Sioux Falls, a draftsman for a precast outfit, said, "We get together with other divers, and that's really nice. You're with people who are interested in your own sport and that's pretty rare out here."

"We're all nuts!" shouted another diver, and a chorus of voices seconded his assessment.

The divers plunged into the water in search of booty. Two men struggled up the rocky bank with a heavy, waterlogged tree trunk, only to learn it was disqualified. "Only manmade items qualify for the Ecology Dive," said Tom.

The gar grabbers were more fortunate. A school of probably three thousand sluggish fish was discovered and soon hundreds of gar were being brought up.

132

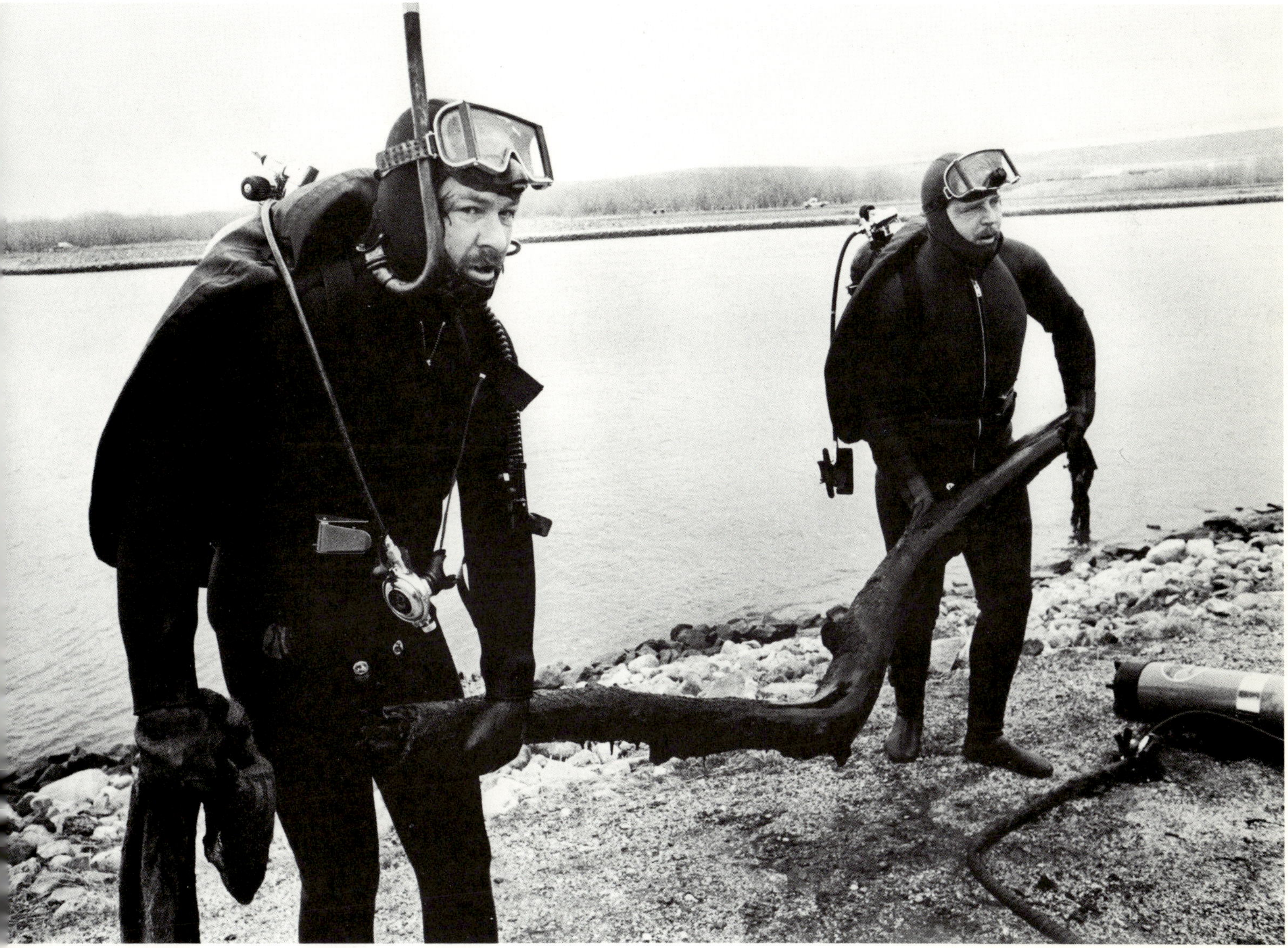

I saw Cliff Jorgenson (right) shortly after he got out of the water. His face was beet red and he looked ready to pass out. What was it like, I wanted to know.

"Fantastic," he replied. "In the winter we always try and dive down here once a month, unless the roads are so bad we can't get down. It's a two-hundred-and-fifty-mile drive, but it's worth it when we get here and shoot the bull with other divers and have a pretty good time."

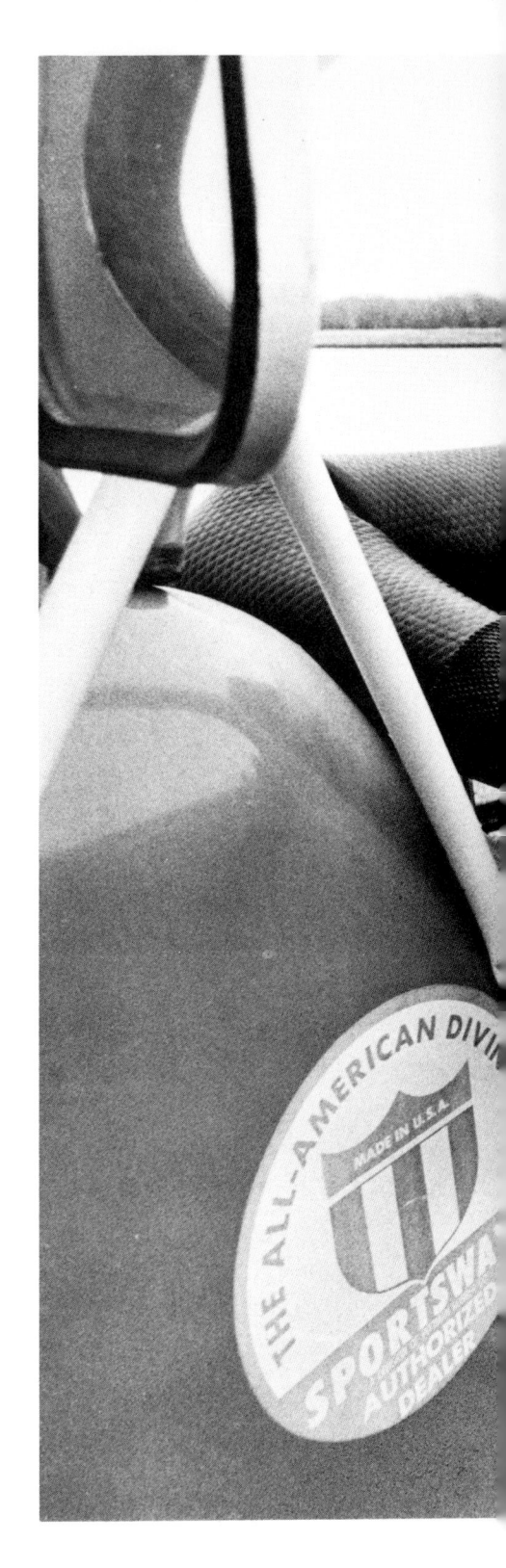

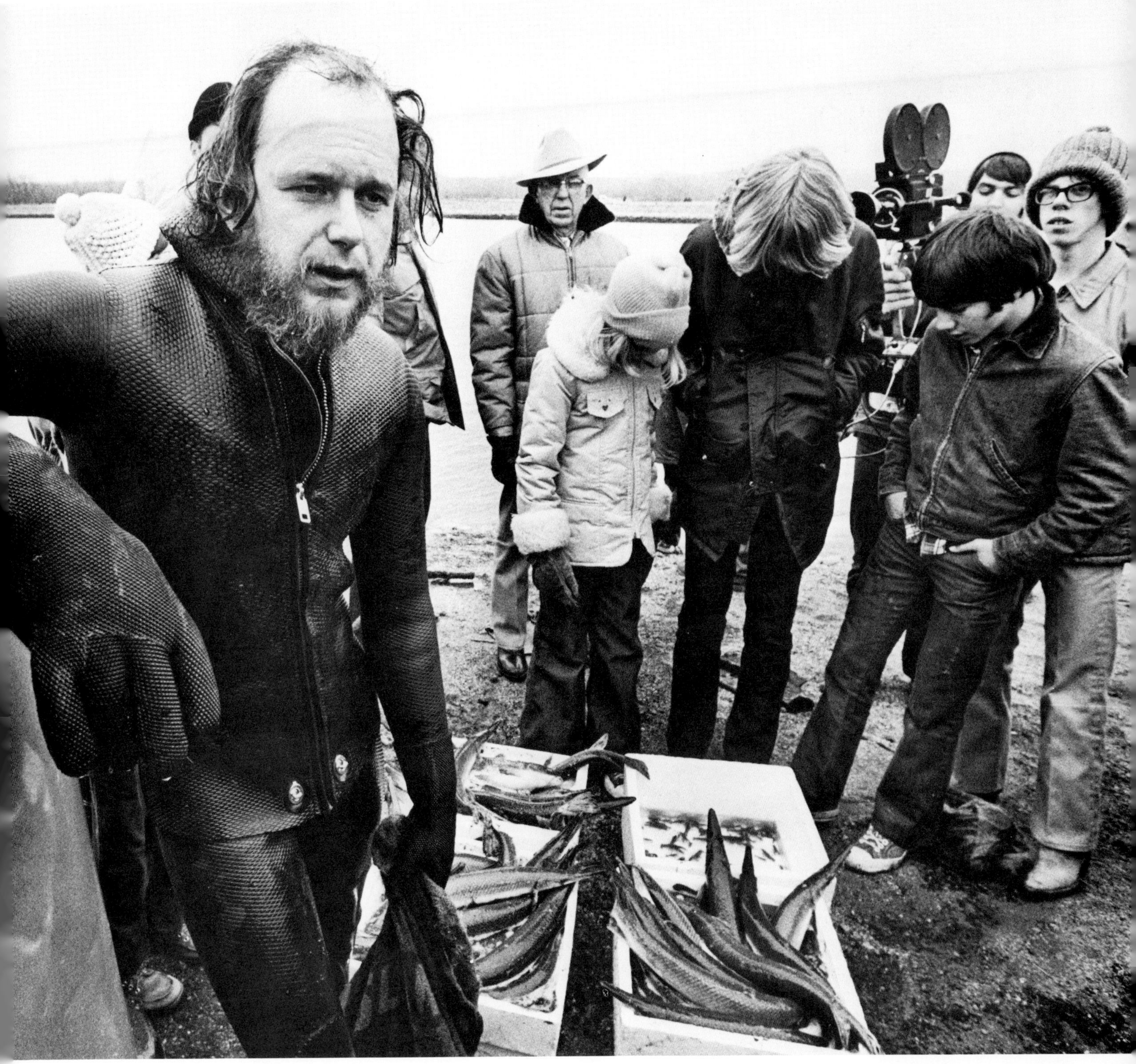

136

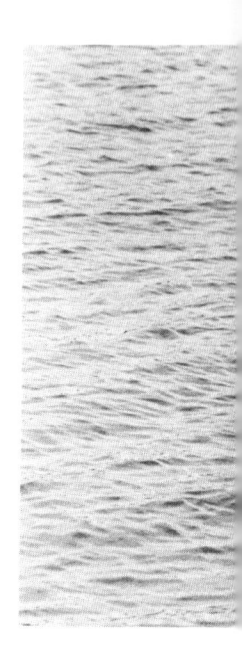

While most of the divers were under water looking for gar, trash, or buffalo skulls, two men laboriously outfitted themselves in the most elaborate equipment at the dive.

Then they moved into chest-deep water and spent the afternoon discussing the merits of the latest underwater diving equipment.

Back at Tom's shop, with dry clothes on and the heat turned up, the divers broke out the beer and began reminiscing about the day's dive, other dives, past dives, future dives. Clearly, the chance simply to get together with other divers was a major attraction of the event.

Mary Jorgenson, who dives with her husband, came over and said, "You must think we're crazy."

"No," I replied. And then I realized that I had goofed. The Oahe winter divers might be eminently "normal" people, but the appeal of their leisure activity was that it was different, bizarre, unusual—even weird. They wanted it to be "crazy"; that was the whole purpose.

Quickly, I tried to make amends. Thinking of my editor standing in the doorway with his grin, I added, "But back in New York they really think you're crazy."

When I decided to visit the National Rattlesnake Hunt in Morris, Pennsylvania, my preconceived notion was that there I'd really find a bunch of whackos; that anyone who goes out in the woods with the sole purpose of picking up live, lethal rattlesnakes has got to be nuts.

Morris is a tiny hamlet, nestled in the rattlesnake-filled mountains of north central Pennsylvania. The first thing I saw when I arrived at the hunt was a sign reading "NO POISONOUS SNAKES TO BE HANDLED OUTSIDE OF PIT AREA." The snake hunts, which are sponsored by the Morris Volunteer Fire Company, have been held for some twenty years and now attract over five thousand people. "They come from all over," said an official, "Canada, Ohio, West Virginia, Virginia, D.C., Maryland, New Jersey, New York. Most people are here because they're curious. They say, 'Now I can go home and tell my friends and neighbors I was at a rattlesnake hunt.'"

Anyone is welcome to go on the hunt. The only requirement is to pay a dollar to the fire company. For neophytes, one of the guides will either actually pick up the rattler or demonstrate the proper technique.

The day I joined the hunt (in the group pictured above), the guide was Irving "Beezer" Briggs, a soft-spoken, instantly likable father of two who had been on almost all the annual hunts.

The other members of the group were equally normal and pleasant, and represented a cross-section of ages and vocations. "I've had three professors, schoolteachers, state police, just about every type of person you can think of," Beezer said, describing a typical snake-hunting group. "Maybe this guy's just a logger and the next guy is a million-dollar businessman; but when we're out, we're just all sportsmen on a snake hunt."

"I've met some of the nicest people in my life on snake-hunts," he added. "I wouldn't exchange my years as a guide for anything in the world."

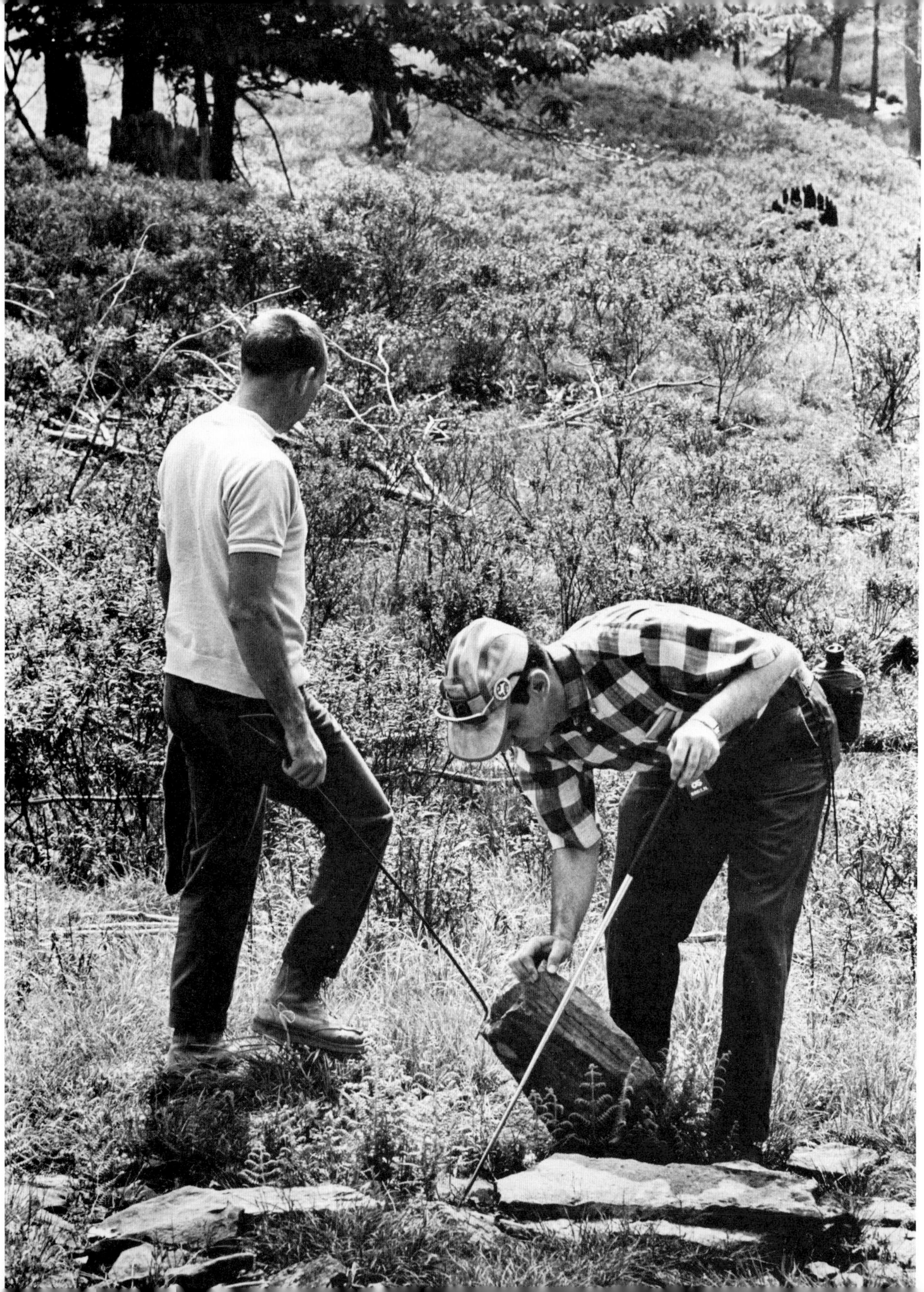

"To catch a rattlesnake, you pin his head with your catcher," said Beezer, when the first snake of the day was discovered, "then get your thumb and forefinger and index finger on the head. You also hold him by the tail to more or less support the weight of the snake. You'll injure him by picking him up by the head with the weight hanging.

"Their most vicious time is when they're first caught," he cautioned, "so getting your snake in the open is important. What makes it so dangerous is that when you grab the snake by the head you might have ferns or leaves or grass or something along with the snake, and that will give him a chance to get loose."

"Did you ever have one get loose at that stage?" I asked.

"The one that bit me in nineteen-sixty-five got loose at that stage," Beezer replied.

142

Fortunately, Beezer was hit with only one fang from a fairly small snake. One of the group "operated" on him and he got to a hospital within an hour, where antivenom serum was waiting. He refused to stay in the hospital, and on his way home stopped by the hunt headquarters.

"I went to the ballgrounds and handled a rattlesnake that very afternoon," he said, "for the simple reason that I love the sport, and I knew if I didn't it would start working on my mind and I'd get scared and not want to handle them. So I went there that afternoon and proved to myself that I would handle them.

"Then for the next two weeks I didn't care what happened. I was so darn sick, from the bite and from the serum, that you couldn't believe it.

"I'm really more concerned about people having heart attacks and overexerting themselves than I am about getting bit by a snake," Beezer confided. The real killer at a rattlesnake hunt often turns out to be walking up a mountain in ninety-degree heat.

"I had a fellow have a stroke back on the mountain," he said. "He just went and I didn't think the man was alive when I went back to the vehicle to get a blanket to make a stretcher. But it turned out it was a heat stroke. He'd been up most of the night at the hotel and he hadn't eaten breakfast. He was a man fifty-two years old and he was in the hospital three days."

A group based in Akron, Ohio, formed the Waterbugs of America Racing Association. A waterbug is a Volkswagen beetle, its top removed and its body sealed to make it watertight. A propeller is hooked to a shaft attached to the car's crankshaft so the boatmobile can move over the water at speeds of seven to ten knots.

145

MEDINA
Body by DENNY
Power by GERRY
Ballast by RANDY
SCHWIM-WAGEN
by
MEDINA

At Portage Lakes, Ohio, the waterbugs started on land and charged into the water with a splash when the gun went off. Then they circled a course that was sometimes 150 feet deep.

At the annual Diaper Derby in Atlantic City, New Jersey, a lady told me, "Sure this is nonsense, but with all the hassles, and crises in the news everyday, people want something crazy."

The Diaper Derby, billed as the "Olympics of the Infant Set," features bare-kneed babies from several states who crawl along a thirty-foot course. Parents or trainers may entice a child with a bottle or cookies or open arms to crawl faster.

The event was attended by a large crowd of spectators, television crews, and reporters, with much shrieking and clapping.

No one told the babies how much fun it all was.

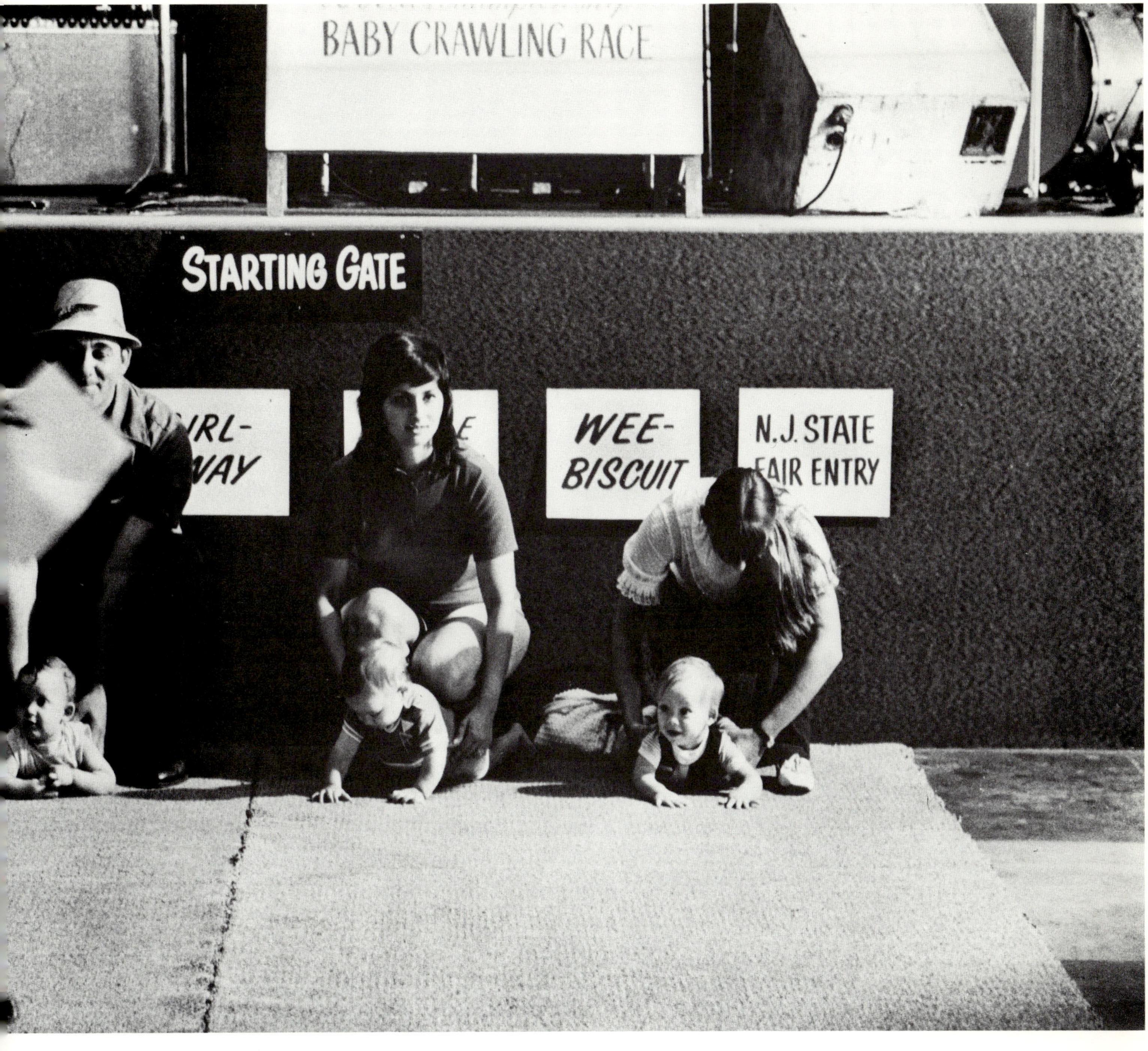
BABY CRAWLING RACE
STARTING GATE
WEE-
BISCUIT
N.J. STATE

150

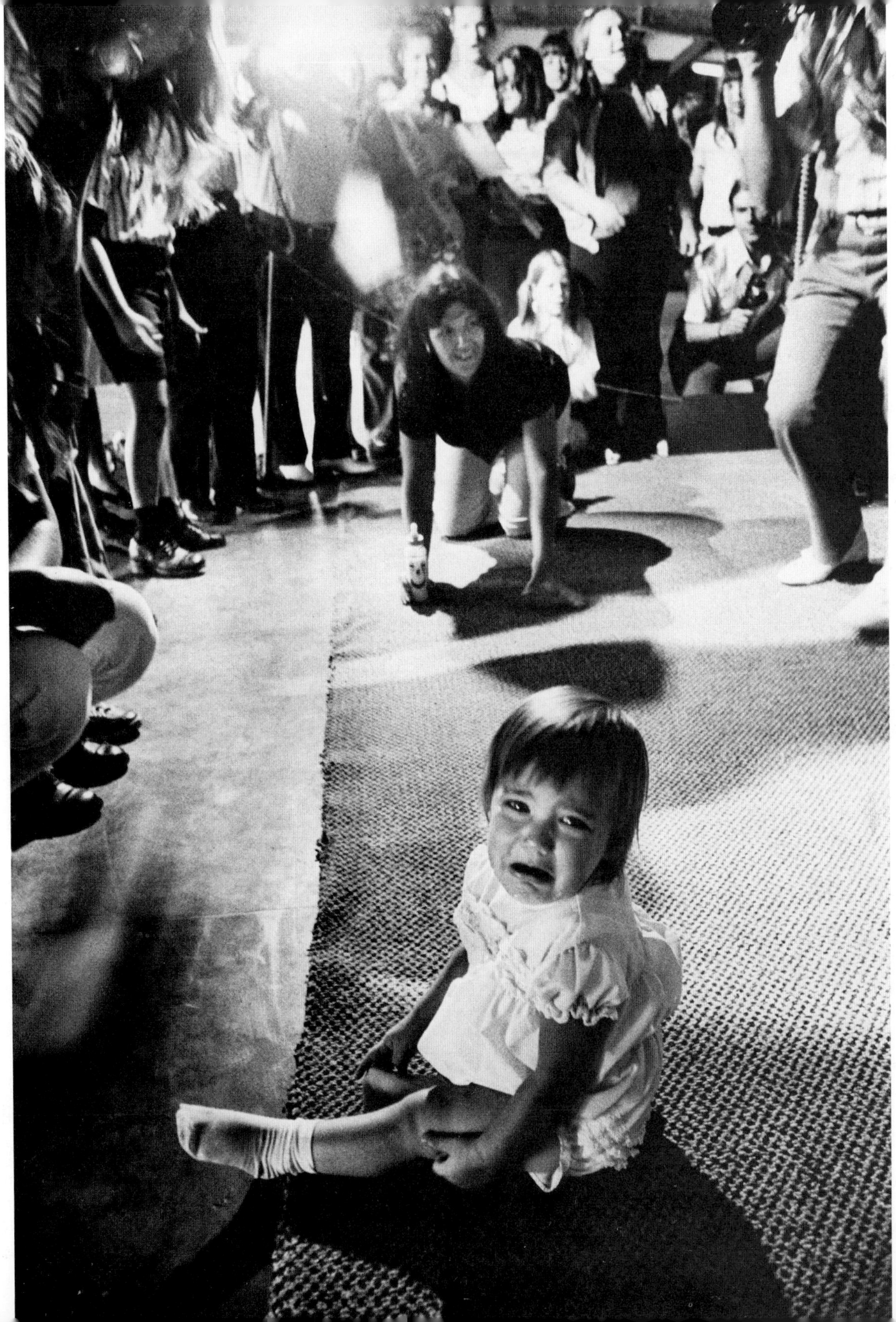

152

153

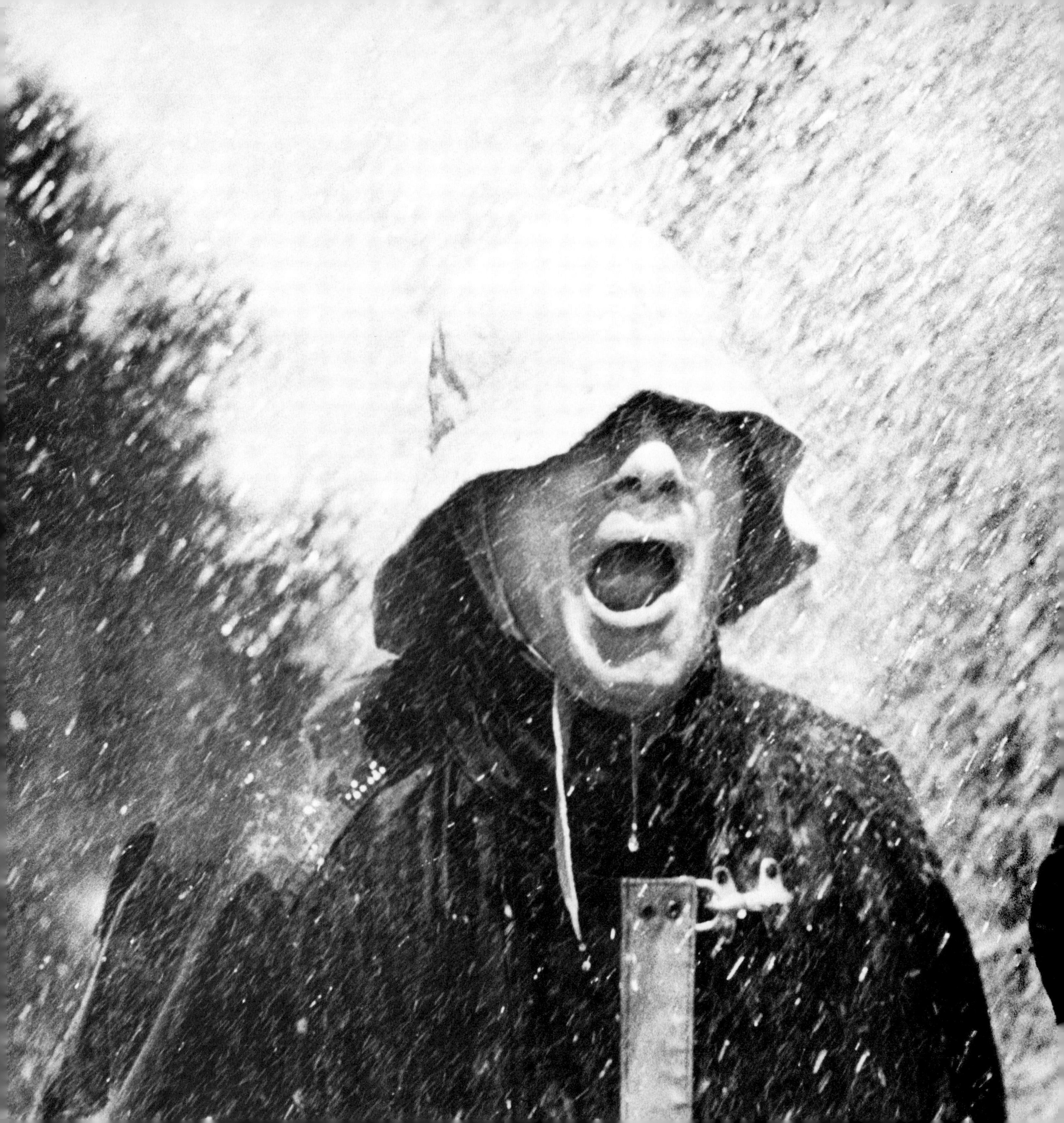

In Pittsfield, Maine, I photographed a sport called water battle, which began as a traditional muster event among volunteer fire companies. It's so appealing, however, that both women and children now want to participate with teams of their own.

"In water battle, you get four men on a team standing forty feet apart," explained Dave Ludden of Pittsfield. "Each match is three minutes long, and the team that gets the most water on them at one time loses. If anybody moves, he's disqualified. The winner is decided by a panel of judges."

"We use a 2½-inch hose on a 1⅛-inch tip with twenty-five pounds of pressure," he continued. "It used to be thirty-five pounds of pressure, but the State Federation cut it back to twenty-five because too many guys were getting hurt. You know, like losing their hearing.

"In three minutes you're figuring between five to seven hundred gallons of water on you, and that's a big drink. That's quite a beating to take. You've got to be some kind of a nut to get into it and enjoy it.

"It hurts, I'll tell you, when the water hits you. But you got to stand there and take it because if you move, your team is going to lose."

"People ask me, 'Why do you get into this thing? What sense is there in it?'" said Bernard Williams, assistant chief of the Pittsfield fire department.

"Well, I don't know. What makes any competition fun? The fact that you've got a chance to beat the other guy. Maybe there isn't any sense to it at all. But there're a lot of games played that there isn't any sense to really. If you stop and look at baseball and golf, there really isn't much sense to them—but they're something people enjoy doing and something people enjoy watching. And the crowds we get when we have water battle must enjoy watching it.

"If we have a lot of fun doing it and other people think we're foolish because we go out and get into this, well, we're having the fun. If a fellow can't have a little fun, he might as well just hang it up."

157

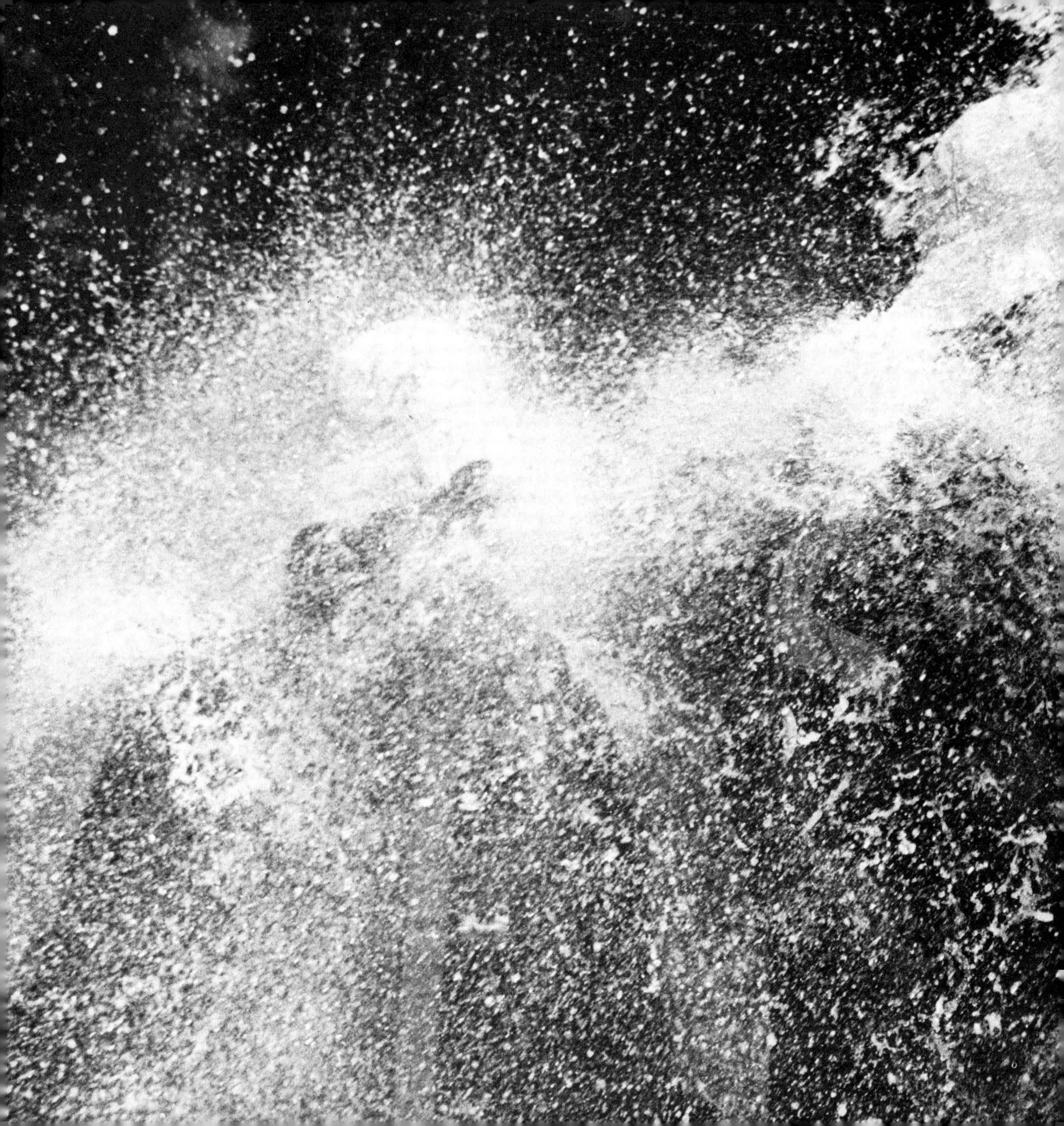

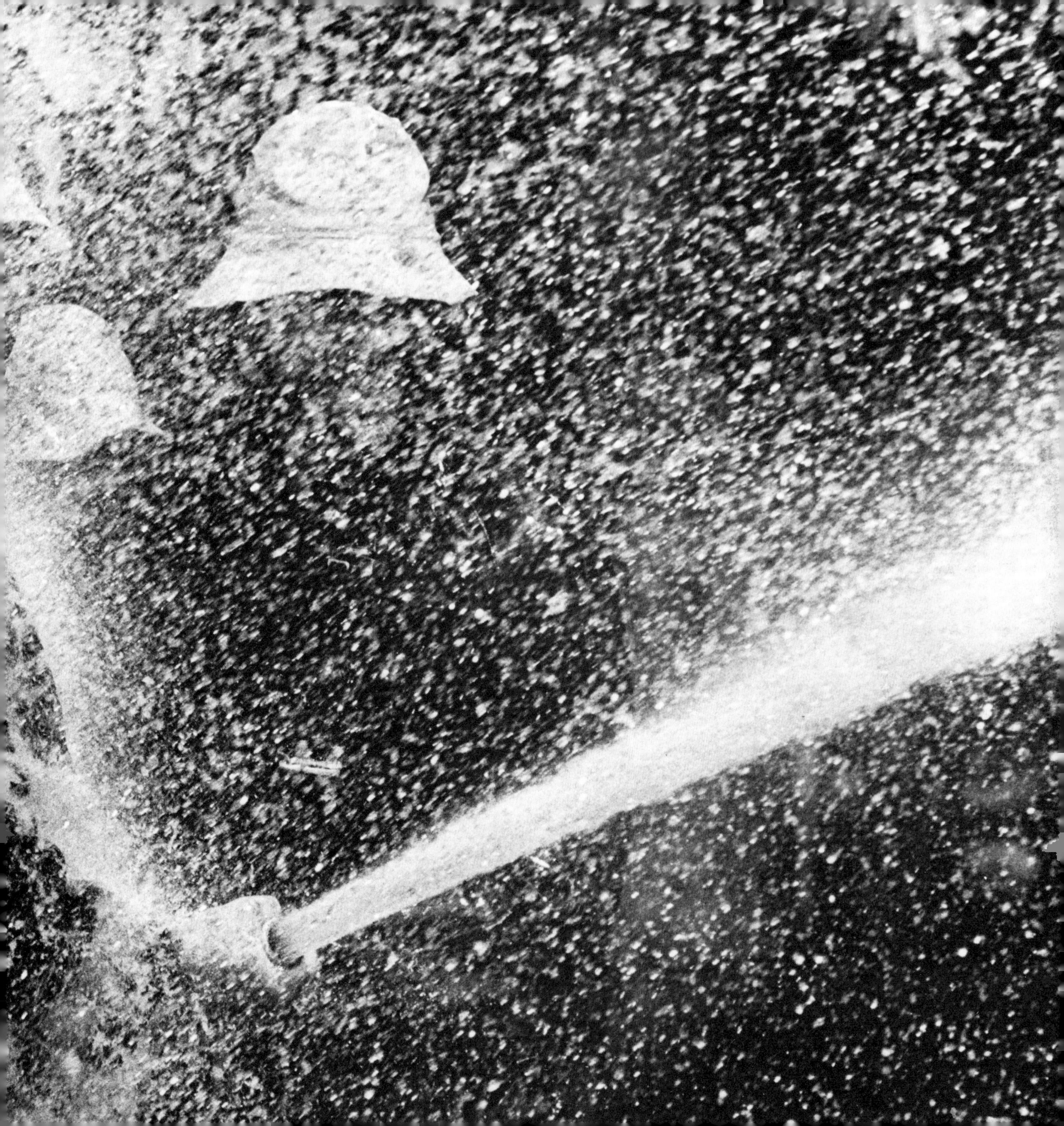

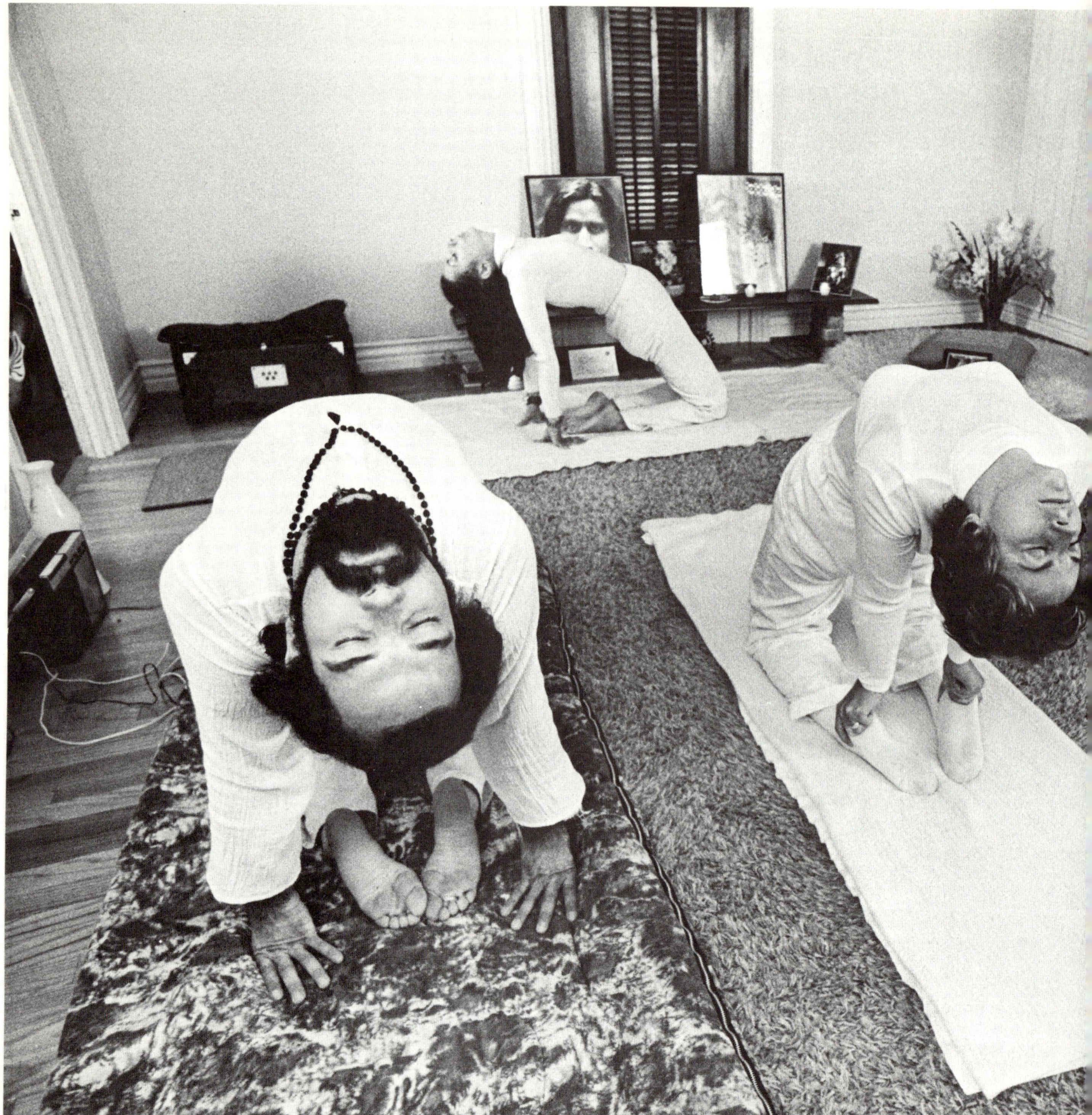

The Future of Leisure

As I write this in early 1977, millions of Americans are rejecting the traditional spare time pursuits of competition, gadgets, and bigger and better toys for what counterculture historian Theodore Roszak has called "the biggest introspective binge any society in history has undergone."

Nine years ago Cindy Casterella learned about yoga at a "relaxicizer" class taught at the YWCA in Watertown, New York, an isolated community in the northern part of the state. Today, she heads the Kripalu Yoga Fellowship of Northern New York, a branch of Yogi Amrit Desai's global Kripalu Yoga Ashram. The fellowship has instructed hundreds of pupils in yoga and has purchased a ten-room house as an ashram.

162

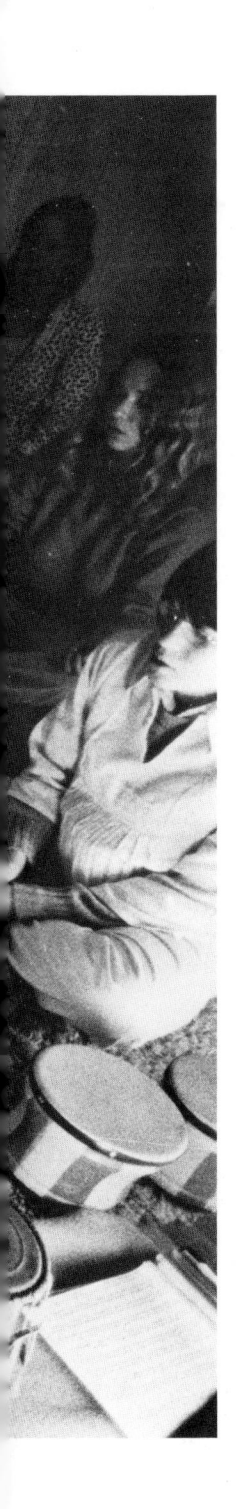

"We're different from other ashrams in that there are no residents here," said Cindy Casterella (above). "We're housewives, we're students, we're professional people, and we're still doing this in spare time here—but all the time wherever we are.

"But it's not a hobby for me, it's not just a way of weight reduction, it's not a way to even 'get high' or relax—it's something that's changed my whole life. People notice it, too—my kids, my husband, my friends. It's nice.

"We don't feel this is a fad. We feel that we're pioneers. We feel that the universe is ripe for this and actually someday there will be thousands coming here—I mean this seems strange for Watertown and it takes our breath away when we're told we're at the grass roots of this enormous thing that's coming. But I think eventually this will spread and there will be centers where people will dedicate their whole lives to this."

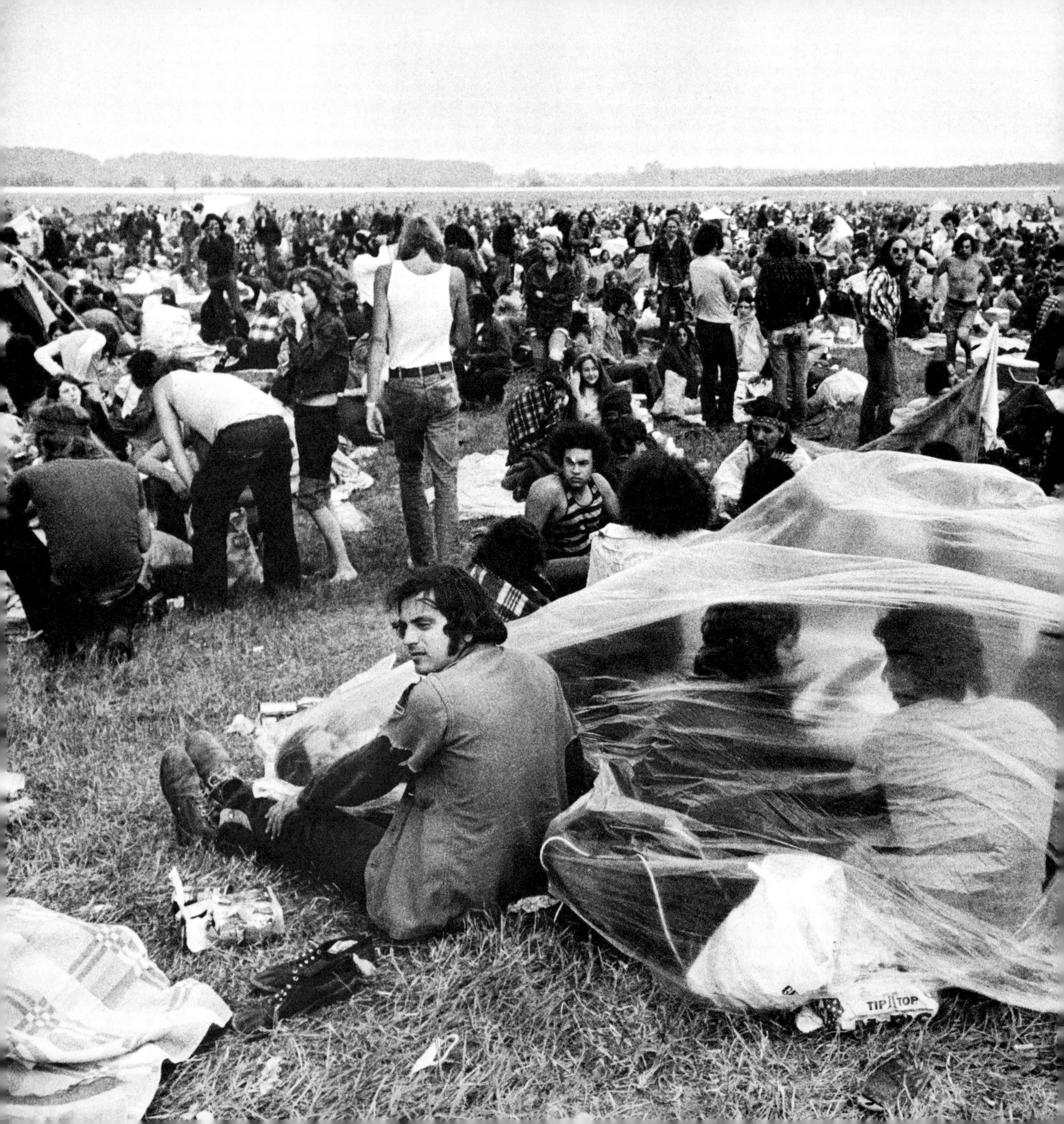
TIP TOP

I'm not convinced that the consciousness boom represents a possible new direction for American spare time. Once before, during my six-year documentation of leisure, there was a seemingly dramatic departure from normal spare time activities, by a large segment of the population.

At the Woodstock Festival in August, 1969, an instant and famous city of five hundred thousand people showed up for three days of mud, music, and spontaneous "togetherness." It appeared that a generation had turned its back on the materialism of its elders and found a leisure outlet that required hardship rather than increased creature comforts.

"The crowds that gathered at this festival, part of an affluent generation that has seldom been cold or hungry except by choice, found the hardships exhilarating," wrote anthropologist Margaret Mead. "I do not think the Woodstock festival was a 'miracle'—something that can happen only once."

166

I was caught up in the momentum of the times and photographed a number of rock concerts as representing a new way to "get away from it all." But festivals after Woodstock all turned out to be debacles—or worse—and a half dozen years after Woodstock, the type of rock concert it's name implied was dead.

While traveling throughout the country, I asked people why such a promising idea had failed. Answers ranged from "It was a fad—a thing to do at the time" to "We were all crazy, nobody would put up with a rock concert now."

But almost to a person, their leisure still included attending concerts. As Tom Davidson of Stroudsburg, Pennsylvania put it, "I like to walk into a place, take my seat, and enjoy listening to the music. You can't enjoy it when you have to fight for position and when people are falling on you—drunk, stoned, throwing up on you."

168

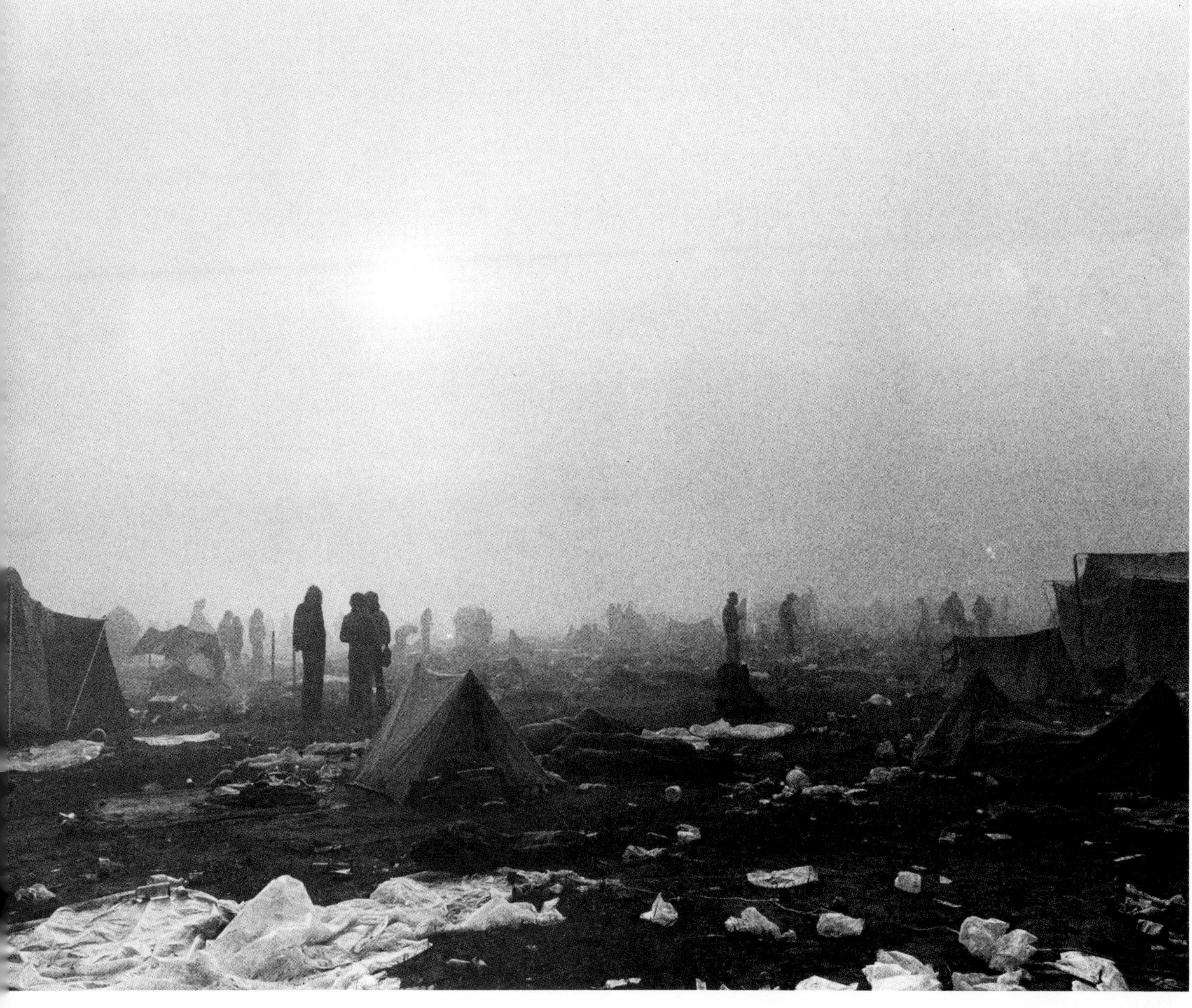

In February, 1977, I sat in a back table at the Pier House Beach Club in Key West, Florida, shuffling the rock festival prints that now seemed oddly dated. I was joined by an editor friend, and we wondered if the rock concert would ever be revived—maybe as a nostalgic thing.

I was holding a print that showed a young man obviously into the music and the atmosphere, his right hand tightly clutching his crotch. I threw the picture across the table and said to my friend, "Where is this guy now?"

"Wait a minute," he replied and went to his room. He returned holding a full-page ad from *The New York Times* that read: THE PLAYBOY READER. HIS LUST IS FOR LIFE. The picture in the ad showed a well-dressed young accountant behind the wheel of an expensive boat that rested on a trailer. His hands gripped the wheel, his eyes were closed, he was savoring the feeling of ownership as the salesman stood next to him ready to write up the order.

"Some didn't hold out much hope for them a few years ago," my companion read from the ad, "Rioting, Burning draft cards, Tearing up campuses. Pot. Painted vans. Beards and long hair."

He paused, then continued reading "Which brings us to the relatively quiet 70's. Where did all that energy go? All that drive that brought on the most explosive decade in modern history. It's still there. But it's been redirected. Toward making up for lost time. Toward making up for all the things that were given up in the 60's. 'The new materialists' Yankelovich calls this new breed."

"There he is now," said my friend, jabbing his finger at the picture of the accountant skimming across the imaginary waves.

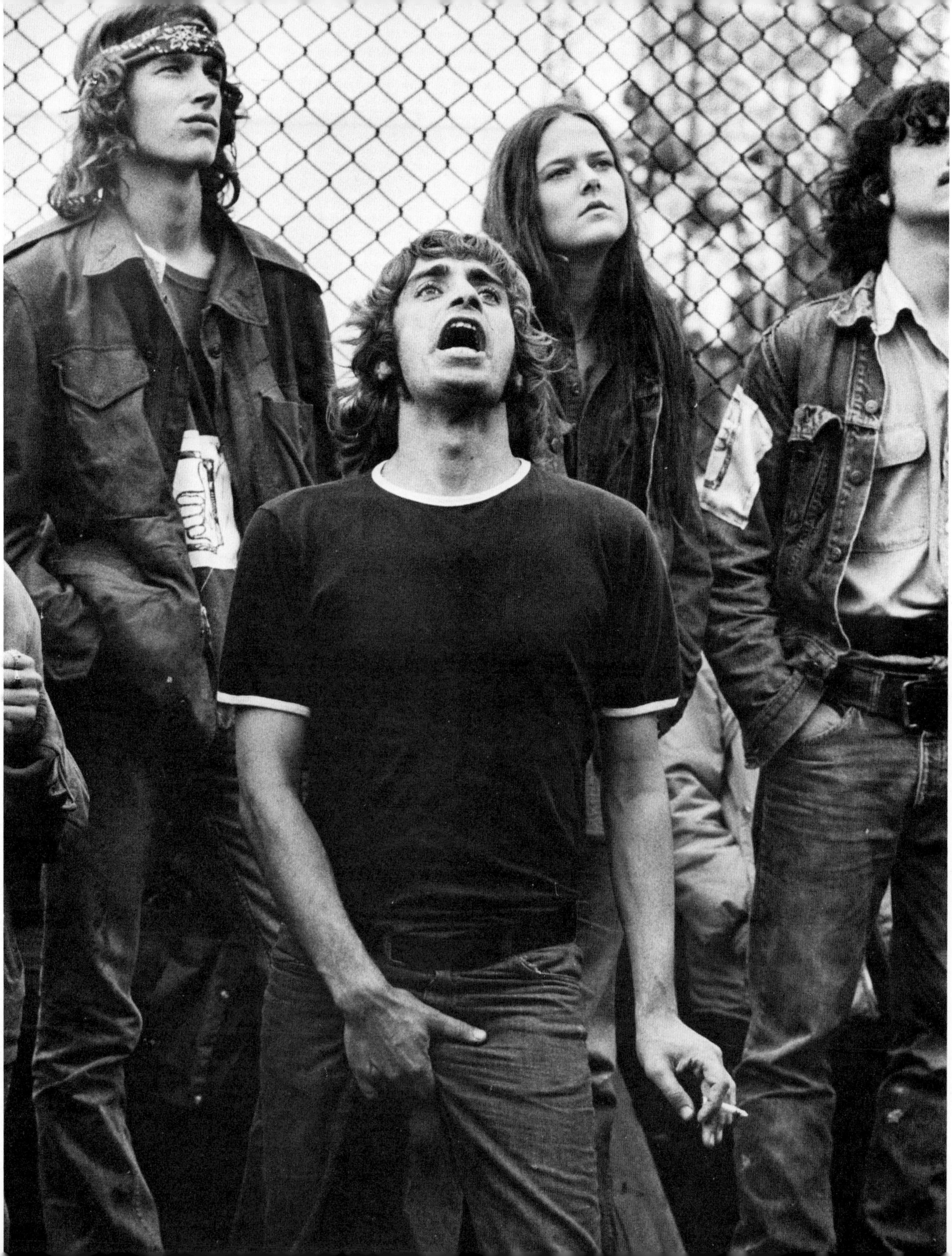

172

The future of leisure in America defies the imagination. Babies at the Bromley Mountain, Vermont, ski area spend weekends in communal cribs while the very young children press their noses against the window, periodically shrieking "There's my mommy! I see my mommy!" as a ski-togged lady smartly glides down the run.

By the time the kids are in the first grade, however, they are completely outfitted and out on the slopes enjoying the activity themselves.

The millions of children growing up in the leisure environment depicted in this book—with an ever increasing amount of time off—will create a leisure world of their own.

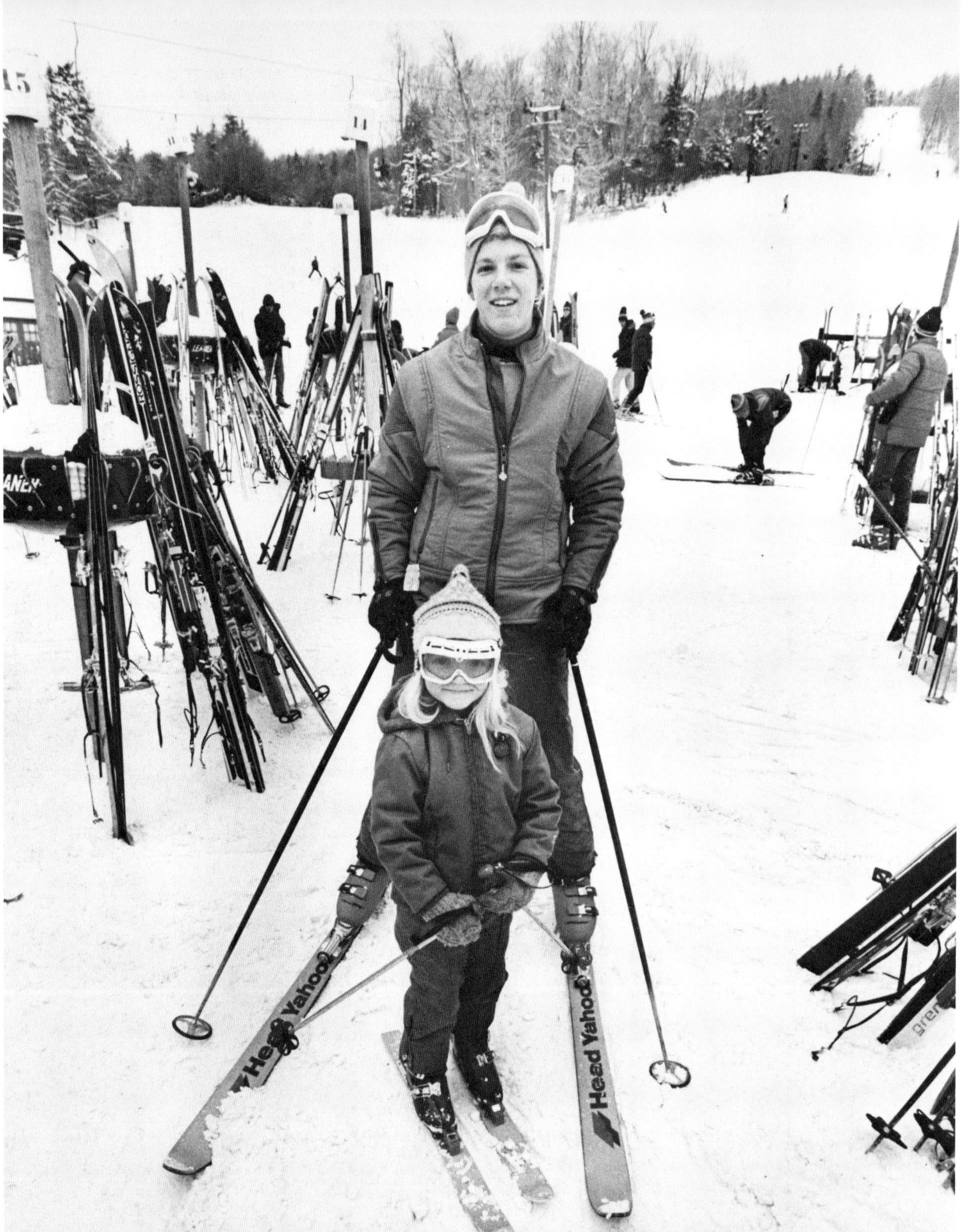
Head Yahoo
Head Yahoo

175

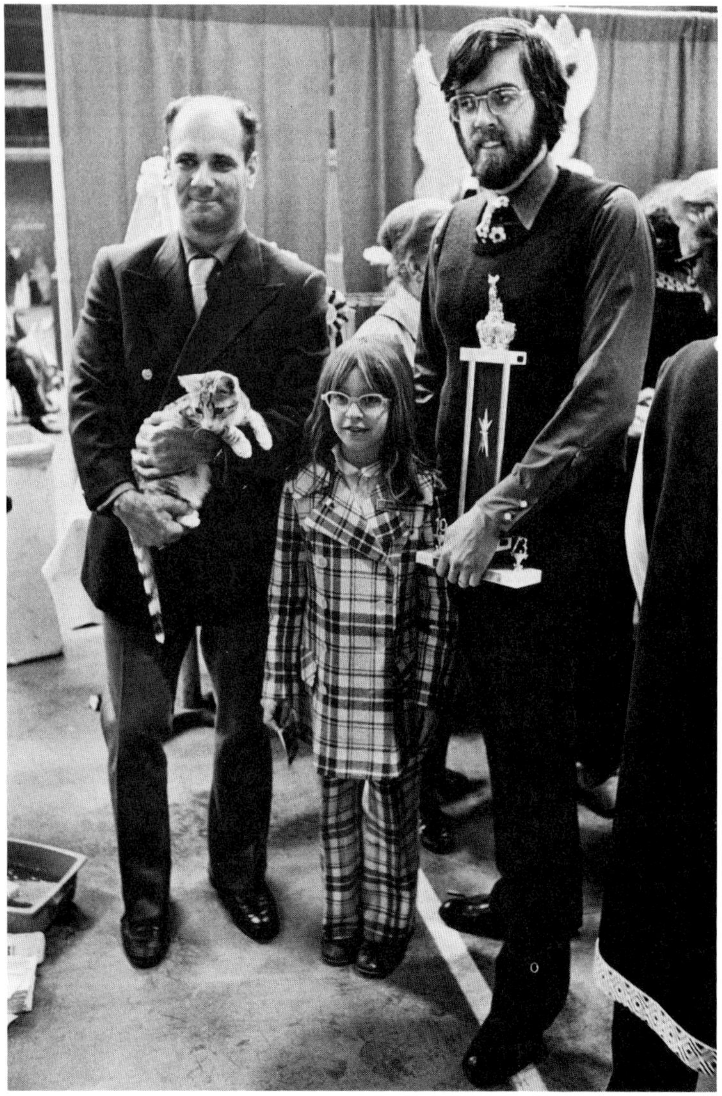

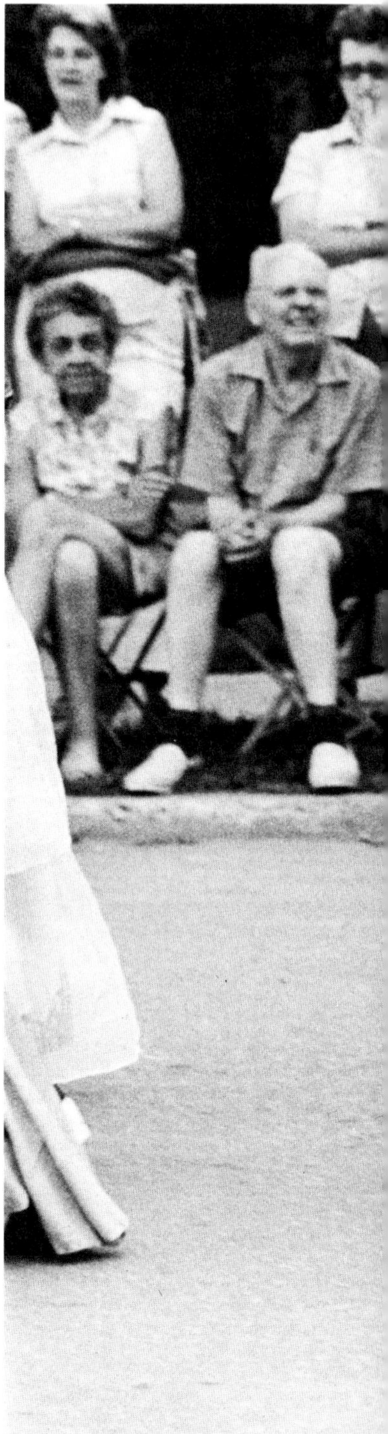

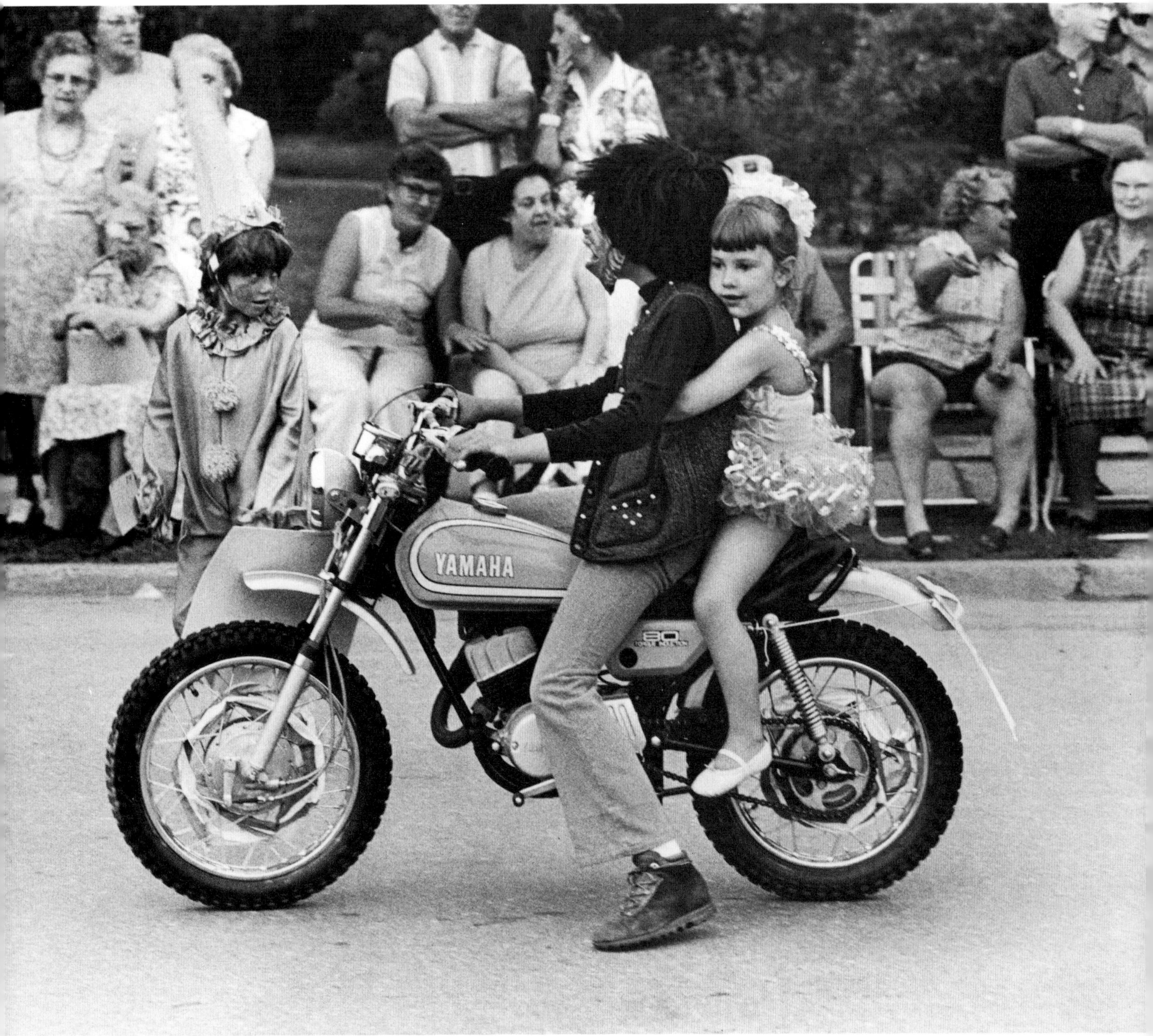
YAMAHA

At the bus rally on Cape Cod, hundreds of kids—whose day had consisted of visiting the beach, riding dune buggies, playing football, and visiting Provincetown—were part of the group. Early in the evening, one bus owner announced he would show a movie for the children. His rig included an ultra-sophisticated video system, and he lifted one of the luggage compartment doors to expose a large color television set.

From his library of four hundred feature films, the kids chose *Willie Wonka and the Chocolate Factory*. At first a large crowd clustered around the set, but they soon started drifting away until only a handful remained—and about half of those were adults.

I went over to a group of kids and asked them why they weren't watching the movie.

"We've seen it," one said.

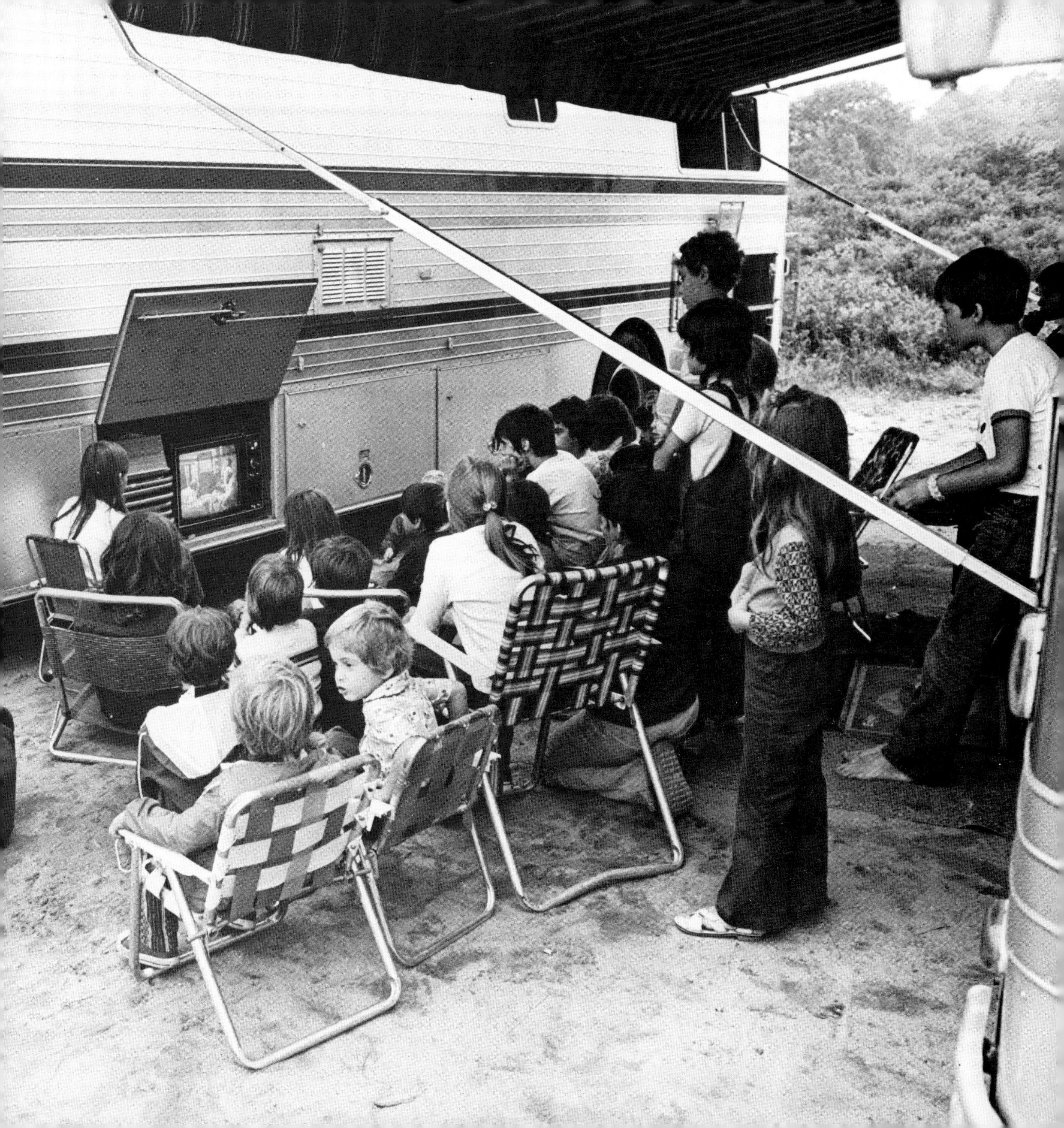

180

Epilogue

During the preceding six years, I'd experienced the gamut of leisure activities in America—but none enticed me into becoming a convert. My own leisure activity remains undefined.

Dr. Alexander Reid Martin, former head of the American Psychiatric Association's committee on leisure, has said, "Our culture puts great emphasis on productivity. We feel we must always be doing something constructive with our time. We see a child swinging on a gate and we say, 'Go find something to do.' We fail to realize that he's already doing something—he's swinging on a gate. Inevitably, when we grow up, instead of swinging on gates when we feel like it, we go out and 'find something to do.'"

I've decided that I'm just a gate swinger.

However, there is one leisure event that does sort of stand out from all of them—a day-long competition that in retrospect seems to embody the essence of the Age of Leisure. It's the activity I would put in the time capsule if I wanted to give future generations a one-shot look at this era.

It's the World's Chicken Plucking Championship, in Spring Hill, Florida. Thousands of Americans drive to this community, forty miles north of Tampa, for one intense day.

"Welcome, ladies and gentlemen, to our Annual Chicken Pluckin' Championship," booms announcer Bill Hatfield, formerly the voice of Lucky Strike cigarettes. Then the Leesburg high-school band, under the direction of Mr. Charles Caudill, plays the national anthem, while the crowd of some five thousand respectfully faces the flag.

It's still early, so we walk around, getting a chicken dinner from the Lion's Club men, wishbone fizz from the V.F.W.'ers, and chicken-bones ice cream from Beta Sigma Chi.

Chicken plucking may well be on its way to becoming an accepted new sport. Since the first meet, when two teams competed, the event had grown to ten teams by Super Pluck IV. Incidentally, there's no worry about professional chicken pluckers cleaning up—chickens have been plucked commercially by machines since the 1940s.

Now the judges are taking their places—a U.S. congressman, the producer of the television show "To Tell the Truth," and a retired U.S. Marine Corps colonel who's now vice-president of a bank.

The preliminary events begin. The members of the Spring Hills Presbyterian Church choir, wearing rubber beaks and attired in formal wear, make up the Chicken Concerto—they cluck in harmony to Rossini's "William Tell Overture" and Offenbach's "Gaité Parisienne."

Evil Kchicken attempted to leap across Lake Hunter on a pedal-powered sky cycle one year. And every year there's the Miss Drumstick Contest. Local teenagers are covered from head to thigh with baking sacks and the judges rate the . . . drumsticks.

"Okay, Mr. Chicken," intones the announcer, "lead these lovely ladies around the ring. And remember, you're judging the drumsticks!"

As the preliminary events draw to a close, an expectant hush falls over the crowd. It's time for the main event:

183

"ANNOUNCER: Now, will all the adult chicken pluckers please come to the right of the stage. While they are getting ready, ladies and gentlemen, we are going to read you the chicken-plucking rules, which are approved by the International Board of Chicken Pluckers:

"One: We're going to soak the birds in a pot of boiling water—a hundred and forty degrees—for thirty seconds, until all the feathers are wet.

"Two: We will test the longest wing feather, because that should pull easy. If necessary, we will resoak the bird for fifteen seconds.

"Three: When a contestant finishes her birds, she may assist her teammates.

"Four: Judges will particularly note the three resisting areas of the tail feathers, wing, and neck for cleanliness.

"Five: One penalty point will be assessed for any bird mutilated severely. We don't want to hurt these birds too much because they're just dead, you understand.

"Six: The plucked birds will be given to some worthy organization afterward. They have been killed legitimately, thanks to our friends at the Society for Prevention of Cruelty to Animals.

"And here they are—the Senior Chicken Pluckers! (Wild applause from the crowd.) You've seen them on the Johnny Carson Show and "What's My Line" on national television.

UPI RADIO MAN BROADCASTING NEXT TO US: "We're right down here by ringside, folks, giving you the play-by-play. Here come the chickens. They've all been scalded."

ANNOUNCER: "They're putting up the twelve chickens now. Okay, girls, back off two steps so you don't get that blood on you. And put your hands above your heads. Are you ready, timers? On your mark! Get set! Go!

There's pandemonium and wild screaming. A voice from the crowd shrieks "Plucker Power!" The announcer's voice barks over the tumultuous din:

"HURRY! HURRY! HURRY! CLUCK! CLUCK! PLUCK! PLUCK!"

UPI RADIO MAN: "We now have fifteen seconds gone and

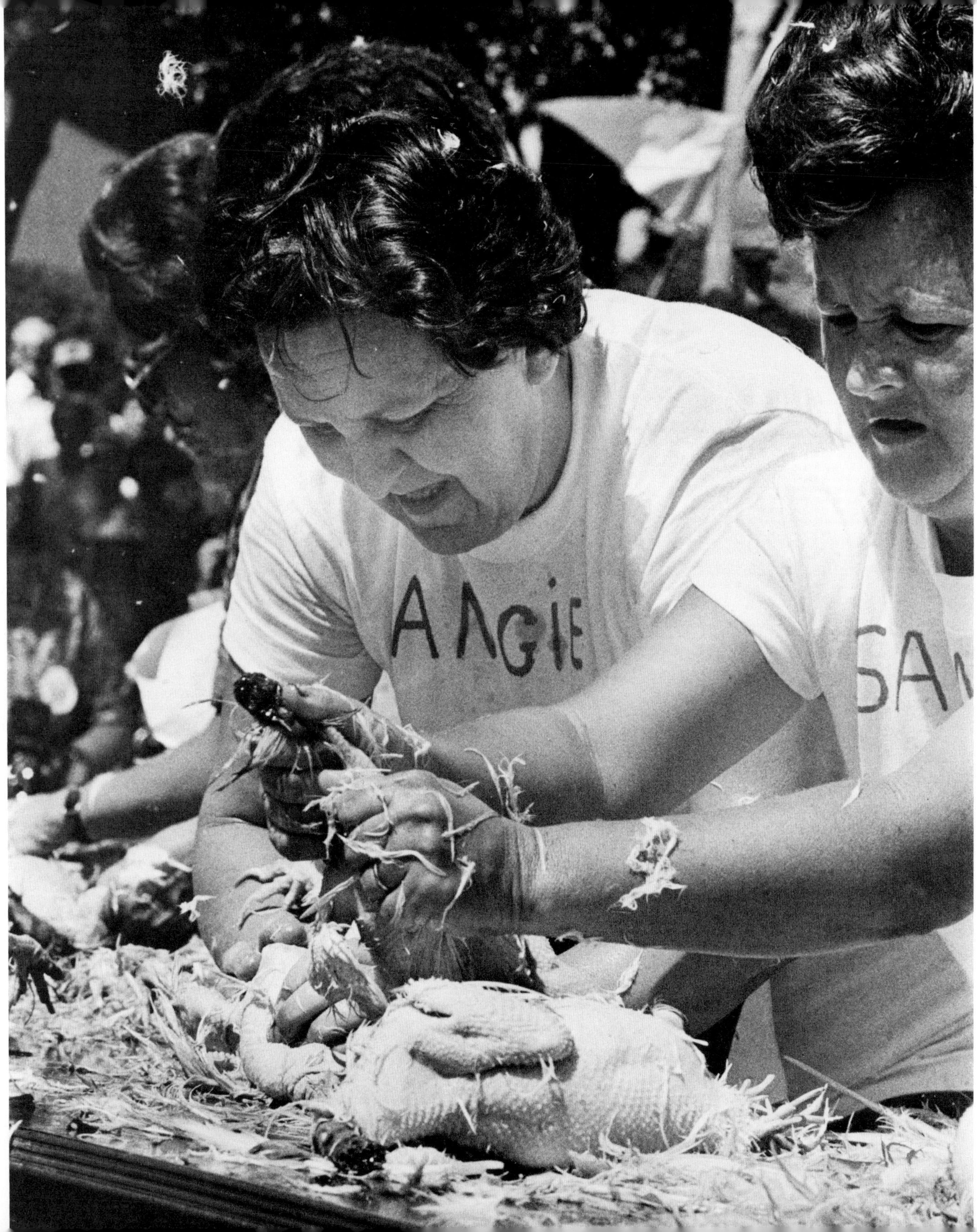
ANGIE

the crowd is going wild. Remember, this is for the World's Championship! It's a real battle. A real battle."

ANNOUNCER: "HURRY! HURRY! HURRY! HURRY! LOOK AT 'EM GO!"

UPI RADIO MAN: "It's now one minute and thirteen seconds and there are feathers all over the place!" (Hoarsely.) "They're right down to the final chicken! One chicken left on each side!" (Hysterically.) "It's going to go right down to the last pinfeather!"

There's an enormous roar from the crowd.

UPI RADIO MAN: "They all practically threw up their hands at the same time, so we'll have to wait for the judges' decision to see who's won."

VOICE FROM BEHIND US: "This has got to be ridiculous."

UPI RADIO MAN: "They were two seconds apart and it looks like Masaryktown is the winner, but it's not official until the judges inspect the chickens. I repeat, it's not official until the judges inspect the chickens. But as of now, Masaryktown is the winner."

"LADIES AND GENTLEMEN, THE WINNER, AND NEW WORLD'S CHAMPION, OF THE INTERNATIONAL CHICKEN PLUCKING CONTEST, IS MASARYKTOWN!"

187

188

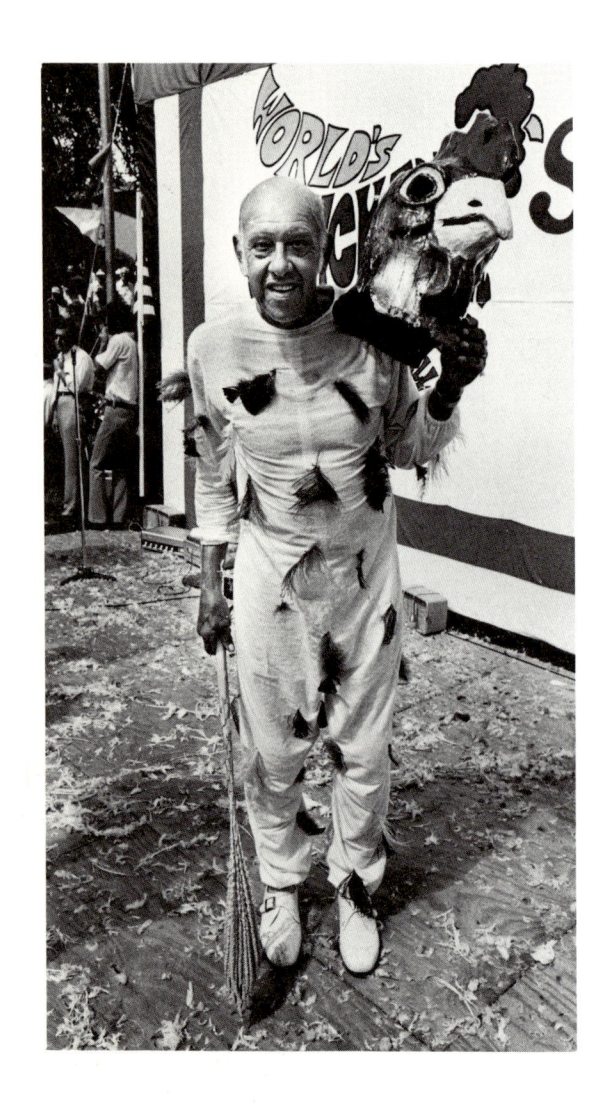

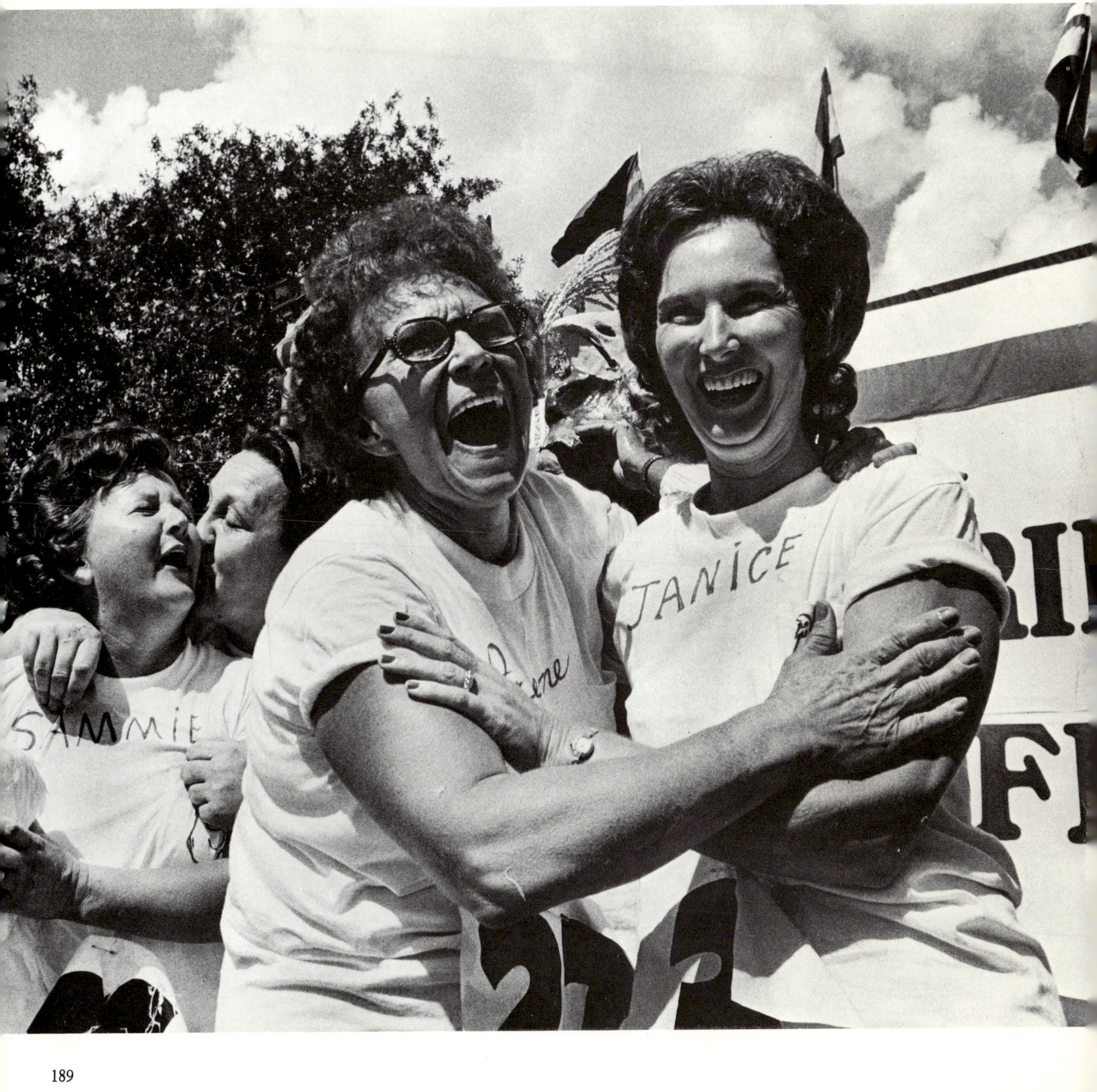
SAMMIE
JANICE

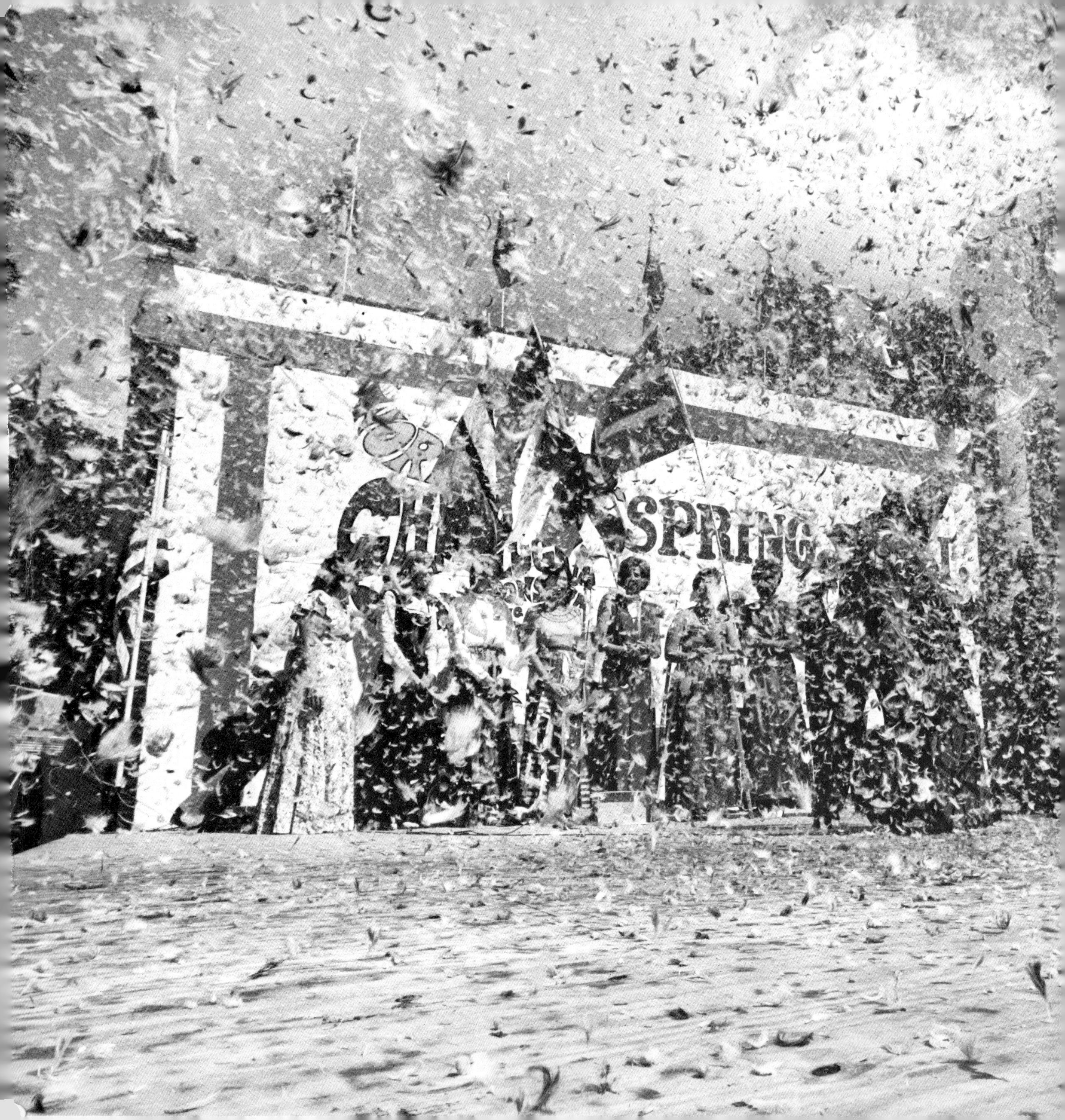
SPRING

The excitement will not subside. Feathers are still falling all over the place. The crowd is buzzing. A lady walks by with a dazed look on her face, wearing a Chicken Plucking eyeshade and carrying a live chicken!

I retreat from the crowd and move to a grassy knoll where I begin unloading my cameras. Another photographer sits down with me and asks, "Are you with a newspaper?"

"No," I reply, "actually I'm taking pictures for a book I'm doing about America at leisure."

"Leisure!" he snorts. "That's where it's at."

He tells me that he's very much into leisure and on alternate weekends he does serious backpacking and equally serious dirt bike racing.

After all these years I should have known better, but I ask him if he thinks there is any incongruity in his choice of leisure activities.

"Back in the sixties," he says, by way of answering, "I was really into the radical trip. You know, outraged by the repression, the injustice, the pollution, the shit in America. I was ready to throw a bomb. Really, man, I was thinking that this was about the worst society going.

"Then I started dating this lady whose parents had come from Denmark and one night at her house I did my thing and her parents went crazy. They had been in Germany when the Nazis took over and, man, they had the stories and the tattoos—and they really did a number on my head. After a couple of months I got to thinking that America was probably the greatest society going."

He stood up, picked up his camera and started back toward the stage. Then he paused and said, "Finally I just quit thinking."

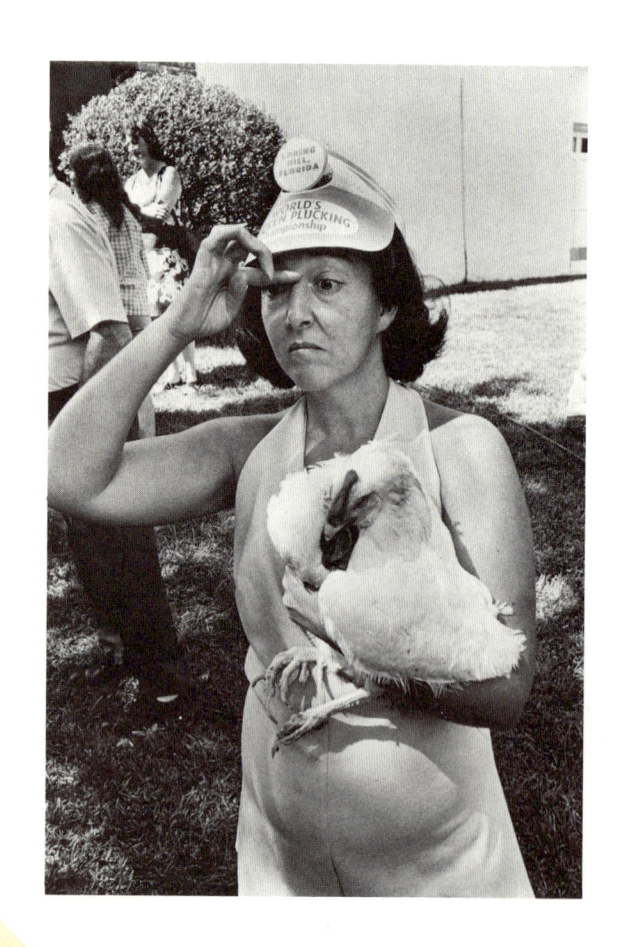

GV
53
.J87

Jury, Mark
    Playtime! :
Americans at leisure

The two Voyager missions in the late summer of 1977 were the climax of the planetary probe series. Their purpose was to explore Jupiter and Saturn as closely as possible by means of photographs and other measurements. Different in their courses and speeds, they collected an incredible amount of information about the two planets. Among their more startling discoveries are these: There is a ring around Jupiter, similar to the familiar rings that circle Saturn. Instead of having six rings, as was believed, Saturn really has hundreds of separate, thin ringlets, as the scientists call them. Also Saturn has at least twenty-one moons, eighteen more than was previously believed. Phoebe, one of Saturn's moons, seems to be rotating in the

The September 5, 1977 blast-off of Voyager 1.

opposite direction to all the other moons. Some experts believe, therefore, that Phoebe is not a moon at all, but a comet that was captured by Saturn's gravity. Eight volcanoes were found in photos of Io, one of the moons of Jupiter, including one in the midst of an eruption. A pocket of gas located near Saturn is the hottest gas known in the solar system. It is up to one million degrees Fahrenheit (560,000 degrees Centigrade), over 300 times hotter than gases in the sun's corona.

By now, Voyager 1 has lost radio contact with earth. It is believed to be flying out to the edge of the solar system and beyond, into the far reaches of space. But Voyager 2 is still active. Heading toward Uranus for an expected 1986 fly-by, it will then possibly fly on to Neptune, nearly 3 billion miles (5 billion km) from earth, for an expected arrival around 1989.

The Voyager space shots mark the close of the first stage of space exploration. At this point in the space program the scientists were prepared to undertake stage two—the Space Shuttle.

The southern hemisphere of Jupiter, with the moon Io in front, as photographed by Voyager 2 on June 25, 1979, when the spacecraft was 8 million miles (12 million km) from earth.

SHUTTLES

5
COUNTDOWN

Count Time

T – 12 years   *Set national space goals*
A Space Task Group is appointed by President Richard Nixon in September 1969. It recommends several goals for space research. Chiefly it aims to achieve a balance between manned and unmanned space efforts and to develop new systems of space transportation.

T – 11 years   *Explore possibility of a Space Shuttle*
In early 1970, NASA begins engineering, design, risk and cost studies of a booster rocket and manned orbiter vehicle that can be recovered and reused. In-depth studies show that the Space Shuttle is a practical idea.

T – 10 years   *Begin development of a Space Shuttle*
Actual planning starts on a Space Shuttle that really will be three vehicles in one: At launch it will be a rocket. Once in orbit it will be a true spacecraft. On return to earth it will land like a glider, a powerless aircraft. And this same craft will make not one, but at least 100 trips into space.

T – 3 years   *Start astronaut training program*
Two astronauts, John W. Young and Captain Robert L. Crippen, are chosen for the first Space Shuttle flight and enter upon their training program. Before launchtime, they will spend 600 hours in the simulator and will learn

Astronauts John W. Young (left) and Robert L. Crippen were chosen to fly the first Space Shuttle mission.

to handle the 2,210 separate dials, controls and displays they will be using during the actual flight.

T – 25 months   *Deliver orbiter to Kennedy Space Center (KSC)*
The orbiter spacecraft, *Columbia,* is flown piggyback on a 747 jet airliner, from California, where it was built, to the KSC in Florida, site of the launch. The *Columbia* looks like a combination of an ordinary delta-wing airplane and a rocket, with its three giant rocket engines in the tail. Less obvious are the forty-six smaller rocket engines for maneuvering in space.

T – 21 months   *Deliver external tank to KSC*
The huge separate tank that carries the fuel and oxidizer is attached to the underbelly of the orbiter.

T – 17 months   *Deliver solid rocket boosters to KSC*
Two additional rockets will be attached on either side of the external fuel tank, beneath the orbiter's wings. They will supply the tremendous thrust needed to raise the orbiter off its launch pad.

T – 5 months   *Mate orbiter, external tank and solid rocket boosters*
The three parts of the Space Shuttle—orbiter, external tank and solid rocket boosters—are hooked up and attached in the KSC's immense Vehicle Assembly Building (VAB). Standing 525 feet (160 m), as high as a 52-story skyscraper, the VAB is the second-largest structure in terms of volume in the world.

T – 4 months   *Test complete Space Shuttle*
Still within the VAB, a whole battery of tests is run on the mechanical, hydraulic and electrical connections between the various units. The on-board flight systems are also tried out.

T – 106 days   *Move Space Shuttle to launch pad 39A*
The assembled Space Shuttle is moved from the VAB to the launch pad on a mobile launcher platform. The mobile launcher covers the distance of 3.5 miles (5.6 km) at the speed of one mile an hour.

T – 53 days   *Test fire engines*
Twenty-second test firing of the orbiter's engines takes place.

T – 30 days   *Rehearse countdown and launch*
The two astronauts in the orbiter and the 200 members of the team in Launch Control Center go over all the steps of the countdown and liftoff. Over the next few days, there are many more practice sessions. The different systems are checked and serviced in preparation for the actual launch.

T – 87 hours   *Call to stations*
Everyone connected with the launch is present for the final four days of the countdown.

T – 77 hours   *Pressurize maneuvering engine tanks*
Fuel and oxidizer are added for the on-board rocket engines that will be used to adjust orbit.

T – 70 hours   *Test fuel cells*
The three batterylike fuel cells that will provide all of the orbiter's electrical

power as well as water during the mission are tested. A fuel cell combines hydrogen and oxygen to produce electrical power, along with water.

T – 68 hours   *Load and test on-board computers*
The five computers in the orbiter that monitor and control the flight are fed the programs for the mission and are tested.

T – 56 hours   *Position solid rocket booster deflectors*
Special flame deflectors are set in place to protect the pad and equipment from blast damage due to heat and flames during launch.

T – 42 hours   *Test payload bay doors*
Behind the cabin is the payload bay where satellites or scientific equipment can be carried. The payload bay doors must be able to be closed for launch and reentry and to be opened during the mission.

T – 18 hours   *Check tracking stations*
Final tests of the network of tracking stations and data collection points scattered over four continents are made. All are equipped with antennas, to maintain two-way communication with the Space Shuttle, and with 126 computers, to process the data they receive.

T – 14 hours   *Retract service structure*
Over the next two hours the part of the tower that is up against the Space Shuttle is slowly moved out of the way.

T – 7 hours   *Clear pad for final countdown*
All service and support personnel, as well as equipment, are taken from the pad. Only those directly involved with the launch remain.

T – 4 hours, 20 minutes   *Begin liquid oxygen fill*
Supercold liquid oxygen, the oxidizer, is pumped into the external tank.

T – 4 hours, 10 minutes   *Begin liquid hydrogen fill*
The liquid hydrogen, the fuel, is pumped into a separate section of the external tank.

T−2 hours, 15 minutes   *Crew wake-up*
The two astronauts are awakened. After breakfast they have a final medical examination, get a briefing on the weather, and are suited up. Inspection and evaluation of the external tank follow.

T−1 hour, 50 minutes   *Crew entry*
The crew enter the orbiter. Their three-level crew quarters contain 525 cubic feet (71.5 cu. m), as much space as a room 14 by 14 by 14 feet (4.3 by 4.3 by 4.3 m). The top level is the flight deck. It contains the controls and displays to pilot the craft and operate all parts of the Space Shuttle. Also located here are monitors to keep a running check on all of its systems.

T−20 minutes   *Start on-board computers*
Computers are set to prepare for launch.

T−9 minutes   *Go for launch*
If no problems are discovered, all systems are made ready for launch.

T−7 minutes   *Retract access arm*
The final connection with ground service is removed.

T−5 minutes   *Start auxiliary orbiter power unit*
The external tank and solid rocket boosters are prepared for firing.

T−3 minutes, 30 seconds   *Start orbiter on internal power*
The fuel cells in the orbiter are activated.

T−2 minutes, 55 seconds   *Pressurize external tank liquid oxygen*
Liquid oxygen is added to the external tank to bring it up to flight pressure.

T−1 minute, 57 seconds   *Pressurize external tank liquid hydrogen*
Liquid hydrogen is added to external tank to bring it up to flight pressure.

T−25 seconds   *Orbiter computer takes control*
The on-board computer is put in charge of final seconds of the countdown.

T−11 seconds   *Release water on launch pad*
The base of the launch pad is flooded with water to absorb the noise and heat of the blast.

T−10 seconds   *Go for launch*

T−3.8 seconds   *Start main engine*

T−0.   *Ignite solid rocket boosters—lift off*

T+6 seconds   *Clear tower*

T+2 minutes, 12 seconds   *Release solid rocket boosters*
After two minutes, when the Space Shuttle is at a height of 30.8 miles (50 km), the fuel of the two solid rockets has been used up. The two empty containers are blasted free of the Shuttle, and fall into the Atlantic Ocean to be picked up and used again.

T+8 minutes, 32 seconds   *Cut off main engine*
At an altitude of 73.6 miles (118.5 km) and a speed of 16,697 miles per hour (26,715 km/h) the orbiter's main engines automatically shut down.

T+8 minutes, 50 seconds   *Release external tank*
At 74.2 miles (118.7 km) from earth and moving at 16,694 miles per hour (26,710 km/h), tiny controlled explosions free the huge, empty external tank from the orbiter. It falls to earth in the Indian Ocean, but is not recovered.

T+10 minutes, 32 seconds   *Ignite orbit maneuver engines*
From time to time, over the next twenty-four hours, the orbiter engines are fired to place the spacecraft in orbit, first at an altitude of 152 miles (245 km) and then at 172 miles (277 km).

T+25 minutes   *Adjust ejection seats*
On achieving orbit, there is no longer any need for the ejection seats, which are useful only in an emergency just before or after liftoff. The seats are stowed out of the way.

T+2 hours   *Test payload bay doors*
The astronauts open and check the payload bay doors. Future missions depend on being able to open and close the doors while in orbit. The open doors also help to get rid of the heat that has built up in the orbiter.

T+5 hours   *Eat meal*
The astronauts take a three-quarter-hour break for lunch.

T+5 hours, 45 minutes   *Test cabin air quality*

T+7 hours, 30 minutes   *Check flight control system*

T+8 hours, 20 minutes   *Check rocket engines*

T+9 hours, 5 minutes   *Take TV pictures*
The astronauts use a hand-held TV camera to film the inside of the cabin. The images are transmitted to earth.

The payload bay doors are opened during flight.

T+9 hours, 50 minutes   *Eat dinner*

T+13 hours   *Sleep*
The crew slumbers for eight hours.

T+22 hours, 45 minutes   *Eat breakfast*
Food, rest, tests and checks of the various instruments and systems of the orbiter occupy the crew for the next thirty hours.

T+53 hours, 27 minutes   *Prepare for reentry*
The orbiter rockets are fired to move out of orbit and start the return trip to earth.

T+53 hours, 56 minutes   *Enter earth's atmosphere*
Passing through the blanket of air that surrounds our planet raises the outside temperature of the orbiter as high as 2,700° F (1,482° C).

T+54 hours, 27 minutes, 43 seconds   *Touchdown*
The orbiter comes in for a landing on the solid bed of Rogers Dry Lake in the Mojave Desert of southern California, at a speed of 215 miles per hour (346 km/h), twice the normal touchdown speed of an airliner. At exactly 1:21 P.M., on April 14, 1981, the highly successful 36-orbit, 54-hour, 21-minute first test flight of the *Columbia* is over.

Touchdown!

6
THE SPACE SHUTTLE

The idea for the Space Shuttle originated in 1969, just a few months after the first manned landing on the moon. The design called for a vehicle that could be launched into space as many as 100 times. Its main purpose was to deliver satellites into orbit, make repairs in space and return satellites to earth.

The artificial satellites the Space Shuttle carries into orbit are used for communication, weather forecasting, scientific observations and military operations. The Space Shuttle crew also checks, services, repairs and returns to earth satellites that have already been placed into orbit. The remarkable Shuttle can even carry into space the materials needed to build space stations or solar power satellites.

At times, the Space Shuttle is a platform from which to observe major events on earth, such as storms, floods, earthquakes, erupting volcanoes and forest fires. It is also a laboratory for scientific experiments. Astronomical observations are free from distortion caused by the earth's atmosphere. What's more, physical and life science research experiments are conducted in a state of zero-gravity.

On a standard mission the Shuttle is launched into low earth orbit where it remains for seven days. During that time the crew carries out its assigned tasks. Then the main part of the spacecraft, the orbiter, returns to earth.

The three parts of the Space Shuttle are the orbiter, with its dark underside, the giant external fuel tank, and the pair of solid rocket boosters.

Within a month, the orbiter is repaired and refitted, and made ready for another flight.

The three main units of the Space Shuttle are the orbiter, the external tank (ET) and the solid rocket boosters.

The orbiter is the main part of the Shuttle. Stretching 121 feet (37 m) long, with a wingspan of 79 feet (24 m), it is about the size of a DC-9 airliner. It carries a crew of two to seven astronauts, and a payload of up to 65,000 pounds (29,500 kg). Before it is fueled, the craft weighs about 150,000 pounds (68,000 kg).

About 31,000 heat-protection tiles cover the outside of the orbiter. The

Two workers make some repairs on the orbiter's glass tiles.

tiles act as a shield during the Shuttle's return to earth, when the temperature reaches +2,700° F (1,482° C). They also protect the craft from the temperature differences in space, which range from +400° F (+200° C) when the sun's rays strike the orbiter to −330° F (−200° C) when it is shaded by the earth. These tiles are quite remarkable. They can be glowing red hot on the outside, yet be cool enough to touch on the inside!

The crew's living quarters are at the very front of the orbiter. The top level is the flight deck. Here are located the controls and displays needed to operate and monitor all the orbiter's various flight, communication and life-support systems. There is seating for up to four crew members on the flight deck.

The mid deck contains a living area with additional seating and a toilet. On this level, too, is the galley, or kitchen, where the astronauts' food is prepared. Nighttime accommodations consist of sleeping bags that are either attached upright to the wall or lie flat in horizontal compartments. When you are weightless, it doesn't matter if you are upright or horizontal. Astronauts who are not zippered into these bags actually float about the cabin while asleep.

To get to the payload bay, the astronauts must pass through the airlock found at the rear of the mid deck. All the equipment necessary for keeping a comfortable environment in the cabin, and a temperature that lets the astronauts work in shirtsleeves, is found on the bottom deck.

The giant payload bay, 60 feet (18.3 m) long and 15 feet (4.6 m) in diameter, is situated behind the crew quarters. It is big enough to house the largest unmanned satellite or a complete space lab unit. The payload bay area is covered by doors that are closed during launch and landing, but usually remain open while the Shuttle is in orbit.

The three huge liquid-fuel rocket engines at the extreme rear of the orbiter are used only for launch. Each one has a thrust of 470,000 pounds (2 million newtons). Forty-six smaller rocket engines at various points around the outside of the craft are used to make midflight adjustments or come out of orbit. They vary in power, producing anywhere from 25 pounds (111 newtons) to 6,000 pounds (27,000 newtons) of thrust.

The orbiter's main engines are powered by fuel that is carried in the external tank (ET). This immense shell is the height of a fifteen-story building—154 feet (47 m) long—with a diameter of 28.6 feet (8.7 m). The one and one-half million pounds (700,000 kg) of liquid hydrogen (the fuel) and liquid oxygen (the oxidizer) are kept in the ET. The oxidizer is necessary, since the fuel cannot burn in space without oxygen.

The two booster rockets, each 149 feet (45 m) long and 12 feet (4 m) in diameter, hold a solid fuel that is different from the liquid fuel used for the orbiter's engines. The solid fuel is made up of 1.1 million pounds (500,000 kg) of aluminum powder (the fuel) and ammonium perchlorate powder (the oxidizer). The mixture looks and feels like the white eraser at the end of your pencil. When ignited, each solid rocket booster provides 2.6 million pounds (12 million newtons) of thrust.

At launch, both the orbiter's main engines and the solid rocket boosters provide the thrust that lifts the Space Shuttle off the pad. After only two minutes or so, the solid rocket fuel is all burned up and the two empty rocket shells separate from the orbiter. Parachutes automatically open and carry the rocket shells slowly down to a landing in the Atlantic Ocean, about 160 miles (257 km) east of the Kennedy Space Center. Here United States ships await their arrival. Later, they are restored and used again. A new pair of boosters costs $50 million; $14 million buys a refilled pair.

After their fuel is burned up, the two solid rocket boosters are released. They fall into the Atlantic Ocean, where they are recovered by waiting ships.

About eight minutes after launch, the orbiter engines have burned up all the fuel in the ET. The empty tank separates and disintegrates as it falls harmlessly into the Indian Ocean. The ET is the only part of the Space Shuttle that is not saved and put into action again.

The astronauts use the orbiter's small rocket engines to get into the exact orbit in space that they desire. The Space Shuttle's highest orbit is about 600 miles (1,000 km). While in orbit the crew carries out the various tasks of the mission.

To return, they fire the orbiter's engines, which push them out of orbit, and the first leg of the journey down to earth begins. On entering the earth's atmosphere the orbiter changes from a spacecraft to a glider. Without any power of its own, the craft is brought down gently for a landing on smooth ground.

The *Columbia,* the first orbiter ever built, was used for all early flights in 1981 and 1982. More advanced orbiters—*Challenger, Discovery* and *Atlantis*—have now come into service. NASA estimates that these four craft, with a turnaround time of about one month, will be able to meet all of the country's space shuttle needs until the year 2000.

About one-third of the Shuttle's cargo space will probably be used for military satellites. The remainder will be available to private companies and government agencies. The cost, though, will be high. Payment for use of the entire payload bay in *Columbia* in the first flights amounted to an "early bird" special price of about $4 million. The regular expense, starting around October 1985, will be a cool $90 million.

In May 1983, a special study group recommended that private citizens be allowed to go along on Space Shuttle flights, the first passengers being writers, broadcasters, photographers and poets. Before this is possible, though, Congress will have to change NASA's charter, which forbids private passengers on any space flights.

7
SHUTTLES AT WORK

STS-1

April 12, 1981, marked the first launch of the Space Shuttle *Columbia,* with astronauts John W. Young, fifty, a test pilot, and Captain Robert L. Crippen, forty-three, a research pilot in the U.S. Navy, on board. The flight, called STS-1 (Space Transportation System-1), though a spectacular success, was not without its minor problems.

Just before launch an on-board computer was found to be forty thousandths of a second out of synchronization with the other four computers. Then during launch the force of the blast knocked 17 of the 31,000 protective heat tiles off the *Columbia*. The loss was not serious enough to cancel the mission, however.

At one point while in orbit, the cabin temperature dropped to a bone-chilling 37° F (2.7° C). "I was ready to break out the long undies," joked one of the astronauts. But a radio signal from earth sent warm air through the cabin's heating tubes, bringing the temperature up to a comfortable level.

Matters had hardly settled down on board when a flight recorder mysteriously stopped working. The astronauts tried to make repairs, but the cover had been screwed on so tightly they were unable to open the case. They had to get along without it.

Later on, the heating unit for the hydraulic system that operates the landing gear and other flight control equipment went out of order. Since there were two back-up heaters, there was no immediate danger. Nevertheless, the astronauts were able to get the broken unit to work again.

One final mishap occurred during the landing. The *Columbia* kicked up pebbles from the dry lake bed, chipping a number of tiles. The damage, though, was slight.

These unimportant "glitches" aside, the Space Shuttle proved to be a triumph for NASA's engineers and scientists. As Crippen modestly put it, "That was one fantastic ride."

STS-2

On November 12, 1981, *Columbia* became the first space vehicle to be launched into space a second time. Aboard were Joe H. Engle, forty-nine, U.S. Air Force, and Captain Richard H. Truly, forty-four, U.S. Navy.

Despite a number of problems that delayed the countdown, the liftoff was perfect. But then, about one hour into the flight, difficulties arose. One of the three suitcase-sized fuel cells that provide the *Columbia* with electric power and water showed too high temperature and acid levels. The trouble persisted even though many attempts were made to correct it. The craft could probably have carried out its mission with two working cells, but according to safety rules the mission would have to be aborted after 54 hours at the most, if the fuel cell was not repaired. It was not, and the planned 124-hour mission was cut short.

Most of the flight down was automatically controlled by computer. As the craft was leveling off Engle asked to take over the controls. He glided the *Columbia* to a perfect touchdown on November 14 at Edwards Air Force Base in California.

Even though their time in space had been cut in half, Engle and Truly achieved about ninety percent of the goals set for STS-2.

Among the most important were tests that involved the $100-million mechanical arm. This Canadian-made device has joints at the shoulder, elbow and wrist, just like a human arm. Fully extended it is 50 feet (15.3 m) long and 15 inches (38 cm) wide. The "hand" consists of a wire mechanism that can grasp payloads, such as satellites. The arm is equipped with its own

A backward glance at planet earth from Columbia's *orbit in space.*

lighting system and closed-circuit TV. This gives the crew a good view of what they are doing. It can also be used to reach around and examine various outside parts of the *Columbia*. Although the astronauts did not move loads with the arm, they did use the TV camera to film them holding a sign that read "Hi, Mom!"

One disappointment of the STS-2 had to do with an experiment growing sunflowers in zero-gravity. Because the time in space was cut short, the seeds did not grow enough to enable the experimenters to tell whether they were disturbed by being weightless.

Other scientific instruments aboard the shuttle were also tested and found to work well. Experiments showed that radar and infrared sensors carried on the craft could be used to search out geological features on earth, such as deposits of oil or minerals. In fact, on this flight the astronauts found a 3-mile-wide area of the Baja California desert that showed rich deposits of gold, silver and other metals. Several months later, scientists flew in helicopters to the isolated site and confirmed the shuttle's findings. From their position in space, Engle and Truly also took photos of lightning bolts that will help scientists understand severe storms on earth.

STS-3

Launched on March 22, 1982, STS-3 became not only the longest and busiest Space Shuttle test flight but also the most difficult. By the close of the eight-day flight, astronauts Colonel Jack R. Lousma, forty-six, U.S. Marine Corps, and Colonel C. Gordon Fullerton, forty-five, U.S. Air Force, had completed 129 orbits (a distance of 3.9 million miles [6.24 million km]), and performed nearly all the tests they set out to do.

This third flight of *Columbia* began only four months after the end of the STS-2 mission. One of its main goals was to expose the craft to the maximum limits of temperature. The tail was pointed toward the heat of the sun for a thirty-hour period and later the nose for eighty hours. Finally the top of the shuttle, with the payload bay doors open, was exposed for twenty-six hours.

The crew used the robot arm to move measuring instruments outside and inside the payload bay to sniff and sample the space environment. And they tested the steadiness of the arm and grip while they made the *Columbia* roll and pitch by firing the small rocket engines. The results were favorable. The arm barely shook; its grip remained tight.

Loaded with an array of astronomy and space science payloads in its cargo bay, STS-3 gathered a lot of information on the effect of *Columbia*'s movement on the gases in the space environment through which it passed, and the buildup of electrical and magnetic charges on its metal skin.

On its mission, *Columbia* carried experiments to study the x rays emitted by solar flares and to gain more information about solar radiation. There was research, too, into the makeup and behavior of micrometeorites, the tiny bits of space dust that strike every object in space.

Eighteen-year-old Todd E. Nelson, from Southland High School in Adams, Minnesota, won a contest for an experiment that could be run on STS-3. He wanted to learn how weightlessness affects the flight of insects, such as flies, moths and honey-bees. The astronauts observed the cages of insects while in orbit. They reported that the insects did not fly at all. Instead they clung to the sides of their plastic cages unless disturbed by one of the men.

Early in the mission, the crew of the STS-3 encountered a few annoyances.

Counted in the trouble was motion sickness, an overheated power unit, a cabin that was either too hot or too cold, loud radio static when they flew over a certain part of Asia, and a toilet that didn't work right. Fortunately, most of the difficulties were cleared up by the third day and the rest of the trip went without a hitch.

Touchdown came on March 30 at White Sands, New Mexico. Heavy rains had soaked Rogers Dry Lake bed in California's Mojave Desert, the usual landing field for shuttle flights, forcing the change. Still far from retirement, the *Columbia* was returned to the Kennedy Space Center to be refurbished for its fourth and final test mission.

STS-4

The last test flight of the *Columbia*, June 27 to July 4, 1982, was virtually trouble-free. All major systems worked satisfactorily in orbit. The astronauts, Captain Thomas Mattingly II, forty-six, U.S. Navy, and Henry W. Hartsfield, Jr., forty-eight, a former Air Force test pilot, cruised around the earth at an orbit altitude of about 185 miles (297 km).

During their first day in orbit, the *Columbia*'s astronauts tested some equipment for preparing super-pure drugs. The experiment's purpose was to learn whether working in zero-gravity would help to obtain a high level of drug purity. Johnson and Johnson, the drug manufacturer who sponsored the project, is most pleased with the results and is planning more research in space.

A top-secret package of military experiments was also aboard. It is believed that among them were sensing devices designed to track enemy missiles and navigational instruments to assist military planes and ships.

New to the STS-4 was the first set of Getaway Special experiments. These are a group of small, self-contained scientific and technological experiments that can be run in space for a fee of from $3,000 to $10,000. The STS-4 bore a cluster of nine experiments devised by Utah State University students.

Following up on previous astronauts' observations of storm clouds and associated lightning, the STS-4 crew photographed and recorded the lightning within storm clouds. Their methods may prove useful in understanding pictures taken by weather satellites.

As the shuttle neared the end of its flight it was hailed as the smoothest ever. For the entire night before the landing, the *Columbia* was put into its "barbecue mode." That is to say, through periodic firings of its control rockets, the spacecraft rolled slowly around and around. All points on the craft were exposed to equal amounts of sun and shade, heat and cold. The purpose was to smooth out any unevenness on its surfaces.

After seven days of orbiting, the astronauts steered the winged spaceship to a perfect touchdown on July 4, 1982. It was the *Columbia*'s first landing on a concrete runway, at Edwards Air Force Base.

It took ten years of development, fifteen months of test flying, 9 million miles of orbital tests, and over $10 billion to prove that *Columbia* was a spaceworthy craft. Now the vehicle was ready to be operational. It was ready to earn its way by making regular runs into and back from space.

STS-5

The STS-5, *Columbia*'s first operational flight, lasted five days, from November 11 to 16, 1982. It differed in a few ways from the four test flights that had come before.

The STS-5 had a job to do. The shuttle was to carry up and launch into their own orbits two communication satellites, each weighing about 7,000 pounds (3,175 kg). Eight hours after launch the first satellite, SBS 3, owned by Satellite Business Systems, Inc., was ejected by a powerful spring from its holder in the open cargo bay. When it had drifted about 16 miles (26 km) away from the shuttle, its own rocket motors were fired. The SBS 3 soared to an orbit altitude of 22,300 miles (35,900 km), high above *Columbia*'s 185-mile (297-km) orbit. The following day another, similar satellite, Anik 3, owned by Telesat Canada, was launched in the same way. The two satellite owners paid NASA a fee of $18 million for the launchings.

Instead of the usual two crew members, the STS-5 had four. The commander and pilot were Vance D. Brand, fifty-one, an astronaut for sixteen years, and Colonel Robert F. Overmyer, forty-six, of the U.S. Marine Corps. There were also two mission specialists, Joseph P. Allen, forty-five, and William B. Lenoir, forty-three. Before they became astronauts, Dr. Allen was a staff physicist at the Nuclear Structure Laboratory at Yale University and Dr. Lenoir served as professor of engineering at the Massachusetts Institute of Technology.

On Sunday, Lenoir and Allen were scheduled to go for the first EVA—extra-vehicular activity—in the shuttle program. The two mission specialists were to spend three hours in the open cargo bay testing new space suits and practicing skills required to repair or service satellites on future missions.

Each space suit cost about $2 million. They were much better than those used for earlier space walks and on the moon. The new suits were more flexible, allowing the astronauts to do many more activities, and had highly advanced life support systems.

On this mission, however, they did not work well. Allen found that the fan that was supposed to circulate the oxygen in his suit did not function properly. And Lenoir's suit did not reach the correct pressure. What makes these findings so surprising is that each suit had been pretested 220 times!

Following the advice of experts on the ground, the astronauts tried to repair the suits. But their efforts were in vain. Finally, and with great reluctance, the EVA was scrubbed.

The rest of the flight was uneventful. The descent and landing were textbook perfect. The four tests and the operational flight convinced everyone, beyond a doubt, that the Space Shuttle really worked. A new era in space had indeed begun.

Challenger

In April 1983, the *Challenger*, lighter and more powerful than *Columbia*, became the second Space Shuttle to start regular flights into space. Despite nearly three months of delay due to engine problems, the flight itself was perfect. The only difficulty was that the communication satellite it launched did not reach the proper altitude. Radio signals from earth that fired the

Dr. Sally K. Ride with fellow STS-7 crew members, from left to right: Robert Crippen, commander; Dr. Norman Thagard and John Fabian, mission specialists; and Frederick Hauck, pilot.

satellite's own small rocket engines finally placed it in the right orbit.

The two highlights of STS-7 in June 1983 were that Dr. Sally K. Ride, thirty-two, an astrophysicist, was on board, becoming the first American woman in space, and that for the first time the robotic arm was used to release into space and then retrieve a 3,200-pound (1,450-kg) satellite. This was a rehearsal for future missions to capture and repair satellites already in space.

On and on the Space Shuttle flights go—more and more often. By 1990, NASA estimates, it will be launching thirty missions a year—about one every twelve days!

52

SATELLITES

8
INTRODUCTION TO SATELLITES

In astronomy, a satellite is a body that orbits or revolves around a larger body or planet. The moon is a natural satellite of earth. Most of the planets in the solar system have satellites circling around them.

Until 1957 the moon was the earth's only satellite. But then, on October 4 of that year, Russia sent Sputnik 1 aloft. Sputnik was the world's first artificial satellite. For about four months it continued to orbit around earth. Soon after Sputnik's flight ended, the United States launched its first artificial satellite, Explorer 1, on January 31, 1958.

Since then nearly 5,000 artificial satellites have been launched. About 500 are still in orbit and in use today. Most of the rest have drifted out of orbit; a few have fallen to earth.

Satellites come in all sizes and shapes. They don't have to be streamlined, since they do not move through the air. Their orbits are all above the earth's atmosphere where there is no air pressure. They are sent up for many different purposes. The main ones are communication, scientific research, weather observation and military guidance and surveillance.

All satellites are launched from earth by rockets. In the past, the method was to place the satellite in the rocket's nose cone. Then, when the rocket reached the proper height, the satellite was ejected into orbit, and the rocket fell back. But starting in November 1982, satellites have been carried

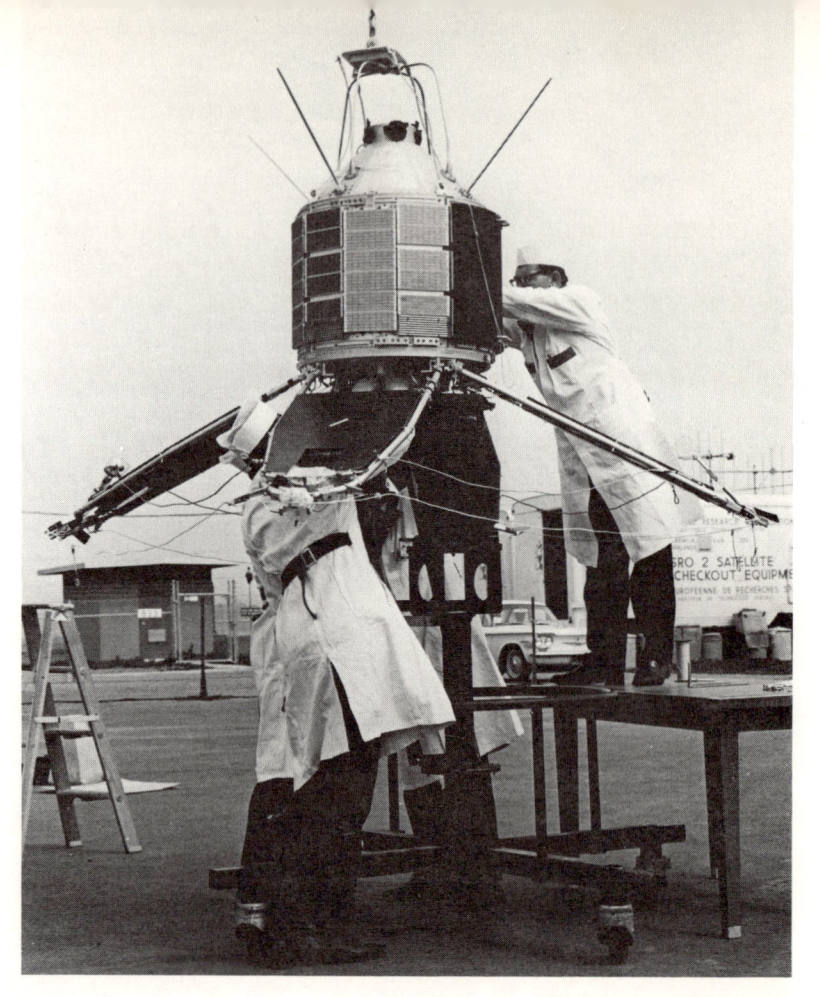

Technicians check a satellite in preparation for launch.

up above the earth's atmosphere by the Space Shuttle. From an altitude of around 150 miles (240 km) the satellite is ejected from the Shuttle's payload bay. Small rocket engines on the satellite then raise it to the desired altitude.

The satellites are all linked to earth by radio signals. The signals from earth can be TV or radio programs, telephone conversations, words, numbers or pictures, data from computers, or commands that direct the satellite's movements and operations. Communication satellites merely take in the signals they are sent, and beam them back to different points on earth. The scientific, weather and military satellites carry out the instructions they receive. Then they radio down the results, which can be data of various sorts, images of earth, views through a telescope, or whatever.

The satellites are circling earth in orbits at various heights or altitudes. Nothing "holds up" the satellites. They are able to stay in orbit because they strike a balance between the speed of their forward motion and the downward pull of gravity. The lower the orbit, the greater the pull of gravity. Therefore, the greater must be the orbit speed of the satellite.

Take a satellite in an orbit 200 miles (320 km) high, for example. The satellite must have a speed of over 17,000 miles per hour (27,350 km/h) to remain in orbit. But at an altitude of 22,000 miles (35,400 km) the satellite need be traveling only at 7,000 miles per hour (11,260 km/h). The particular altitude chosen for each satellite depends on the job it is to do.

Satellites stay in orbit by striking a balance between their forward speed and the downward pull of gravity.

9
COMMUNICATION SATELLITES

Satellites that are lifted into orbits thousands of miles above the earth for the purpose of sending radio, TV, text, pictures and other signals to different parts of the world are called communication satellites. Signals are beamed to these satellites from transmitting stations on the ground by means of special antennas. Then the satellites send the signals back to earth. The signals can be received at stations thousands of miles away from the transmitting station.

Communication by satellite avoids the problems of radio or television broadcasting. When radio waves are sent from the transmitter antenna, they travel out in all directions. Some go up into the sky and are reflected back to earth by an electrically charged layer in the sky called the ionosphere. The ionosphere is from 60 to 300 miles (97 to 483 km) above the earth. By bouncing back and forth between the ground and the ionosphere, these radio waves can travel distances of hundreds or even thousands of miles. But the greater the distance, the weaker the signal.

Television broadcast waves are even shorter than radio waves. They are not reflected at all by the ionosphere. They go straight out into space. To pick up a TV signal, the receiver has to be in a line of sight with the transmitter. Unless you live within 100 miles (160 km) or so of the TV transmitter, you cannot receive the programs.

For greater distances, the signals must be beamed between microwave towers that are no more than about 35 miles (56 km) apart. Antennas on each tower receive the signal and pass it on to the next tower or to the receivers in the area. The only other way to carry TV signals farther is to send them through cables or wires. Both microwave towers and cables, however, are expensive and difficult systems to build and keep up.

The idea of using a satellite for long-distance radio communication first arose in the mid-1940s. Some German scientists sent a signal up to the earth's natural satellite, the moon. Due to its shape, the moon reflected back only about seven percent of the original signal.

The next year, scientific visionary and writer Arthur C. Clarke suggested the idea of orbiting artificial satellites. The satellites would receive radio signals from earth and rebroadcast them over a wide area on earth.

A satellite in orbit at an altitude of 22,300 miles (35,900 km), Clarke said, would always hover over the same spot on earth. Just as a mark on a revolving car tire is always over the same point on the wheel hub, the satellite is always fixed over the same site on earth. Such a satellite is said to be in geosynchronous or geostationary orbit. But before Clarke's vision could become a reality, many scientific advances had to be made.

The first step came late in 1958 when the U.S. Army Signal Corps launched the first test artificial satellite, called SCORE (Signal Communication Orbit Repeater Experiment). SCORE was not in geosynchronous orbit. As it passed over the transmitter on earth, signals were sent up, which were automatically stored on tape. On its next pass over the area, SCORE rebroadcast the signals back to earth. After thirteen days of operation, though, its batteries went dead and SCORE stopped working.

SCORE was called an active communication satellite, because it included a receiver to pick up signals from earth, an amplifier to strengthen them, and a transmitter to broadcast them back.

In 1960 NASA launched another kind of satellite. It was Echo 1, this nation's first passive communication satellite. Such satellites merely reflect signals beamed in their direction, much as a mirror reflects light.

Echo 1 was nothing more than an immense plastic balloon, the size of a ten-story building, thinly coated with shiny aluminum. The entire 100-foot (160-km) satellite weighed just 135 pounds (61 kg) and folded into a holder the size of a beach ball for launch. In space, it automatically inflated to its full size.

The radio signals that are sent to a passive satellite must be quite strong to begin with because they weaken as they make their way to space and back. The satellite must also be very large to reflect enough radio energy. And receiving stations must be very sensitive to pick up the weak reflected signal.

While Echo 1 was less advanced than SCORE, like other passive satellites it did not depend on batteries that could go dead or electronic equipment that could fail. Passive satellites such as Echo 1 have the added advantage of being able to reflect signals from many ground stations at once.

The first message sent via Echo was transmitted by President Eisenhower during the satellite's first orbit. Then a telegram was beamed from America to France, followed by the transmission of a photograph, line by line, from Iowa to Texas. On April 24, 1967, the silvery satellite transmitted a TV signal for the first time in history.

Echo 1 completed more than 40,000 orbits over the next seven and one-half years. During that time many of the tiny meteorites that speed through space pierced the thin skin of the balloon. It lost gas gradually until the spring of 1968, when it entered the earth's atmosphere and burned up.

The U.S. Army sent up several active satellites during the 1960s. Courier 1B, launched in the fall of 1960, was not powered by batteries, like SCORE, but was covered with solar cells, which changed sunlight directly into electricity.

The Army put on an amazing show of Courier's skill. Actors made a thirty-six-hour tape recording of the entire Bible. The tape, played at high speed, was transmitted to Courier during fourteen minutes of one orbit, while the satellite was in sight of the ground station. On its next overflight, the satellite was instructed to broadcast back the signals it had received. When

Panels of solar cells provide the newer satellites with energy from the sun.

played back, the result was a perfectly clear thirty-six-hour recording of the Bible.

A mechanical defect led to the failure of the Courier after less than one month. But in that short time it had relayed nearly 120 million words and about sixty pictures.

In 1962, for a fee of $3 million, NASA launched the first private communication satellite for American Telephone and Telegraph (AT&T). Called Telstar, it was a small, active satellite that weighed 170 pounds (77 kg) and had 15,000 separate parts, including 1,064 transistors and 3,600 solar cells. It could carry sixty two-way telephone conversations at the same time.

The success of the experimental communication satellites led fourteen nations around the world to band together in 1964 to form the International Telecommunications Satellite Consortium or Intelsat. The first Intelsat, called Early Bird or Intelsat 1, was placed into geosynchronous orbit over the Atlantic Ocean in 1965. Weighing 83.5 pounds (38 kg), it could carry either 240 telephone calls or one TV program at a time between the United States and Europe. By 1969 three Intelsats were in space, one each over the Atlantic, Pacific and Indian Oceans. These three satellites alone served the entire globe, except for some areas around the north and south poles.

Today there are nine Intelsat satellites in orbit. Each is designed to remain

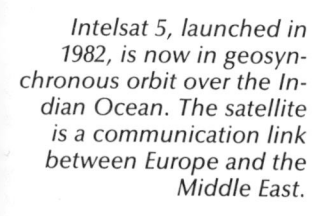

Intelsat 5, launched in 1982, is now in geosynchronous orbit over the Indian Ocean. The satellite is a communication link between Europe and the Middle East.

aloft for seven to ten years. Every one can handle 12,000 telephone conversations or twenty color TV transmissions at one time. About two-thirds of all international communication among the 105 nations that now belong to Intelsat is handled by these satellites. And new models are being designed that will more than triple the capacity of each one.

Numbers of satellites are needed because single satellites can serve only part of the earth at one time. Altogether about seventy communication satellites hover over the equator at this time. Even though they are at least 450 miles (724 km) apart, there is danger of overcrowding as new ones are launched. Scientists believe if they get any closer to one another than 200 miles (320 km), the signals will interfere with one another.

A new use of communication satellites began in the early 1980s, with the Satellite Master Antenna Television (SMATV) and Direct Broadcast Satellite (DBS) services. Both send TV programs to people's homes directly from satellites; the signals are received on dish-shaped antennas facing up toward the satellite. From the antenna the TV signals pass over wires to each TV set.

SMATV is designed to serve a large number of families in a house or apartment complex. It is already in use at several residential communities in Florida, Texas and Arizona. DBS is still in the planning stage, with service expected to begin about 1985. Here each house will have its own two-and-one-half-foot (0.76-m) dish antenna on the roof to receive the satellite signals.

To make sure the SMATV and DBS programs are received only by paying customers, the electronic signal is sent in a scrambled form. Subscribers have a built-in unscrambler that changes the jumbled signal into clear pictures and sounds. All others get only a scrambled image and noise.

For now, and for the immediate future, there are more communication satellites in space than any other type of artificial satellite. Communication satellites can spread news of important events throughout the world in a matter of seconds. They are such powerful tools of information and education, in fact, that some nations are trying to set up international controls on the operation of communication satellites in their lands.

10
SCIENTIFIC, WEATHER AND MILITARY SATELLITES

Scientific Satellites

The first American scientific satellite, Explorer 1, was launched on January 31, 1958. This satellite is given credit for having discovered two very important doughnut-shaped regions of charged electrical particles around the earth called the Van Allen belts. Dozens of scientific satellites since then have collected additional stores of information, both about earth and about space.

Take the basic shape of the earth. It was long believed to be the shape of a globe. Satellite studies show that it has a slight pear shape, and is not completely round. To add to the new view of the earth, the equator is an ellipse, not a perfect circle.

Map makers always complain about mistakes found in about seventy-five percent of all maps. These maps, which are often based on the findings of explorers traveling on foot, have features that may be dozens of miles off.

For some time it has been known that the best way to make an exact map is to use aerial photos, taken from airplanes. But about one million individual photos are needed to cover just the continental United States. Today the job of preparing maps is being done by satellite pictures. With only 400 photos, all the most important features of the country, coast to coast, can be seen.

In recent years, the demand for oil, metals and other minerals has vastly increased. Satellites have been put to work searching out new deposits. In some cases, satellite photos have pointed out particular geological formations, such as folds or faults in the earth's surface, that scientists know are associated with some mineral deposits.

In other instances, underground deposits produce heat, which the satellite can discover with special temperature-sensitive instruments. Certain minerals that glow can be spotted from satellites. And ore deposits in the ground cause a weaker gravity force over the spots where they are located. Satellites are able to measure differences in gravity where they exist.

Satellites study the earth's water resources. They can measure currents, temperature, ice conditions, fish movement and tidal waves in the ocean. By monitoring the flow of water in rivers, the water level in lakes, the amount of melting snow and conditions of flooding, they can help determine the best places for dams. Satellites can check for water pollution and even trace it back to its source.

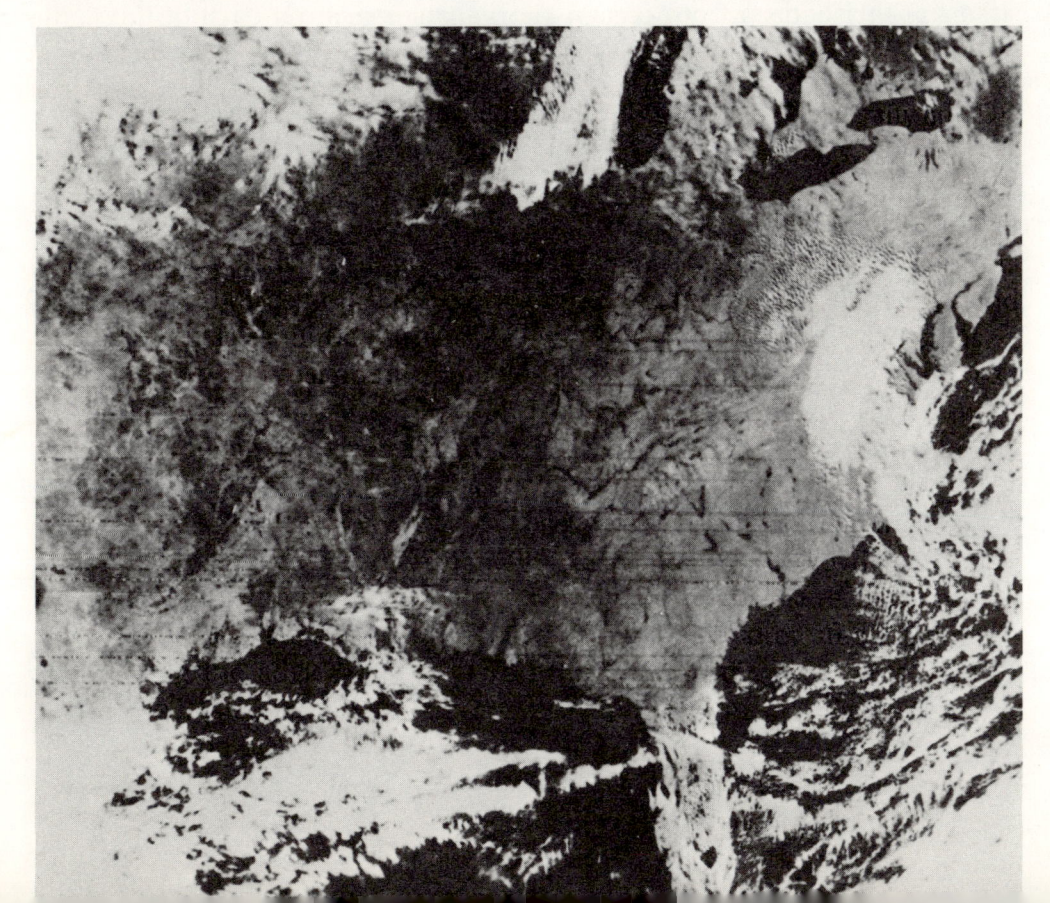

This satellite view of the United States clearly shows many of the nation's lakes and rivers.

Farmers and foresters worldwide have taken information from satellites and put it to good use. The data gathered by these devices can show the number of acres devoted to each crop, the plants that are suffering from disease, drought or insects, the presence of soil erosion and the level of moisture in the soil.

Plans for building housing and factories, installing transportation systems, creating recreational areas and providing other land uses can most easily be made with satellite photos. Even the movements of large herds of animals, or of particular creatures with radio transmitters attached to them, can be followed by satellite.

Perhaps you already know some of these general uses of satellites. But are you aware of satellites that are used for very specific scientific purposes?

Lageos (Laser Geodynamics Satellite), for example, makes accurate measurements of the tiny movements or drift of the continents on earth. On the Lageos surface are 426 reflectors to bounce laser beams back to earth. The lasers are flashed up from certain spots scattered about each of the continents and are reflected back to the source. By knowing the exact location of Lageos, and carefully computing the time for the round trip, scientists can

A worker conducts the final tests on the Lageos satellite, with its 426 reflectors. In space, Lageos is used to measure the tiny movements of the earth's crust.

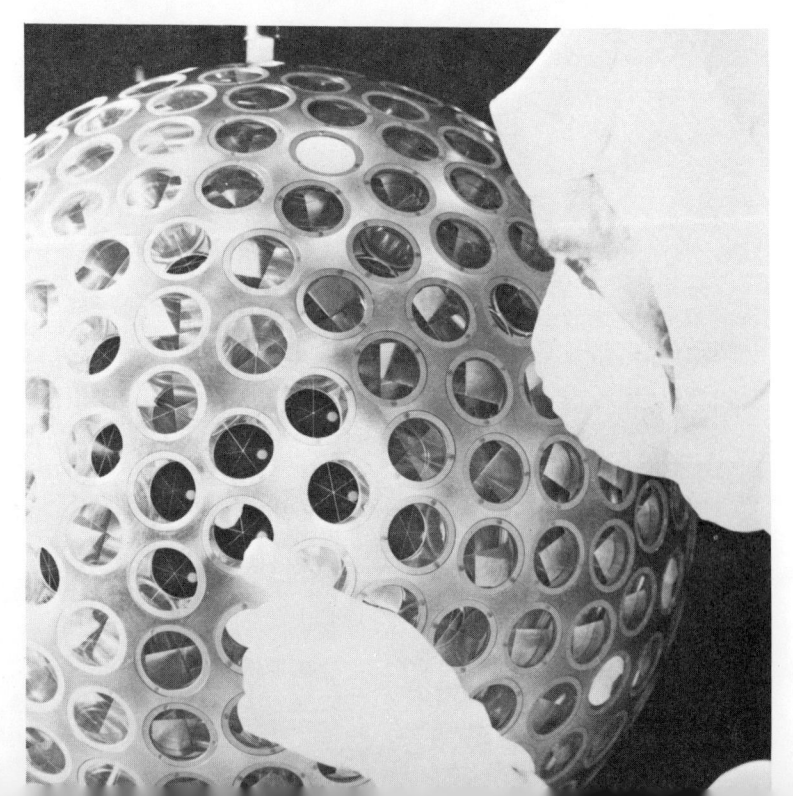

pinpoint the source to within two inches. Since the movements of the continents are measured in tiny fractions of an inch each year, this is a long-term project. Lageos will probably stay in orbit for at least fifty years.

The two Dynamic Explorer (DE) satellites, which were launched in August 1981, were planned to study the worldwide effect of energy emitted from the sun. These sensitive devices note changes in the earth's atmosphere, in the weather and in the long-range climate. Recent findings are telling us more about the sun's effect on radio signals.

The DE 1 and 2 are traveling in polar orbit, that is, they fly over the poles rather than the equator. The orbit of DE 1 is at 14,000 miles (22,500 km); DE 2 is at 800 miles (1,300 km).

Of all recent scientific and resource measurement satellites the Landsats are most outstanding. Four of them were put into orbit by NASA from 1972 to 1982.

The latest one, Landsat 4, is quite a remarkable piece of equipment. With a weight of 4,273 pounds (1,938 kg), and designed to stay aloft for three years, it is able to "see" the earth below. The actual term is "remote sensing." From its orbit at 438 miles (705 km) it takes photos, or rather builds images, of a strip of earth 115 miles (185 km) wide. Each image covers an area about the size of the state of Maryland; it takes 570 combined images to picture the entire continental United States.

Like the earlier Landsats, the most recent version has a Multispectral Scanner (MSS). Passing over the earth, it picks up four wavelengths or colors of light: visible red, green, and two lengths of infrared light. The Thematic Mapper (TM), a special feature of Landsat 4, is sensitive to seven different wavelengths. This advanced model gives back images that are many times clearer and sharper than MSS.

From the images created at each wavelength we get various kinds of information: This forest has mostly pine or maple trees; that farm is growing wheat; the lake water is clear here and clouded there; large numbers of fish live in those tidal waters; the soil is eroded on the western slope of this mountain; plants are blooming later than usual in the valley;

the urban area is spreading to the east; strip mines cover 200,000 acres; and so on.

Landsat 4 radios these images to earth as individual bits of data. They flow down to ground stations at the rate of 100 billion bits a day. Electronic equipment changes these data into images on film, which look like photos. Scientists, farmers, public officials, people who fish for a living and mineral prospectors in over 100 countries study the photos and use them to plan for the future.

The atmosphere that makes life on earth possible makes looking at the sky very difficult for astronomers. The air that surrounds the earth distorts the appearance of the stars and planets as they are seen through telescopes. Also, it completely blocks several kinds of radiation from the various bodies in space.

Over the years, astronomers have placed telescopes and various measuring instruments in orbit above the atmosphere. These automatic devices make observations through the emptiness of space, and radio the results down to the scientists on earth. A good many astronomical discoveries have been made based on these observations.

Weather Satellites

Scientists use weather satellites to help them forecast the weather and learn more about how weather conditions are produced.

Early in June 1972, photos taken by a weather satellite showed the formation of a tropical storm in the Gulf of Mexico. Weather scientists, called meteorologists, at the government's National Oceanic and Atmospheric Administration (NOAA) watched it very carefully. By June 14 the storm showed signs of turning into a hurricane. It was named Hurricane Agnes. The satellite pictures showed that the hurricane was moving up over Florida. The meteorologists then warned the people in the path of the storm to prepare for high winds and heavy rains.

Over the following days, the weather scientists kept a careful watch on Hurricane Agnes—tracking its movements, and giving people very precise information on where and when it would strike. Agnes proved to be a very severe hurricane. Winds raged over 150 miles per hour (240 km/h) and about 28 trillion gallons (106 trillion liters) of rain fell over the eastern United States.

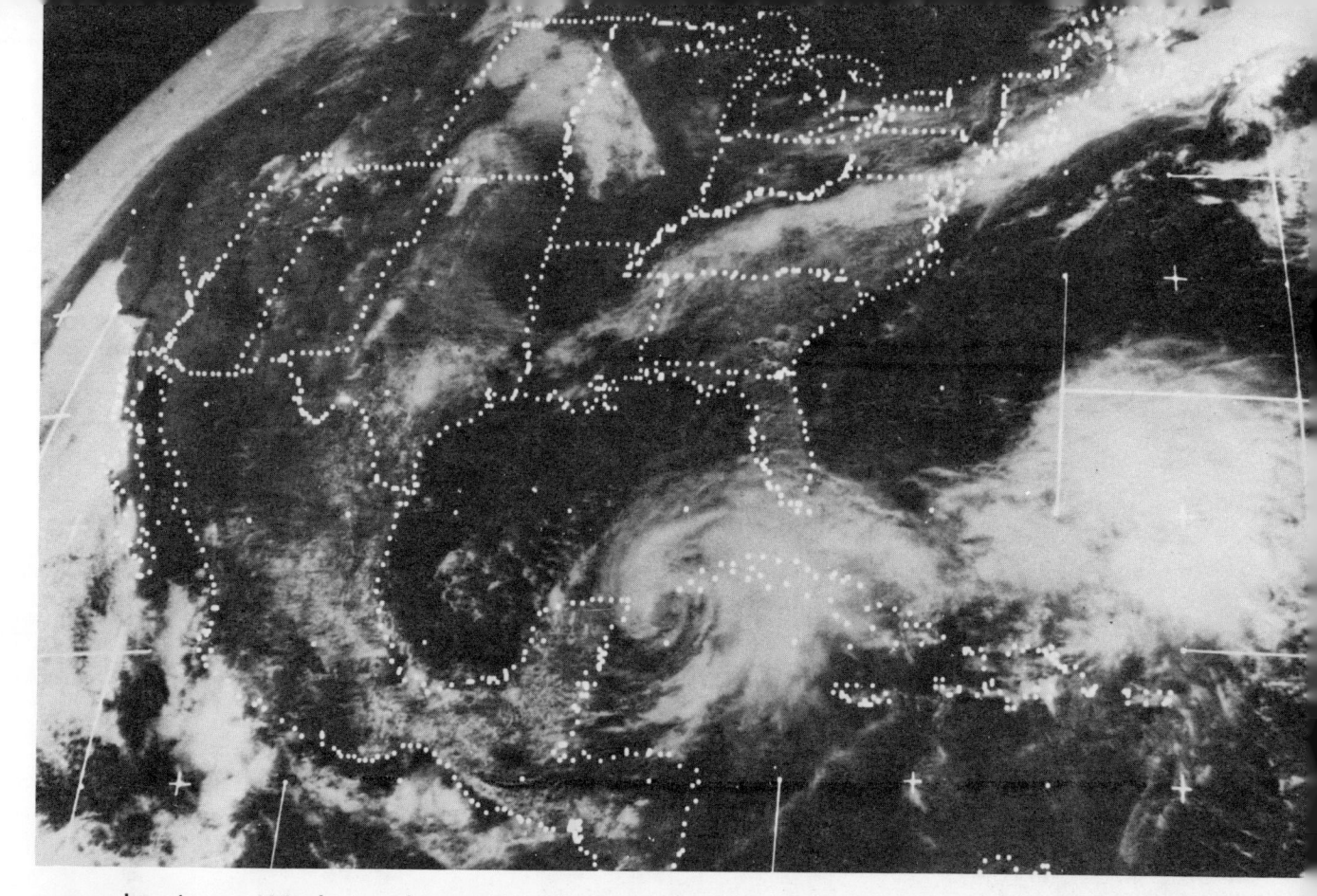

The storm killed 129 people and destroyed an estimated $3.5 billion worth of property. As awful as these figures are, meteorologists guess that without early satellite warning perhaps 5,000 would have perished, and damage would have been two or three times as great.

NASA, working with NOAA, has launched two main series of weather satellites. TIROS (Television and Infrared Observation Satellite) was first, on April 1, 1960. Four years after, the NIMBUS (Latin word for rain cloud) satellite was placed in orbit. Since then, a succession of TIROS and NIMBUS satellites have been lifted into space.

Pictured here by satellite are the swirling clouds of Hurricane Agnes as they start to cover the southern tip of Florida.

All weather satellites work in the same basic way. They are in a polar, north-south orbit, at an altitude of about 500 miles (800 km). The TV cameras that they carry are pointed toward the earth. They film the earth's surface during each orbit. Sensors measure heat and light waves coming from earth. Because of the rotation of our planet, each orbit carries the satellite over a slightly different part of the world's surface. In the course of a day, a satellite can photograph and take measurements of weather conditions over the entire globe.

From time to time pictures and data are transmitted to ground stations by radio. Hundreds of weather stations around the world receive the signals from orbiting weather satellites on sensitive antennas. A NIMBUS satellite, for instance, can transmit about 667 million bits of global weather information to earth each day. Such weather information is available to anyone with a receiver equipped to pick up the satellite signal.

Besides regular weather-watch duties, some satellites perform search and rescue. The first use of such satellites came in September 1982. A single-engine plane with three men aboard crashed in the wilds of northwestern Canada. A satellite, with a radio receiver tuned to the international distress

In orbit the TIROS opens up and gathers weather data, which it radioes to earth.

frequency, picked up the weak signal from the tiny downed plane. The message was relayed to the ground station in Ottawa, Canada. A computer used the signal to calculate the exact location of the plane. A helicopter was sent and rescued the men, injured but alive. Canadian officials said that the area was so wild and rugged that it would have been impossible to find them without the satellite.

Starting in 1982, NASA weather satellites put into operation a special long-range research project on the effects on the world's weather of the eruption of El Chichon, a volcano in Mexico. The study began soon after the eruption spewed an immense cloud of dust and gas into the atmosphere.

The radio signals from TIROS are received by sensitive ground antennas.

Already the scientists have learned that the cloud of volcanic dust is 6 miles (9.6 km) thick on average, and between 13 and 18 miles (21 to 29 km) in altitude. It is spread out over a large portion of the earth. In time it will probably cover the entire Northern Hemisphere as well as large parts of the Southern Hemisphere.

Generally, the lower layers are moving from west to east, but the upper levels often move in the opposite direction. Within this cloud, too, there is a "sloshing around," as local winds move parts back and forth.

Meteorologists are making various predictions based on the satellite findings on the El Chichon cloud: The amount of sunlight reaching the earth's surface will go down about five percent; the average temperature of the Northern Hemisphere will drop by as much as one degree over the next few years; and there will be early frosts over the next few years.

No one knows how long these effects, if they occur, will last. The latest estimate, though, is from two to seven years.

Military Satellites

The armed forces use artificial satellites for communications, to help pilots and sailors navigate, and to make observations of the lands of potential enemies. The year 1982 marked a turning point in the history of the military space effort. Although military space activities are kept secret, it is known that in 1982, for the first time, the space budget of the Department of Defense ($6.4 billion) exceeded that of NASA ($5.5 billion).

The military competition between the two superpowers, the United States and the Soviet Union, now includes a race for supremacy in space. In 1967 both nations signed an Outer Space Treaty, which bans the placement of any weapons of "mass destruction" in space. It also forbids the use of the moon or any planet other than earth for military purposes.

As far as is known, neither country has violated this treaty. But there is little question that both powers are developing weapons designed to destroy enemy satellites in space and enemy missiles and rockets on the ground or in the air. These are considered weapons to destroy enemy arms, not weapons of mass destruction.

Experts estimate that there are about fifty United States military satellites in space. A good number of them are just like civilian communication and weather satellites. The main difference is that these military satellites are intended to be used just by the armed forces.

Another group of satellites provides navigational aids for the military. These satellites beam down radio signals that contain coded information

A U.S. Navy communication satellite is weighed and balanced before being placed in the nose cone.

about their direction, distance, speed and position. Instruments aboard ships and aircraft and on movable ground stations pick up the signals and feed them into a computer. Knowing the satellite's position, the computer can calculate its exact location on earth. With this information, it can also figure out what course to steer for a destination and what speed to use to arrive there at a certain time.

Before the introduction of navigational satellites in the 1950s, pilots and sailors, in particular, found their exact positions by using the stars. An accuracy of location within 10 miles (16 km) was considered good. With the latest satellite navigational system, location is accurate to within 30 feet (9 m)!

The advantages to the military are obvious. The armed forces can use the satellites for controlling the conduct of war scientifically. They can plot air, land and sea courses by the shortest, fastest and least crowded routes to avoid collisions. Information on the exact location both of our ship, plane or missile, and of the enemy target, makes it possible to score direct hits. One day, equipment that receives the satellite signals may be placed in a backpack or worn on the wrist. This way soldiers on foot, in tanks or in trucks can always know exactly where they are.

A good number of military satellites are known as "spies in the skies." Their job is to gather information or intelligence on the enemy. The TV cameras and electronic equipment in these devices can collect a storehouse of facts that are helpful in planning wartime strategy. They can take valuable photos of army and navy installations, troop movement, and weapon production and storage.

The latest spy satellite, called Big Bird, weighs 11 tons (10 metric tons) and is the size of a railroad car. It has a wide-angle lens that lets it see a vast area at once. When something suspicious appears, ground control can direct the satellite to use a telephoto lens for a closer look. One expert has stated that Big Bird is able to focus on a golf ball from an orbit height of 150 miles (241 km)!

Spy satellites that are sensitive to heat and other forms of radiation can spot nuclear bombs and even pick up warm spots in ocean waters where nuclear submarines are passing through. They can immediately detect a rocket or missile launching. Even the radio signals used to control rocket and missile firings can be picked up. And they can eavesdrop on radio, telephone and satellite-to-satellite conversations anywhere in the world.

The protection of our satellites in space is most important. Scientists are looking for ways to protect American satellites from attack by a nuclear warhead, a laser beam or a satellite on a collision course. To ward off these dangers, shielding is being built into some satellites to help them withstand atomic blasts. Some satellites have highly reflective surfaces to bounce back laser beams. One day the satellites in space may spin so fast that the laser beam will not be able to focus its energy in one spot. Also, additional small rocket motors built into the satellites may enable them to outmaneuver and escape enemy attack.

Along with better satellites, the Defense Department is working on a group of antisatellite weapons, called A-SATs. Further along, according to published reports, is a missile with an explosive warhead that will be launched from a high-flying airplane. It will home in on the enemy satellite and explode on contact. Laser beams are also in the planning stage, but more research is still needed.

The use of particle beams, which send a powerful beam of energized atomic particles against enemy satellites, is underway. But this requires great amounts of energy. It will probably work only if fired in space, not from earth. Experts tell us it will be several decades before a particle beam will be a practical weapon—if ever.

What is the future of satellites in space? Will there be colonies of people who live and work on giant space stations? Will satellites be used to supply us with more vital information about the earth and space and the universe? Or will most satellites be put to military use as the "high ground" from which new weapon systems will threaten entire continents?

The history of space shots, shuttles and satellites is short, but brilliant. It is up to each of us to work to assure a glorious future in space of positive achievements that will advance knowledge and benefit all of humanity.

GLOSSARY

Antenna   A solid dish or arrangement of metal rods and wires that is used to send and receive radio waves.

Artificial satellite   *See* Satellite.

Astronauts   The men and women who fly the spacecraft launched from earth. On Space Shuttle flights, the astronauts are either pilots, who are responsible for controlling the flight itself, or mission specialists (also known as payload specialists), who handle the various operations and scientific experiments of the mission.

Communication satellite   An artificial body that receives radio signals from earth and transmits them to stations located at various distances from the original sending station. The signals can carry radio or TV broadcasts, telephone calls, or data in the form of words, numbers or pictures.

Data   Facts and figures that are used in reaching conclusions; plural of datum.

Docking   The process whereby one spacecraft becomes attached to another in space.

EVA   An acronym for extra-vehicular activity; it refers to anything done outside the spaceship while in flight.

External tank   A tank containing fuel and oxidizer that is found outside the spacecraft.

Firing   The act of turning on a rocket engine.
Fuel   Any material that produces useful heat or energy. The fuels used in space are usually either aluminum powder or liquid hydrogen.
Fuel cell   A source of both power and water on space missions. By combining hydrogen and oxygen in a fuel cell, electricity is produced, with water as a byproduct.
Geosynchronous orbit   An orbit at the altitude of 22,300 miles. In this orbit, a satellite always remains over the same spot on earth.
Glider   An aircraft without any source of power. The Space Shuttle orbiter functions as a glider as it returns to earth.
Launch pad   The structure from which space shots are sent into space. Most launch pads are at the Kennedy Space Center at Cape Canaveral, Florida.
Liquid rocket fuel   Liquid hydrogen is the most common fuel in space. In the rocket engine it is combined with liquid oxygen, the oxidizer.
Manned   A spacecraft containing a man or woman; the opposite of unmanned.
Military satellite   A type of satellite that is devoted to military purposes, such as communication, guidance or surveillance.
Mission   The practice of sending one or more people to accomplish a particular set of tasks; the purpose or purposes for each space launch.
Mission specialist   See Astronauts.
Module   A separate unit of the spacecraft. Many of the planetary probes had a lander module that dropped to the planet surface and a command module that continued to orbit around the planet.
NASA   The acronym for National Aeronautics and Space Administration. NASA was established in 1958 by the United States government to develop and oversee the nation's space efforts.
On board   Anything carried in or on the spacecraft.
Orbit   The regular path followed by one body around another body.
Orbiter   Any vehicle that is designed to go into orbit around earth or another planet.

Oxidizer   A source of oxygen for the fuel that is burned in rocket engines.

Payload bay   The part of the Space Shuttle, behind the crew quarters, where scientific equipment or satellites are kept.

Payload specialist   See Astronauts.

Pilot   See Astronauts.

Planet   Any body in space that revolves around a central star.

Rendezvous   The meeting of spacecraft in space without actually becoming attached.

Rocket   Any device that is pushed forward by gases that are produced by burning fuel; the exhaust gases escape through a rear vent.

Rocket booster   A separate rocket that is used at the start of a spacecraft launch to get the craft off the pad.

Satellite   A natural or artificial object that orbits around a planet. The moon is a natural satellite that orbits around the earth. Many artificial satellites have now been placed in orbit and also revolve around the earth.

Scientific satellite   A satellite that performs scientific experiments or makes observations in space. Scientific satellites map and study the planet earth and use telescopes and other measuring devices to explore outer space.

Simulator   A replica of the spacecraft cabin that astronauts use to practice the various tasks they will be performing during an actual flight.

Solar cell   A device that changes sunlight into electrical current.

Solar system   The sun and all the planets and smaller bodies that revolve around it.

Solid rocket fuel   One type of fuel used to power rockets. Aluminum powder is a common solid rocket fuel. It is usually packed with ammonium percholate powder, which supplies oxygen for the combustion of the aluminum.

Space   The vast region that extends out beyond the earth's atmosphere.

Space shot   Any object, manned or unmanned, that is launched into space from earth.

Space Shuttle A reusable spacecraft that is designed to carry objects or people into space and return them to earth; parts of the Space Shuttle can be reused many times.

Tracking stations A number of sites scattered around the world that receive and send radio signals to spacecraft.

Unmanned A spacecraft that does not contain a person; the opposite of manned.

Weather satellite A satellite that observes and photographs weather conditions and radioes the information down to earth.

Zero-gravity A state of weightlessness, without gravitational pull. An orbiting spacecraft is in zero-gravity because of the particular orbit it follows.

INDEX

Airplanes, 14
Allen, Joseph P., 51
Apollo, *see* Project Apollo
Anik, 3, 50
Armstrong, Neil, 22
A-SATs (Antisatellite weapons), 73
Astronaut, 9–13, 18, 19, 20, 21, 22, 23, 25, 26, 31, 35, 37–38, 39, 40, 41, 42, 44, 45, 46–47, 48, 49, 50
   mission specialist, 9, 10, 51
   pilot, 9, 50
   training, 9–12, 31–32
Atlantis, 44

Balloons, 14
Big Bird, 72
Brand, Vance D., 50

Chaffee, Roger B., 22
Challenger, 44, 51
Clarke, Arthur C., 57
Columbia, 32–38, 44, 45–51
Command module, 22
Conrad, Jr., Charles C., 26
Cooper, Jr., L. Gordon, 192
Courier 1B, 58–59

Crippen, Robert L., 31
Cross-training, 12

Discovery, 44
Dynamic Explorer, 65

Early Bird, 60
Echo 1, 57–58
Eisenhower, President Dwight D., 6, 58
El Chichon, 69–70
Engle, Joe H., 46, 47
EVA (Extra-vehicular activity), 20, 51
Explorer 1, 6, 18, 53, 62

Fuel, 32, 33, 34, 35, 42–44
Fuel cell, 20, 33–34, 35, 46
Fullerton, C. Gordon, 48

Gagarin, Yuri, 17
Gemini, 6, 19–21
Geosynchronous orbit, 57, 60
Getaway Special, 49
Glenn, John H., 18, 19
Goddard, Robert H., 16
Grissom, Virgil I., 22

Ham, 18
Hartsfield, Jr., Henry W., 49
Hurricane Agnes, 66–67

Intelsat, 60–61
Ionosphere, 56

Jupiter, 28, 29–30

Kennedy, President John F., 19, 25
Kennedy Space Center, 32, 33, 49
Kerwin, Joseph P., 26

Lageos, 64–65
Laika, 17
Landsat, 65–66
Launch Control Center, 33
Launch pad, 20, 33, 34, 36
Lenoir, William B., 51
Lousma, Jack R., 48
Lunar module, 22
Lyndon B. Johnson Space Center, 9, 10, 11

Mariner, 6
Mars, 27–28
Mattingly II, Thomas, 49
Mercury Project, 6, 18–19
Mission Control Center, 12
Mission specialist, see Astronaut
Moon, 6, 19, 21, 22–23, 53, 57

NASA (National Aeronautics and Space Administration), 6, 9, 10, 12, 23, 25, 27, 31, 44, 57, 59, 67, 70
Newton, Sir Isaac, 16
NIMBUS, 67, 68
Nixon, President Richard, 31
NOAA (National Oceanic and Atmospheric Administration), 66, 67

Orbit, 17, 18, 19, 20, 22, 25, 36, 39, 44, 48, 49, 53, 55, 58, 60, 65
  polar, 65, 68
Orbiter, 9, 32–33, 35, 36, 38, 39–44
Outer Space Treaty, 70
Overmyer, Robert F., 51

Payload bay, 34, 37, 42, 48, 54
Payload specialist, see Astronaut
Phoebe, 29–30
Pioneer, 6, 28
Project Apollo, 6, 19, 22–23, 25

Ride, Dr. Sally K., 52
Rocket, 12, 14, 16, 17, 20, 53
  Agena, 20
  ancient China, 16
  fuel, 16
  Saturn, 22

Satellite, 7, 39, 44, 52, 53–73
  astronomy, 66
  communication, 50, 51, 54, 56–61
  mapping, 62
  military, 54, 70–73
  navigational, 71–72
  scientific, 54, 62–66
  spy, 72–73
  weather, 54, 66–70
Saturn, 29–30
Schirra, Jr., Walter M., 19, 21
SCORE (Signal Communication Orbit Repeater Experiment), 57, 58
Shepard, Jr., Alan B., 18
Simulator, 12, 31
Skylab, 25–26
Spacelab, 52
Space shot, 6, 18, 19, 21

Space Shuttle, 6–7, 9, 31–52, 54
   engine, 32, 36, 42, 43, 44
   external tank, 32, 33, 35, 36, 42, 44
   robot arm, 46–47, 48, 52
   solid booster rocket, 32, 33, 36, 42–43
Space suit, 51
Space Task Group, 31
Sputnik, 6, 17, 53
STS (Space Transportation System), 45–52
   1, 45–46
   2, 46–47
   3, 48–49
   4, 49–50
   5, 50–51
   6, 51–52
   7, 52

Telstar, 59
TIROS (Television and Infrared Observation Satellite), 67
Truly, Richard H., 46, 47
Tsiolkovsky, Konstantin E., 16

VAB (Vehicle Assembly Building), 33
Van Allen belts, 62
Viking, 6, 27
Vostok, 17
Voyager, 6, 29–30

Water survival, 11
Weightlessness, see Zero-gravity
Weitz, Paul J., 26
White II, Edward H., 20, 22

Young, John W., 31

Zero-gravity, 10, 26, 39, 42, 47, 49